*Language, Discourse, Society*

General Editors: **Stephen Heath, Colin MacCabe** and **Denise Riley**

*Selected published titles:*

Michael O' Pray
FILM, FORM AND PHANTASY
Adrian Stokes and Film Aesthetics

Denise Riley
'AM I THAT NAME'
Feminism and the Category of 'Woman' in History

Moustapha Safouan
SPEECH OR DEATH?
Language as Social Order: a Psychoanalytic Study

Moustapha Safouan
JACQUES LACAN AND THE QUESTION OF PSYCHOANALYTIC TRAINING
*(Translated and introduced by Jacqueline Rose)*

Stanley Shostak
THE DEATH OF LIFE
The Legacy of Molecular Biology

Lyndsey Stonebridge
THE DESTRUCTIVE ELEMENT
British Psychoanalysis and Modernism

James A. Snead, edited by Kara Keeling, Colin MacCabe and Cornel West
RACIST TRACES AND OTHER WRITINGS
European Pedigrees/African Contagions

Raymond Tallis
NOT SAUSSURE
A Critique of Post-Saussurean Literary Theory

Geoffrey Ward
STATUTES OF LIBERTY
The New York School of Poets

**Language, Discourse, Society**
**Series Standing Order ISBN 0–333–71482–2**
*(outside North America only)*

You can receive future titles in this series as they are published by placing a standing order. Please contact your bookseller or, in case of difficulty, write to us at the address below with your name and address, the title of the series and the ISBN quoted above.

Customer Services Department, Macmillan Distribution Ltd, Houndmills, Basingstoke, Hampshire RG21 6XS, England

# The Force of Language

Jean-Jacques Lecercle and Denise Riley

First published 2004 by
PALGRAVE MACMILLAN
Houndmills, Basingstoke, Hampshire RG21 6XS and
175 Fifth Avenue, New York, N. Y. 10010
Companies and representatives throughout the world

PALGRAVE MACMILLAN is the global academic imprint of the Palgrave Macmillan division of St. Martin's Press, LLC and of Palgrave Macmillan Ltd. Macmillan® is a registered trademark in the United States, United Kingdom and other countries. Palgrave is a registered trademark in the European Union and other countries.

ISBN 1–4039–4248–X

This book is printed on paper suitable for recycling and made from fully managed and sustained forest sources.

A catalogue record for this book is available from the British Library.

Library of Congress Cataloging-in-Publication Data

Lecercle, Jean-Jacques.
  The force of language. Jean-Jacques Lecercle & Denise Riley.
    p. cm.
  Includes bibliographical references and index.
  ISBN 1-4039-4248-X (cloth)
    1. Language and languages--Philosophy. I. Riley, Denise. II. Title.

P107.L43 2004
401--dc22                                                2004051676

10   9   8   7   6   5   4   3   2   1
13  12  11  10  09  08  07  06  05  04

Printed and bound in Great Britain by
Antony Rowe Ltd, Chippenham and Eastbourne

# Contents

# Acknowledgements

The original conception of this book was pursued with the backing of a British Academy grant awarded by its Overseas Policy Committee to the authors in 2002.

Denise Riley's chapters were completed thanks to her study leave from the School of English and American Studies at the University of East Anglia in the autumn of 2002, and to a successive term of leave funded by the Arts and Humanities Research Board in the spring of 2003: she is most grateful for their support. She owes warm thanks to those in the Department of Rhetoric, University of California at Berkeley who heard part of 'A voice without a mouth' in April 2003 and who generously offered her their suggestions, David Copenhafer especially. The chapter here on 'Bad Words' grew out of an exchange with Judith Butler, to whom she is, as always, greatly indebted. She also owes much to Jon Cook, Mladen Dolar, Colin MacCabe, Moustapha Safouan and Joan Scott.

An earlier version of 'Bad Words' appeared in *Diacritics*, vol. 31 no. 4, 2001 and as a part of Denise Riley's *Impersonal Passion: Language as Affect*, Duke University Press, 2005.

# Introduction

*Jean-Jacques Lecercle*

Consider the following sentence (it comes from an old rugby song):

Oh, Sir Jasper, please do not touch me!

Traditional linguistics, or the mainstream philosophy of language on which it is based, has a number of analyses to offer in order to account for such a sentence. We could, for instance, suggest a syntactic analysis: the sentence is in the imperative mood, it has also been the object of what was once called the negative transformation. We could, in the style of functional grammars or of enunciation linguistics, account for the presence of the grammatical marker 'do', that is, account for the mental operation which it inscribes within language. We could also speak the language of pragmatics, and show that the speech-act of which the sentence is the bearer is an indirect one: the imperative suggests the sentence is an order, but the presence of 'please' suggests that, on the contrary, it is rather a prayer (even as the canonical 'please could you pass me the salt' appears to be a request for information when it is really a disguised or weakened order). Lastly, we might try and account for the name as a rigid designator, in the approved manner of Kripke.

But there is one element of the sentence that traditional linguistics, and the philosophy of language that underpins it, will not account for: the 'oh' that begins our sentence.

It is the object of this book to account for aspects of language, such as this 'oh', which mainstream conceptions neglect or reject – aspects of language in which what is deemed irrelevant by traditional linguistics, such as the expression of emotion and affect, is central. It is the object of this book to take into account the incarnated word, the word made flesh.

1

In order to enter this new field, we must leave traditional linguistics and its rational calculus, and indulge in the dubious devices in which those wild and demented linguists, known as *fous littéraires*, revel.

Here is such a device. What happens if we repeat the sentence, cancelling each time the last word? What happens is the following series of sentences:

> Oh, Sir Jasper, please do not touch me!
> Oh, Sir Jasper, please do not touch!
> Oh, Sir Jasper, please do not!
> Oh, Sir Jasper, please do!
> Oh Sir Jasper, please!
> Oh, Sir Jasper!
> Oh!

Where it appears that my sentence is far from innocent: it is in fact an old 'joke', of a blatant male-chauvinist nature, a weapon, using the indirect route of laughter, in the struggle between the sexes, and a token of the oppression of one sex by the other. The device, based on the contingent (and apparently irrational) possibility of what poeticians know as 'sentences within sentences', has revealed aspects of the workings of language which rational calculus ignores. Let us name a few.

The most obvious is, of course, the masculinist violence of the so-called joke: this is a fine instance of the three-way game of sexual jokes, as analysed by Freud – a game based on exclusion (of the woman who is the butt of the joke) and alliance (betweeen the two men who 'share' the joke and laugh). Language here is not a neutral instrument of communication and the exchange of information, it is a weapon in a symbolic struggle, the object of which is the creation of a *rapport de forces*. There is violence in this sort of laughter: the violence of identification through exclusion.

But the device also discloses the importance of the first word of the initial sentence, of this 'oh' which traditional linguistics cannot account for. It suggests that utterances, even in their graphic form, are always also expressions of the affections of the body and the affects those affections provoke. For the initial 'oh' cannot be pronounced in the same way in the first and in the last stage of the game. In fact, its changing tones punctuate the story the series of sentences narrates: it inscribes the changing affects in the speaker, and is thus the most important element, not for the calculus of the meaning but for the interpretation of the sense of the sentence.

The sentence, once it has been fully deployed, tells a story, a rather banal story of seduction, but one which is told with a certain rhetorical and poetic efficacy: this is where the aura of sense goes far beyond the meaning parsed by linguistic analysis. For in fact, there is a line missing in my series. Another application of the device will cancel the 'oh!' which is the last remaining element of my sentence: so silence is an integral part of the series, it is the goal towards which it tends, it embodies the moment when language becomes totally incorporated, when the silent language of embracing bodies no longer needs articulated utterance. But silence as a relevant moment of language is hardly something that mainstream philosophy of language enables us to understand.

Lastly, because my sentence tells a story, it has a certain relationship with the world: its analysis cannot be content with the immanent account which rules of grammar provide. And the world in question is a social world: the sexual relationship is always a social relationship, a question of gender rather than sex. The story is not any story of seduction: it involves an aristocrat ('Sir Jasper'), which is a quaintly archaic name that smacks of the eighteenth century, and the speaker is therefore a servant girl. An intertext, the banal story of the woman seduced and abandoned, is therefore convoked. The Victorians revelled in the tragic consequences of this story, prostitution or death. The eighteenth century likes the comic version, where the servant girl captured her seducer and was raised to the nobility through marriage. Intimations of *Pamela* and *Joseph Andrews*, but also of *Adam Bede*, are immediately perceived.

We need, therefore, an account of language that accepts the fact that language tells us a story of bodies and affects, of oppression and liberation, of struggle and *rapports de force*. In that account, it will be clear that 'bad words' are more important than the blameless transmission of neutral information. We need an account of language that does not start with an individual speaker who translates her thoughts into articulated utterance, an account of language which radically rethinks the usual contrast between 'inner' and 'outer', which is prepared to start from the collective and consider private consciousness as the internalisation of public linguistic intercourse, rather than the usual reverse. We shall therefore have to revisit, not only the question of insult and spoken injury, but the ancient but neglected question of the nature of inner speech.

The first part of the book, written by Denise Riley, does just this. It deals with the voice without a mouth that is inner speech, and with the forensics of spoken injury. The second part, written by Jean-Jacques Lecercle, seeks to formulate the new philosophy of language that we need, starting from the demented theories of *fous littéraires*, proceeding through a critique of the major research programme in linguistics, Chomskyan linguistics, and trying to suggest a number of theses for a new philosophy of language.

# Part I (Denise Riley)

# 1

# 'A voice without a mouth': Inner Speech

Whose voice, no one's, there is no one, there's a voice without a mouth, and somewhere a kind of hearing, something compelled to hear, and somewhere a hand, it calls that a hand, it wants to make a hand, or if not a hand something somewhere that can leave a trace, of what is made, of what is said, you can't do with less, no, that's romancing, more romancing, there is nothing but a voice murmuring a trace.

Samuel Beckett[1]

We might add, perhaps, that the ego wears a 'cap of hearing' [Hörkappe] – on one side only, as we learn from cerebral anatomy. It might be said to wear it awry.

Sigmund Freud[2]

The word is available as the sign for, so to speak, inner employment; it can function as a sign in a state short of outward expression. For this reason, the problem of individual consciousness as the inner word (as an inner sign in general) becomes one of the most vital problems in the philosophy of language.

V. N. Volosinov[3]

## 1   Introduction: Solitude's Talk

If a flower-streaked inward eye could constitute Wordsworth's bliss of solitude, the inward voice has fared less glamorously. Its merest mention doesn't so much conjure up the consolation of inner riches recalled *sotto voce* as the pathos of this chattering internal radio for the anti-social; a poor comforter of enforced solitariness, or some misanthropist's illusion of company on his culpable flight from society. Inner speech is the touchstone of a privacy which needn't depend on the isolation of its silent speaker, for it may mutter forcefully in our ear even when we are among some animated social gathering. The very topic of inner speech conjures an aura of loneliness, whether hapless or wilful. It covers an emotional spectrum shading from the self-consciousness which eavesdrops on itself to the manias of aural possession. There's a thick history to this, intersecting with historical fluctuations in the idea of solitude and its worth. At periods the solitary became decorative; so hermits were hired to grace, hairily, the grottoes of eighteenth-century estates. And if there was an acceptable sex of solitude, this wasn't usually female, unless unsexed by saintliness. But compulsive or enforced sociability is a very modern aim and prescription; on the other hand, some psychoanalytic thought has held to the value of our being able to tolerate being alone.

Our inner speech, if by convention an index of our solitude, is at least faithful to us. It is reassuringly or irritatingly there on tap, and persists quite independently of our faltering memories. It offers us the unfailing if ambiguous company of a guest who does not plan to leave. The fact of its insistent in-dwelling can blind us to its peculiarities, rather in the way that we might no longer want to interrogate some lasting attachment. Among its convoluted qualities, the inner voice, however ostensibly silent, is still able to be heard by its possessor. Where it resonates, no air is agitated. No larynx swells, no eardrum vibrates. Yet if I swing my attention on to my inner speech, I'm aware of it *sounding* in a very thin version of my own tone of voice. I catch myself in its silent sound, a paradox audible only to me. We don't, though, seem to have much of a vocabulary, an odd lack, for this everyday sensation. On what, then, does my conviction of the tonality of my inward voice depend; do I have a sort of *inner ear* designed to pick up this voice which owns nothing by way of articulation? For I can detect my usual accents and the timbre of my voice as soon as I try to overhear myself by trapping the faint sonority of my inner words. But they are audible, if that is the adjective, only in a depleted form which keeps some faint colouration but is far less resonant in the ear than when I'm speaking aloud. (Well, of course! Still, if my inner speech is less loud to me, that's not just because it is not uttered.) It is as if an inner ear is alert to my inner voice, although what happens isn't exactly an instance of *hearing* my own voice speaking. So when I think I can overhear my own inner speech, what do I mean? This silent speech is an apparent oxymoron. Is it more of an ear-voice, which detects it at the same time as it issues it? But I do have the feeling of hearing something, in the same way that I can run a tune audibly through my head, yet without humming it even silently. Or I want to say that I 'hear' it; there's no exact verb for this peculiar kind of hearing something which is not actually sounded, and which evades any measurement of articulation. Yet a kind of hearing it surely is. While for want of anything better, we have to call its instrument inside us our 'inner ear', this expression is habitually allied, not to anything auditory, but to the metaphorical still small voice of conscience.

While the history of solitude remains to be written, an alluring project, at least one of its close companions has enjoyed a separate career in its own right. Inner speech as a phenomenon has proved a severe trial for several philosophies and psychologies, especially in the nineteenth century, as if it provoked a crisis of understanding about language since it seemed to be a manifestation of a paradoxical privacy, where language is usually taken to be communication through articulation and display. But is the inner voice merely a stifled form of outer speech; or is its true origin a meditative state, a mentalese preceding articulation and suggesting that there is thinking prior to words? The ordinary inner voice, that is: the neighbouring case of verbal hallucination is different, often florid, and a specialism of nineteenth-century psychiatry. What is inwardly heard can range from the companionable to the frightening, encompassing the brood-ing censor within, the persecutions of psychoses, furious interdictions, cajoling insistences, the white flash of conversion. The psychoanalyst Otto Isakower, convinced of hearing's dominance in id's sphere, wrote of 'alarming experiences in the realm of hearing: a keen awareness of cadences in the speech of the people around, an importing of deeper meaning into what is heard, falsification of auditory perception and finally auditory hallucinations'.[4] The language of longing and griev-ance alike can grip the mind to pad it with obsessive speculation, as if this pressed in from the outside. There's a strong aspect of linguistic possession to fervent love, as well as to hate. The mind is no theatre for the play of language which we can hiss off stage at will. No leisured affair, linguistic occupation can sometimes be prosaic enough, but can also take the violent shapes of the unwilled reitera-tion of what should be allowed to die down, of verbal post-traumatic disorder, malicious parental injunctions. That these echoes should remain inner is a matter of restraining any slippage in self-managing. Talking aloud to yourself, thereby rehearsing your inner voice in front of others, is by common convention a mark of eccentricity which may eventually conduct to madness. Be seen and heard to do that, and you've pricked the permeable membrane of decorum which partitions speaking inaudibly to yourself from speaking aloud to others. (The use in the street of the hands-free mobile phone has famously shaken this distinction; you tactfully step out of the path of a loud maniac walking behind you, only to overhear him barking orders to his wine warehouse.)

These pages can only brush past some facets of inner speech: its risky closeness to hallucination, its status as the carrier of conscience, and its authority as the apparent source of distinctive style. Mainly, though, they will reflect on the odd topology of outer and inner which the topic of inner speech guarantees, and through which the insinuations of the outside seem to filter inside us, yet without necessarily forcing on us an impression of being invaded. There's no symmetry in practice between the innerness of our silent speech and the outwardness of our articulated speech; these are not opposites, able to be tidily partitioned by strict interiority versus exteriority. And meanwhile my broad sense of what is 'inner' to me turns on this roughest of distinctions between the contents of my own skin and all the rest lying outside it, a distinction which is naturally inconstant and is always being undermined by very many common experiences – for instance the different bodily inversions (as experienced in their relentless temporal sequence) of making love, pregnancy and morning sickness. The following pages will dwell on the ways in which linguistic experiences, too, are utterly disrespectful of the territorial boundaries of inside and out.

Any such train of reflections will soon deposit us in an enduring and classical dilemma in the philosophy of language, which concerns the location of thinking in words. Our thought is not secreted in a realm apart, in some innermost and sealed chamber of our being. 'Thought is no "internal" thing and does not exist independently of the world or of words. What misleads us in this connection, and causes us to believe in a thought which exists for itself prior to expression, is thought already constituted and expressed, which we can silently recall to ourselves, and through which we acquire the illusion of an inner life. But in reality this supposed silence is alive with words, this inner life is an inner language.'[5] This almost Jamesian way of putting it (it is actually Maurice Merleau-Ponty's description) was written in the mid-1960s, over half a century later than William

James's great compendium, *The Principles of Psychology*.[6] Yet substantially the same psychological authorities are gathered behind both. Their depictions of inwardness as vivaciously speech-filled need not, taken on their own, imply any element of surrender to the unwanted incursions of words, or any thrilling submission to their despotic possession, let alone any trace of abjection. These are the emotions of capitulation to language, which have so heavily shadowed other accounts of how words strike at the heart of their subject.[7] If we want to steer clear of espousing such a languorously depressive resignation to the force of indwelling words, we'll need to fight against a strong tendency of inherited supposition here.

## 2   Inner Speech in Neuropathology

How does this seeming linguistic innerness work; can anything about its nature be illuminated by the study of its neural manifestations? Wittgenstein, a philosopher of language who was rather devoted to the outerness of inner speech, was strenuously unconcerned with speculating about the precise physiology of inner thought: 'A hypothesis, such as that such-and-such went on in our bodies when we made internal calculations, is only of interest to us in that it points to a possible use of the expression "I said ... to myself"; namely that of inferring the physiological process from the expression.'[8] But many other devotees of language were not unconcerned, and hadn't been for many decades. Wittgenstein's disavowal marks that break he intended with an earlier and durable philosophy of mind given over to speculation on consciousness and its physical basis, and which had long asserted its cousinship with psychology. Nineteenth century neuropsychology, in particular, had no great impulse to distinguish its own speculative formulations from those of the philosophy of mind, while on the other hand, philosophy of mind itself took introspection as its proper route into the psychology with which it was so intimate.

A faintly forlorn aura hangs about the topic of inner speech today, as if it's no more than a set of old conundrums now abandoned, whose mention may dimly conjure up the nineteenth-century neuropsychologies of Wilhelm Wundt the taxonomist of feeling, Carl Wernicke after whom the brain lesions of particular aphasias are named, Paul Broca who gave his surname to those local lesions which blocked articulation, or John Hughlings Jackson whose work on aphasia Freud respectfully credited. (Some aphasic reading and writing problems scrutinised by the later neuropsychologist Henry Head could indeed attract a predictable Freudian interpretation; 'One of Head's patients could write his own name and address correctly, but he was unable to write his mother's address, though she lived in the same house.'[9]) Aphasia was, in short, responsible for a rich and copious nineteenth-century clinical literature, especially fascinated by those cases where words survived inside the patients' heads despite damage to their powers of utterance. The will to decipher the nature of inner speech which neurologists drew from their cherished topic of aphasia is clear, for instance, in the very title of Ballet's *Le langage intérieur et les diverses formes de l'aphasie.*[10] As Jackson wrote, emphasising the durability of inner language, 'we do not use the expression that the speechless man has lost words, but that he has lost those words which serve in speech. In brief, speechlessness does not mean entire wordlessness.'[11] An anarthria, a disturbance of the power of articulation due to cortical or brain stem lesions, was distinct from true aphasia, the loss of language; 'The anarthriac understands, reads, and writes. His thinking is not impaired, and it is possible for him to express his thoughts in every other way than by the word since his inner speech is not affected.'[12] (This venerable tradition of exploring aphasic disturbance to contribute to a philosophy of language was extended by Roman Jakobson's 1971 study of different aphasias, which he treated as figures of metaphor and metonymy.[13])

An effort to establish the conceptual study of inner language – especially where there was some doubt in its subject's mind as to who spoke it – lay at the core of these animated late nineteenth and early twentieth century investigations of speech disturbances. By 1906 the neurologist James Mark Baldwin could write decisively: 'The doctrine of brain function in speech is now pretty clear – thanks to the teaching, principally, of pathological cases ... With those patients who are able to speak without interrupting the voice which they hear, we have a hallucination of objective speech: they hear what they think is a real voice outside them. While the other class have a hallucination of internal speech. They declare that there is someone inside them, speaking to them.'[14] It was on the terrain of inner speech that pathologies of articulation encountered pathologies of grasping the words' source, just as they continue to meet in modern research on the neural base of schizophrenic auditory hallucinations.[15]

Where aphasia once ruled, schizophrenia later arrived to usurp its dominance, not only clinically but epistemologically – to name distinctions to which the early philosophy of mind had been systematically indifferent. Our sanity, though, has long been popularly taken to be manifest in our realising what the true origin of our inner voice was. Or, in the case of a verbal hallucination, remaining sure nevertheless that we were not at the mercy of some aggressive invasion. That kind of an insistent voice is felt by its sufferer to be quite different from her ordinary inner voice, while at the same time she can realise with perfect clarity that what's vividly resonating in her head does not arise from any external source.[16] This not unusual phenomenon of hearing a voice, where this isn't attributable to schizophrenia, has its own large clinical literature; and here those studies which try to differentiate these ordinary experiences of hearing voices from those symptoms which are classified as psychotic often end up with blurred diagnoses of case histories, in which the officially sane are recorded as voice hearers nonetheless. The official diagnostic measurements are anyway famously unsatisfactory, recognised as always overdue for revision, such as this item on the standard American checklist for schizophrenia: the occurrence of 'prominent hallucinations ... of a voice with content having no apparent relation to depression or elation, or a voice keeping up a running commentary on the person's behavior or thoughts, or two or more voices conversing with each other'.[17] In clinical practice, though, the working distinction between delusion and sanity can be far less confidently deduced from the presence of inner conversation, and so the test becomes, not the hearing itself of inner voices differing from ordinary inward speech, but the hearer's own capacity to recognise that these are still self-generated voices, even where they are experienced as peremptory invasions.

What physically happens in our brains during the activity of inner speech had long absorbed neurological investigation, which eventually came to pin its site down to the left inferior frontal region. Long after this broad consensus about the material basis of inner speech – and rather as if this unsatisfied preoccupation of a nineteenth-century philosophy, which had eventually abandoned it, had migrated to the latest neurology – the neural location of self-consciousness itself has been declared traceable.[18] What is more, recent neurological research has suggested that 'the brain regions involved in self-awareness are identical to the regions responsible for inner speech'.[19] The old preoccupation with speech pathologies has been reinvigorated by the newest technological advances; so for instance, according to some neurophysiologists, even inner speech itself can fail (here one supposes that the test of this must be the absence of detectable neurological activity) when someone suffers from severe anarthria.[20] The development of magnetic resonance imaging, or MRI, has permitted

the fine localisation of brain functions. So with the study of the delu-
sions of some psychotic disorders, of inner voices as emanating from
someone else, it is poor or distorted neural communication between
those pathways of the brain which monitor inner speech which is
now thought responsible for these distressing hallucinations.[21]

   Such extraordinarily precise work of the neural geographers of inward
speech, newly permitted by the advanced scanning which records its
materiality, by no means exhausts the range of inquiry about it.
Questions of the philosophy of language have always flourished not
despite, but at the very heart of these neurological researches; and they
are not rendered redundant today. So, for instance, intense arguments
over the existence of 'mentalese' (the syntactical frame for a wordless
thought, which precedes and which must be translated into inner language) continue in debates on the 'language of thought hypothesis'.[22]
Its adherents pursue their new account of language *vis-à-vis* thinking,
which, for them, should possess the very exactness which William
James had felt impossible when he had tried to characterise the feeling
of anticipation in intending to speak: 'The intention *to-say-so-and-so* is
the only name it can receive. One may admit that a good third of our
psychic life consists in these rapid premonitory perspective views of
schemes of thought not yet articulate.'[23] A thought which races ahead
of its solidification into words – this very formulation can still remain a
spur to furious questioning.

## 3   The Inner as the Truer

'Language is, in its very nature, inadequate, ambiguous, liable to
infinite abuse, even from negligence; and so liable to it from design,
that every man can deceive and betray by it,' wrote Bishop Butler.[24]
But conversation with oneself, while admittedly vulnerable to error, is
also crowned as the site of our best proximity to truth. Inner speech is
not only a site of enduring fascination for neuropathology, and an
aspect of a wavering sanity, but it also carries the grave burden of being
the very locus of morality. What self-scrutiny demands from us in
practice is our dwelling within our inner speech; we will try to find out
what we are up to, or what we really feel, by overhearing ourselves.
Then we will tell ourselves. Or as Merleau-Ponty put it, 'we present our
thought to ourselves through internal or external speech'.[25] This is rit-
ualised in the dramatised inner speech which, from ancient Greek
theatre onwards, has been enshrined on stage as soliloquy, from the
medieval Everyman play to the Renaissance and afterwards, when it

was often inflected by Shakespeare's tactic of making his soliloquies soul-revealing devices, rather than plot-elucidating tactics. Off-stage life, too, allows us endless chances to dramatise our inward thought for ourselves as speechifying, and often we do this backwards, by reconstructing what might have been, or what really ought to have been. The familiar feeling of *esprit d'escalier* when, leaving the room and going downstairs, you are assailed, too late, by the vivid realisation of what you *should* have said, is another version of the dramatic soliloquy in which second thoughts about our responses to absent others are rehearsed aloud, run past ourselves. This can then appear to us as the blow of truth unveiled in retrospect. It is the term 'the inner voice', as distinct from 'inner speech', which is almost always used with this connotation of conscience and its revelations, all realised by means of self examination.

This materialisation of conscience is the inner voice which addresses me by whispering forcefully to me. It holds the authority of its separation from me. I know this voice within me is not mine, yet in admitting to hear it, I am at no risk of being judged mad. The aural possession of the self by something else falls, in this instance, on the side of not only sanity but of goodness. Conscience comes from the outside. It is overwhelmingly an instance of importation, announcing the ethical like a messenger – and yet at the same time it is an indwelling authority. The figure of the still small voice depends on this interiorisation of conscience as a form of dictation. Its biblical origin is rather different, though. Here is chapter and verse: 'And He said, Go forth, and stand upon the mount before the Lord. And, behold, the Lord passed by, and a great and strong wind rent the mountains, and brake in pieces the rocks before the Lord; but the Lord was not in the wind: and after the wind an earthquake; but the Lord was not in the earthquake: and after the earthquake a fire; but the Lord was not in the fire: and after the fire a still small voice.'[26] Then Elijah, 'a man of God' and the recipient of all these cataclysmic demonstrations, tells this tranquil divine voice how things stand with him, and the story proceeds. But there is no element anywhere in it of confessing, internalising or unveiling. Only much later did the theologies of guilt supply such resonances to the 'still small voice' and drive it as bad conscience into the interior of the mind; where in the Bible, it was not.

As a metaphor, the still small voice is tenacious, but is not naturalistic. It's striking that this manifestation of conscience is neither still – it is highly active, professionally busy – nor is it so small. If it may whisper, it more often deploys megaphone-like capacities to intervene sonorously, shepherding our attention on to the correct path. Wherever it's even invoked by its bearer, in the same blow it is instantly effective. We do not hear reports of this kind: 'I heard a still small voice inside me telling me what I knew I had to do – then I went and did the opposite.'

There are, then, many differing if often linked notions of the inner voice as the locus of truth; these include its periodic standing as the ultimate confirmation of our being to ourselves, or else as the necessarily conscientious truth of our internal utterance. While our capacity for communicative speech (with others) has often been proclaimed as the sign of the distinctively human, yet the inner voice, as a strong tangible aspect of the self with itself in solitude, can be taken as a reassuring touchstone of my very existence. Here Descartes's *cogito* could be rendered instead as 'I am aware of my inner voice, therefore I am.' Together with its strong sensation of self-immediacy comes the impression, at least, of truth-telling. Socrates emphasised the greater veracity of the inward word as true writing on the soul when he spoke warmly of the man who thinks that 'a written composition must be to a large extent the creation of fancy ... that even the best of such compositions can do no more than help the memory of those who already know; whereas lucidity and finality and serious importance are to be found only in words spoken by way of instruction, or, to use a truer phrase, written on the soul of the hearer to enable him to learn about the right, the beautiful, and the good ....'[27]

My own inner voice does not lie to me. To possess an *in*authentic inner voice is impossible. Self-deception is a different matter; and then the self-deceiver is often described as pulling the wool over her own eyes precisely by ignoring her inner voice. It's as if the possibility of falsehood can only arise with the spoken voice, through the opportunities for lying aloud which stem from my inner voice's ability to say one thing while my uttered voice, intending to deceive, says another. It is in this exploitation of the gap between the inner voice and the outer voice that the lie lies.

Falsity and fluency aren't necessarily intimate. Yet by convention, an easy articulacy hints to us that its possessor may be lying. But the most eloquent discourse may nonetheless be rigorously true; while reticent, hesitant or austere diction, or silence, may well lie. So much for outer speech. The inner avoids such slipperiness. Still, the inverse of this Platonic intuition of the truth of the inner is a long modern history of suspicion of the word, whatever its site; the kind of modernity dating back at least to Nietzsche, and fed by many impulses, ranging from those philosophies of expressivity which espouse a conception of the betrayal or seduction of words, to those fuelled by a dislike of phonocentrism.[28] But as Tristan Tzara once inquired sardonically, 'Must we no longer believe in words? Since when have they expressed the opposite of what the organ that emits them thinks and desires?'[29] The reputation of the word for honesty *can* be salvaged from the hands of the many theorists of linguistic treachery who lie in wait for it, but by now the reputation of language in general for reliability has been terminally compromised. And, to go against the grain of the very last sociologists who keep faith in a benign intersubjectivity, language is hardly reliably communicative. 'Or as Fritz Mauthner put it, it was via language, with its common surface and private base, that men had "made it impossible to get to know each other".'[30] Another tradition of looking darkly at language will invoke the lacunae which hang within personal speech as also shadowing the social. The privacy of hiding, traditionally the province of individual inner speech, can become magnified into a kind of historical silence. If we can accept this way of putting it, here is another instance of the malleability of the inward and the outward in language (to which my discussion will soon turn). There are social anarthrias, and there are historical aphasias. Raymond Williams wrote about those historical silences which are immediately social silences, in the sense that at times the transitions between inner speech and public articulation are unable to happen: 'there are certain language situations which are historically repressive. People talk of language as a means of expression but it is also evidently a means of selection. In certain social–historical circumstances, there are things which could not be said, and therefore, in any connecting way, not thought.' This kind of conviction of the forcefulness of language in its very powers of inhibition is a companion to the idea of its dictatorship: 'Jakobson has nicely remarked that a language is defined not because it permits saying ... but because it compels saying; so every sociolect involves "obligatory rubrics", great stereotyped forms outside which the clientele of this sociolect cannot speak (cannot think).'[31]

## 4  Possession and Occupation

If indeed language compels, how does it compel from within us? There's not so much distance between the experiences of listening to someone else holding forth seamlessly while lecturing or giving a reading perhaps, and of deliberately switching our attention onto our own inner speech. We hear these voices, in both instances, running inside our heads, and the felt distinction between the two may be slight; however, we sense that to turn our scrutiny on to our inner voice at once magnifies and distorts it, as if it's dragged before a microphone which renders it synthetically sonorous. It's denatured simply by becoming the focus of examination. Hence the infamous problem of the method of introspection which so bedevilled earlier philosophical psychology and which resulted in the irritation relayed in Wittgenstein's work, with its empathetic yet antagonistic evoking of James's introspective approach to consciousness.[32] For what was the need for this slippery assumed innerness?

Its study was not questionable on the grounds of its solipsism; to practise introspection, in the armoury of the philosophy of mind, was no act of self-importance. Strenuously attending to oneself speaking was a means of empirical observation which had nothing to do with 'narcissism'; unless, that is, one were to do violence to the quite different dominant concepts of narcissism – to Freud's, and to its source in Ovid's story of Echo and Narcissus; there's a vast gulf between the idea of critical self-presence, and these versions of narcissism as self-enchantment.[33] Wittgenstein's doubt, though, was more concerned with the tacit supposition of a secret which needed to be exhumed before behaviour could be made intelligible to others. On the contrary, this kind of guessing was redundant.

The conception of the inner state as a lucid source for interpreting the buzz of the outer is particularly taxed by the case of inner speech. For even my habitual and unexcited presence to myself is a case of mild possession, in that I'm usually harmlessly owned by my inner speech in its swelling and streaming within me. In addition to this routine colonisation, what we might call an unconscious plagiarism runs from our unintended borrowing of phrases or tones to our unacknowledged and unrealised influences by half-incorporated ideas, to constitute a linguistic occupying power. This can be kindly, as with the mild and educative aspect of verbal exchange; 'There is then a taking-up of others' thought through speech, a reflection in others, an ability to think "according to others" which enriches our own thoughts.'[34] But our saturation in and reiteration of everyone else's words can also become savage, as witnessed by the relentless hallucinations classified by Pierre Janet or recorded by the aurally possessed themselves, like the unhappy Judge Schreber.[35] And then my sane and ordinary inner speech is itself likely to be a swarm of quotations, often from anonymous and vanished others. The dead chatter away as the inner speech of the living. This is well caught in the terse wording of a miners' banner from about 1890 still hanging in Durham Cathedral: 'They being dead yet speaketh'.[36] Reaching past its invocation of those killed at their work underground, this biblical quotation refers to Abel, whose sacrificial act had so irritated his brother, Cain, that he killed him. Abel's sacrifice continued nevertheless after his death to speak as a clear witness.[37] Such supposedly mute reproach and testimony is, like the still small voice, often a loudly reverberating affair.

Even my daily and amiably prosaic mutterings to myself tend to be polyvocal. As to how I inhabit my own inner speech, I am probably more accurately described as talking *with* myself rather than *to* myself. A great deal of what goes on in the head consists of an agitated running self-interrogation; 'What did I just come into this room to get? Oh, I know, I probably left my cup of coffee in here, it'll be cold by now. No, no, I had to telephone someone, but who was it?' That is, there is an internal dialogue, but in these exchanges I appear to occupy both sides of it, and there is no one heavily weighted side to my garrulous split self. Certainly this incessant small talk with myself is not the same as *thinking*. This isn't, though, just because its content is banal rather than reflective. The nature of my thinking simply does not generate the same puzzle for me as does dwelling on my sense of my inner voice. And yet the difference here isn't simply that I will notice my inward voice as it meanders along, whereas cogitation is habitually turned outward to the world and to my being in it. There is a stronger difference, a qualitative difference rather than a simple difference of directedness. As Wittgenstein remarked, ' "Thinking" and "inward speech" – I do not say "*to* oneself" – are different concepts.'[38] For my inward speech doesn't usually speak *to* me.

Still, perhaps at times a sense of dialogue can spring up in me, and I may feel that I'm talking both to and with myself when I notice that I have become my inner companion. Then I can silently calm myself, debate with myself. More censoriously, as my knowing superego I can berate myself, upbraid myself, goad myself along. But very often I do not actually address myself at all, and there is simply talking inside me. *There is a voice.* Questioned as to its origin, I would be in no doubt that it's my own voice, but its habitual presence in me resembles a rapid low-grade commentary without authorship, rather than any Socratic exchange between several loquacious and attentive inner selves. Better Beckett's accurate assertion: 'whose voice, no-one's'.[39]

## 5   Ventriloquy, Autoventriloquy, and Interpellation

How to characterise these various verbose presences within us, but in a way which does not merely reinforce the metaphor of their invasion of our inward and blank innocence? We might say that inner speech itself lives as a state of ventriloquy, in that there is talking within us as if we are spoken from elsewhere; but this state *just is* our main mode of speaking. It's present in the ordinary experience of overhearing myself speaking inwardly in a well-formed voice, whether as an outcome of switching my attention onto my inner speech or of feeling it to have risen and swum forward to claim my attention. Ventriloquy makes this daily inner speech: the state of sensing that words are running through me, across me. There is a kind of 'it is speaking in me' which is not exactly 'it *is* speaking me', but is an unwilled busiedness which I catch and may try to inhibit in myself. Words race across me in polyphonic brigades, constantly swollen by the forces of more inrushing voices, and I can put up only a rear-guard censoring action. But this impression is no fully blown hallucination, for again there is no disowning and projecting of my inner voice, only my feeling of becoming a vehicle for words from elsewhere, much as a ventriloquist's dummy or doll is made to speak vicariously. The real speaker's, the ventriloquist's voice, is thrown as if to issue from the passive doll, seemingly animating it. But the person who is the terrain of imperative inner speech, whether of love or hate or some other force, herself becomes the theatre for the performer and the puppet alike. The performer here is the arch-ventriloquist, language. Its apparently spoken puppet is that aspect of the inner voice marked by echo, repetition and dictation, the aspect which slips into the habitual broader streaming of words so that it would be impossible to distinguish exactly between such driven inner speech and something more 'spontaneous'.

Here, though, it's arguable that the more apparently spontaneous, the more compelled the voice. And it could well be claimed that ventriloquy inheres, anyway, in *any* uttered language use too. But for the moment, I'll restrict this term to an end of a continuum; and my supposition is that ventriloquy is not only a passing and banal companion to any inner voice, but is its incisive constituent. For inner speech is no limpid stream of consciousness, crystalline from its uncontaminated source in Mind, but a sludgy thing, thickened with reiterated quotation, choked with the rubble of the overheard, the strenuously sifted and hoarded, the periodically dusted down then crammed with slogans and jingles, with mutterings of remembered accusations, irrepressible puns, insistent spirits of ancient exchanges, monotonous citation, the embarrassing detritus of advertising, archaic injunctions from hymns, and the pastel snatches of old song lyrics. Here I want to propose a further twist: that as well as all this, some element of *autoventriloquy* also thrives in inner speech. By this lumpy neologism, I mean that anywhere in this densely chaotic onrush of the speech of the outside which courses through my inner speech in such common effects of ventriloquy, there may in addition occur *the effects of an autoventriloquy which disposes or arranges me to speak as if I myself were their source.*

What, though, are these effects and how do they operate? To put it in an unwieldy formula: *within inner speech, autoventriloquy is the name for how interpellation works by deploying a middle voice looped through a circuit of authority.*

To elucidate this, I'd characterise autoventriloquy's working as a special use of the middle voice, a form of the verb which is distinct from the usual active or passive voice. The linguist Antoine Meillet offered a memorably particular instance of this, as used to denote acting upon oneself or for one's own sake; he found a taut form which can only be translated, long-windedly, as 'I carry out a ritual act on my own behalf.' In his *Grammaire du Vieux-Perse*, Meillet discussed some verbs whose inflections or endings were so finely modulated that they distinguished between (what would be translated as) 'I perform a ritual act' (for someone else) and 'I perform a ritual for myself'.[40] So an Old Persian speaker could economically claim, through this appositely inflected voice, that he had managed a ceremony on his own behalf.

Here Meillet drops the matter. But there are repercussions which linger for our enquiry, since this use of the middle voice was more complex than any simple reflexivity like 'I pour myself a drink'. And the moment that he evokes, of a ritual sacrifice, is anyway a vicarious affair from the outset, because it is habitually done in my name by someone else who owns a vested power as my elevated representative. But in this example of my performing it, the act has run instead through the loop of *a self formally distanced from itself.* Instead of the priest, I seize hold of the sacrificial knife to make the prescribed cut on my own behalf. So while I do it myself, I am actually acting vicariously for the priest, whose own action would have been done for me. I still remain a stand-in. Although I physically make the direct gesture, I am nevertheless acting on my own behalf at one remove, in by-passing the priest's authority and imitating it in my person.

How does Meillet's esoteric example of this doing it ultimately for oneself, but through the circuit of authority of another, connect with my suggestion that anyone's inner speech may often incorporate a degree of autoventriloquy? It was Roland Barthes who, pursuing his own conviction about the verb 'to write' as having become a short-hand for an activity neither exactly active nor passive, resurrected Meillet's brief mention of this archaic grammar of priestly ritual.[41] But, leaving aside Barthes's ideas about authorship here, it does seem to me that the Old Persian scenario of pious bloodiness resembles an aspect of inner speech. For inner speech often embodies the characteristic not only of being vicarious from the onset (that is its ventriloquy) but of circling through a linguistic authority which does not reside in me. I, as an actively speaking agent, am also a stand-in for myself. (Interpellation's workings are hovering very close at hand.) For in my inward as well as in my uttered speech, I may well speak ritually, per-forming, as Meillet puts it, a linguistic *acte de culte* on my own behalf. I pick up a ready-fashioned verbal instrument of self-description, and, if confident that it will stand me in good stead, I abrogate its use to myself. All know how a word can become a cosh. A categorical word as a badge of my social group membership can readily be adapted, espe-cially piously, to bludgeon others. If I announce, 'We Celts know intu-itively that ...' or 'Speaking as a mother of three myself, I ...' then I've seized a tool from some stock in the vast storeroom of genealogical cliché, to wield it for myself. When I sign myself up for some appella-tion, or I militantly take up the right of redefinition for myself in asserting my new categorisation, I seem to wrest myself free of the old business of being defined from the outside by another; no longer will I will be spoken but I shall speak for myself, we shall speak ourselves. But my redefinition has deployed some new or more often some disin-terred characterology sanctified by recent fashion, to which I must look for definitional mastery in a circuit which has traced the old route of authoritative language. I stake my claim for myself by following my asserted distance from myself, or my self-alienation, into a collectivity from whence I triumphantly reclaim it as if it now declared my truth. But what *is* the old priest whose actual person I've made redundant, yet whose presence as the priesthood is still necessary for my vicarious action on my own behalf to exist intelligibly? The very syntax of my declarative utterance refers this question straight back to the existence of some Linguistic Enunciator. This is language, or the word.

The linguistic vignette in which I interpose myself to cut the throat of the goat on my own behalf has an unlikely cousinship to a classic 'blonde girl joke'. (As a platinum blonde myself, I can be allowed to recount this example of genre humour.) The blonde girl goes to see her doctor who informs her, to her surprise, that she's expecting a baby. She replies 'How do I know it's mine?'

To make heavy weather out of this joke, on the side of the girl: far from being the dumb blonde of the old hairist-sexist genre of humour, she has studied the vicarious nature of claims to possession all too faithfully, and her fidelity to the principles of indirection and substitution have led her to suppose that she must imitate passing through some diversion by dispossession in order to be able to make an 'authentic' assertion on her own behalf. So she repeats to her doctor what a man traditionally says to you when you tell him you are pregnant. She wants to have a maternity test. While the blonde could have claimed immediate bodily certainty of her future baby as hers (since the stealthy implantation of their embryos by would-be parents into young women while they sleep is a technique in its infancy) she knows that claims to possession tend to be systematically alienated from the start. She is quite right that often there's something impersonal and second-hand embedded in the most seemingly direct of utterances. So she plays safe by seizing the sacrificial knife of the clichéd paternal response 'How do I know it's mine?' This question is thoroughly disabling to have put to you; the blonde girl does brilliantly to grab back its aggression by performing this linguistic rite on her own behalf.

Many other weapons will be offered to the blonde girl for her to brandish, for instance a psychosocial nostrum of today: 'All men are emotionally damaged, and damaging'. Her darker experiences might lead her to assent to this generalisation. Yet if her optimism protested against its totalitarianism, she could not want to. To instead repeat it in scare quotes, and ironically, would at once weaken the nostrum's autoventriloquy by exposing it as functioning through that very mechanism. Having recourse to the irony stemming from repetition reveals that the speaker has grasped that autoventriloquy is at work. (But for its standard reading to work, the punch line of the blonde girl joke has to assume the failure of such irony.)

On the other hand, autoventriloquy enjoys its real triumph when I have so naturalised some description as my own that I'll repeat it to myself with contented conviction, and without meditating on where it originated. A categorical thought races over my mind, and will have its way in me unless I actively throw it out; there's merely a *reactive* will to deal with the unbidden linguistic arrival, to demur or to confirm it, to say yes, I will be that thing, will ascribe that opinion to myself, will take on that sentiment. This resembles the capacity to write, which in practice is far more of a capacity to *edit* than it is to originate, and is often a matter of working retrospectively with or often against the unchosen words that flash across the head. If authorship is more like editorship, then in a similar fashion, my identifications run through a loop in which I engage in a rite for myself, the discursive knife blade ready to hand as I borrow it from the impersonal priestly figure of categorical language. This vicarious stroke need not be any conscious act of triumph. On the contrary, I may eventually sense that I am on weak ground in imagining that I had originated this category which really pre-exists me; so I might well feel uneasy. Such an unease could be fatally soothed, and only temporarily assuaged, were I to join in the choruses of others voicing the same identification and associated plaints and resentments. By this stage, the movement by which I had got hold of the pre-fashioned linguistic instrument to wield in my own cause, *is* the acting of successful interpellation within my inner speech. It is not a matter of an imposition on me from without.

Such a piece of autoventriloquy – my repetition to myself of whatever authoritative positioning I have caught from the world, to 'make it mine' in a rite on my own behalf – is not to be understood as my inexplicable and lamentable submission to the Law. I do not abruptly capitulate, to sag into some black hole of the psychic (even if this is glossed as the Law of Language.) We could instead pursue a materially linguistic account of interpellation's reception by and within its targets, but without needing to fill in any gaps as to how it exploits the vulnerability of its hearers by invoking for our explanation a depth psychology of submissiveness, or abjection. Here again there is no opposition between the linguistic and the psychic. What I've called the autoventriloquy of the inner voice could be read as a description of the working of identification, a term which usually lodges in the vocabulary of psychoanalysis.

As for the prudent question of how our periodic *rejections* of interpellative claims can happen, it should not be forgotten that, after all, the ventriloquist is a comic entertainer and his dummy traditionally a cheekie chappie, whose function is to amuse the audience by pertly answering back to his master, making witticisms at his expense. Pursuing the logic of this metaphor of the staged 'resistance' of the ventriloquist's doll – who will soon be packed away, limp, in a box at the end of the show – would only avoid depositing us at a deeply pessimistic conclusion if we recall that, after all, our great ventriloquist is language. So the possibilities of our being able to answer back to the dictates of interpellation within our inner speech must entail having many more linguistic resources at our disposal. Or rather, to phrase it less optimistically, for someone to have been subjected to such a proliferation of interpellations, and from so many quarters, that these are bound to clash among themselves, giving rise to division and scepticism in their bearer. This is no vision of some solitary and glorious resistance by a discerning subject skirting her way through a minefield of words; but of that person's *over-determination* by so very many words that the determining cover of any single one of them gets blown. (Yet when a thicket of contrary interpellations assails your ears, not only enforced eloquence might ensue, but the dubious resources of linguistic brutality and curtness.)

A further question: but why in the first place *should* anyone ever seize the sacrificial knife; and isn't that a commendably anti-authoritarian attack on the priestly function? Sadly, the logic of this example must end up by depicting it as an ultimately conservative gesture, if with its radical moment, because the verbal weapon stays the same, if in different hands. The description ventured here of autoventriloquy's workings says nothing about any particular historical and political conjuncture. And one can experience interpellation from all ideological quarters, not merely from the conservative enemy, as in Althusser's account; the dictates of so-called identity politics may be equally interpellative and equally demanding of assent. So may the dictates of linguistic love. The margin between being recognised and being interpellated is apt to get perilously blurred.

What this suggestion about autoventriloquy as practical aspect of societal identification can support – a socialist philosophy of language – is itself a broad, if a better, pragmatic characterisation of language, and a negative critique. Any prospect of fleshing out how language operates 'within' people would need to elaborate further, somehow, on the working of inner speech. (Certainly this account of its element of interpellation recalls the ideas of linguistic possession and aphasia beloved by nineteenth-century philosophies of mind intrigued by speech disturbances.) The coinage of autoventriloquy may help to demonstrate how the word, 'the ideological phenomenon par excellence' as Volosinov says, lodges in and does its work in and through its speakers.[42] Yet nothing is uniform here, and a broad brush is unpersuasive. So the question lingers: how is it that people can speak and be spoken so very differently, even after all due allowance is made for educational and social divergences?

## 6   Style is Two Men Plus

Two men at least, that is; and usually many more – here the famous saw *'le style, c'est l'homme'* is far too unassuming. Style's arena is crowded. There's a recalcitrant enigma in how to account for the always wide differences among writing styles, especially if we rely on the model of linguistic importation of verbal material from the outside into the interior of the writing person.[43] How should we explain the often violent idiosyncrasies of what's sometimes, if unhelpfully, called the writer's 'voice' – for instance, Wittgenstein's renowned aphoristic style which often mutates into something else, a Socratic dialogue with himself where questions, elaborations, qualifications, hesitations checks and reassurances are intertwined in rapid succession, the whole thing done in a natural tone of quizzical meditation as if transcribed directly from a tape of his inner speech, so that the reader must follow eel-like twists of thought, glissades into self-interrogation, sharp veerings away, or the snapping of some particular thread. But wherever does such a graphic style emerge from? We'd have, at least according to the usual account, little choice but to suppose that the language of the outside sifts down onto the gaily diversified inside of each solitary head, there to receive its unique colouring and thence to reissue onto the page as a highly individual and finished style. What's unsatisfying about such a description is its adherence to that old standard division which has already given us pause, in which an individual and rich interiority is the refinement of a more lacklustre and uniform outside of language. And on this kind of supposition, the writerly style is what carries the stamp of authorial authenticity. Style is the autograph.

Faced with this seemingly inescapable model of common sense, Volosinov fires at the heart of it with his dialectical retort: a style is indeed founded in interiority but that very interiority is always already social. From the start, the privacy of my inner speech was already abuzz with loquacious inner auditors. I am overheard by an internalised listener, or by many. My constant companion in the shape of my inner speech becomes – to reduce Volosinov's account into the conventional psychological terms – my inner dialogue with an attentive superego, while my style is, in effect, both a response to and a compendium of all the voices I have met in my life:

> It is naive to suppose that one can assimilate as one's own an external speech that runs counter to one's inner speech, that is, runs counter to one's whole inner verbal manner of being aware of

oneself and the world ... A poet's style is engendered from the style of his inner speech, which does not lend itself to control, and his inner speech is itself the product of his entire social life. 'Style is the man', they say; but we might say: Style is at least two persons or, more accurately, one person plus his social group in the form of its authoritative representative, the listener – the constant participant in a person's inner and outward speech.[44]

Hence style is two men. But who these two or more interlocutors may be is not predictable. It would follow that there's a wild card in the style of anyone's inner speech, depending on the nature of their characteristic attentiveness towards the world (the aspect emphasised by Merleau-Ponty), but there's also the effect of their subjection to being overheard and to a concomitant guilt, prone to self-scrutiny (the aspect emphasised by Althusser). These facets of inner speech as the source of writing style do not, though, vie with each other for supremacy. Instead both hold a conception of the idiosyncrasy and the contingency of any social being (who is also any writing being). But this contingency is not in the least at odds with sociality. In his meditation on style, Volosinov's feat is to stay faithful to his conviction of the seamlessly social nature of the inner voice, while not thereby sacrificing its singularity, its remainder of distinctiveness. This he can manage only by slicing across the orthodox absolute contrast of inner and outer speech. These two states are indeed separable; as they must be, else a world thronged with psychotics or with automatons would result, depending on whether dictation from within, or from without, had won the day. But the states are separated by a membrane which is susceptible to the osmotic linguistic pressure of the outside, to the prose of the world.

The outer world, dense with signs, is soaked up inside the head already sign-stuffed. The inner psychic and the social-ideological are continuous; not identical, of course, but virtually inseparable: 'Therefore, *from the standpoint of content, there is no basic division between the psyche and ideology: the difference is one of degree only.*'[45] The sign trespasses all the boundaries of inner and outer, not respecting them, exuberantly indifferent to the unhelpfully contrastive epistemology which supposes that the psychic is completely cut off from the outer ideological. But the psyche is outside from the start:

Psychic experience is something inner that becomes outer and the ideological sign, something outer that becomes inner ... Between the psyche and ideology there exists, then, a continuous dialectical interplay: *the psyche effaces itself or is obliterated in the process of becoming ideology, and ideology effaces itself in the process of becoming the psyche.*[46]

So inner speech is evidence of the sociability of the language which also makes itself at home according to the local oddness of whatever interior it finds, but will be returned to the world. There is no mysterious transmission of ideology to brood over here, since for Volosinov the word is ideological from the start, operating through the generous medium of signs; while the innerness of the voice is experiential rather than theoretically absolute, since this very innerness of speech is merely a different site for the operations of ideology. The orthodox topography of inner and outer is dissolved again, and language floods in everywhere; yet the result is no morass.

To suppose that style lies beyond the dictates of the singular will doesn't necessarily commit us to eyeing it romantically. Here Barthes has a discussion of writing style which instead polemically emphasises its solitariness, its animality, its ahistorical and asocial life:

> Whatever its sophistication, style has always something crude about it; it is a form with no clear destination, the product of a thrust, not an intention, and as it were a vertical and lonely dimension of thought. Its frame of reference is biological or biographical, not historical: it is the writer's thing, his glory and his prison, it is his solitude.[47]

Unchosen, for Barthes it is an uncontrollable organic extrusion, almost triffidlike: 'It is the decorative voice of hidden, secret flesh; it works as does necessity, as if, in this kind of floral growth, style were no more than the outcome of a blind and stubborn metamorphosis starting from a sub-language elaborated where flesh and external reality come together.'[48] This understanding of style in its unfolding blindness accords it a helpless strangeness, and here Barthes has in mind André Gide's recourse to neoclassicism, as an instance of a writing which had decided to back off from the perils of the wilful: 'By reason of its biological origin, style resides outside art, that is, outside the pact which binds the writer to society. Authors may therefore be imagined who prefer the security of art to the loneliness of style.'[49]

This is literary style; or rather, it is one interpretation of what a writerly style is, and which emphasises its wilful outcropping. But the style of inner speech, while an affair of the linguistic unconscious, can also border on something outside the order of the tamed and be a kind of plotting, like a subcutaneous cunning. The interpenetration of the inner and outer sites of words, which is one of the determinants of a style, also includes an automatic constant assessing by their inward speakers. Fragments of a calculating reciprocity are embedded in the apparent spontaneity of inner speech, as Volosinov implies (and here some hint of our old friend, conscience as self-examination, is not so distant):

> The fact of the matter is that no conscious act of any degree or distinctiveness can do without inner speech, without words and intonations – without evaluations, and consequently, every conscious act is already a social act, an act of communication. Even the most intimate self-awareness is an attempt to translate oneself into the common code, to take stock of another's point of view, and, consequently, entails orientation towards a possible listener.[50]

## 7 The Seamless Stuff of Signs

Yet a less generous attention to inner speech's calculation might have noted how its secrecy permits lying, how it allows for the controlled deception of others while it congenitally risks a loss of control of itself, perhaps through compulsive echolalia or worse, through unstoppable persecutory voices. But Volosinov is never concerned with describing the spasmodic darkness of inner speech, rather he aims to settle and clarify its conceptual uses. In his hands the inner voice, far from being a tremulous evanescent thing or a mysterious phenomenon stemming from solitariness, turns out, startlingly, to found an entire theory of ideology as psychic organisation. It works like this: 'Wherever a sign is present, ideology is present, too. *Everything ideological possesses semiotic value.*'[51] This sign is wide in scope and is anchored firmly in the world.

> Every ideological sign is not only a reflection, a shadow, of reality, but is also itself a material segment of that very reality. Every phenomenon functioning as a sign has some kind of material embodiment, whether in sound, physical mass, colour, movements of the body, or the like ... Both the sign itself and all the effects it produces (all those actions, reactions, and new signs it elicits in the surrounding social milieu) occur in outer experience.[52]

Such broadly conceived signs will link themselves continuously to each other, as if in serpentine string theory:

> And this chain of ideological creativity and understanding, moving from sign to sign and then to a new sign, is perfectly consistent and continuous; from one link of a semiotic nature (hence also of a material nature) we proceed uninterruptedly to another link of exactly the same nature. And nowhere is there a break in the chain, nowhere does the chain plunge into inner being, non-material in nature and unembodied in signs.[53]

This ideological chain stretches from individual consciousness to individual consciousness, connecting them together. 'Signs emerge, after all, only in the process of interaction between one individual consciousness and another.'[54] That is, Volosinov's account admits of no gulf filled by a secretive inner expressivity flowing between and underneath these linked signs, since this very innerness would anyway be composed of exactly the same stuff, the always social material of signs.

We're close enough to William James's radical empiricism, his conviction that 'consciousness', if isolated, is a vacuous notion, when Volosinov insists, 'If we deprive consciousness of its semiotic, ideological content, it would have absolutely nothing left. Consciousness can only harbour in the image, the word, the meaningful gesture and so forth. Outside such material, there remains the sheer physiological act unilluminated by consciousness, i.e. without having light shed on it, without having meaning given to it, by signs.'[55] Prominent among the stuff without which consciousness would be vacancy is verbal matter. While spoken words hang between people, they result from buried labours whose working happens, with inner speech, to be at times invisible and thereby consigned to privacy: 'Although the reality of the word, as is true of any sign, resides between individuals, a word at the same time is produced by the individual organism's own means without recourse to any equipment or any other kind of extracorporeal equipment. This has determined the role of word as *the semiotic material of inner life – of consciousness* (inner speech).'[56] Volosinov's lucid polemic maintains that the rest of communication's work is effectively a matter of physiology; but then most physiology can itself be drawn into the wide realm of the sign. 'What, then, is the sign material of the psyche? Any organic activity or process: breathing, blood circulation, movements of the body, articulation, inner speech, mimetic motions, reactions to external stimuli (i.e. light stimuli) and so forth. In short, *anything and everything occurring within the organism can become the mate-rial of experience*, since everything can acquire semiotic significance, can become expressive.'[57]

Inner speech, then, is characteristically mobile and energetically transpersonal. Such a rendering of inwardness as simultaneously social doesn't, though, drive us out into a howling desert of language stripped of individual anchorage. My inner speech may appear to lie on the side of a systematic indifference because it doesn't habitually present itself to me, its listener, although on occasion it may. Yet usually it doesn't seek to address itself to anything. While it trickles like water or dashes along in a babble, this evident *im*personality of my most intimate incarnation, my inner speech, is nevertheless no icy thing to be claimed as evidence for a founding self-estrangement of the human. So I'd rather argue, next, for an innocent *ekstasis* of inner speech. This is really more of an *enstasis* or a standing inside of itself; but in any event, we need not consider it as an unhappy flaw.

## 8   Language as Blameless Ekstasis

Ekstasis, literally being 'out of place' or beside oneself, is the etymo-logical source, filtered through many layers, of the word ecstasy. Ecstasy's modern drift from its devotional and religious associations towards the secular sexual and the psychotropic is starkly displayed on the internet, where a search for the word 'ecstasy' will bring up a flurry of pornographic or of clubbing drug sites, but no saints. Yet despite this heavy sexualisation of the word, ecstasy is still consid-ered a private state. The condition of being in *ekstasis*, or outside yourself, isn't usually read through the consoling dialectic of being inside anyone else instead.

There's been a different ambiguity about ekstasis as a philosophical characterisation of being; is it actually and necessarily realistic to understand yourself as congenitally standing apart from yourself? But against this admission of ekstasis, Michel Henry, a recent philosopher of the immediacy of a self to itself, emphasises the importance of what he calls self-presence. He finds a malevolent redundancy in some modern attitudes to the self:

The intuition buried at the heart of Freudianism, according to which all life is unhappiness, is torn from its contingency when it is referred to its ultimate phenomenological presuppositions – that the inside of the world, the unconscious as such, is separated from reality and thus becomes desire, endless desire. Beyond Nietzsche, Freud once again rejoins Schopenhauer.[58]

Henry implies that our post-Marxist conceptions of an inevitably alienated labour, and the separations of the self from itself in psychoanalytic thought, are cousins, two versions of ekstasis which both derive from a nineteenth-century 'nature philosophy'. The resulting theoretical splitting of the self, and the enthroning of a systematic self-estrangement, enshrine a gratuitous melancholia and fearfulness. And the question of how my own inner speech may periodically seem to confront me, almost to stand against me, would indeed come close to this anxious ekstasis, as Henry senses it. Inward being becomes, but quite falsely, perilous. As he puts it:

> In a proposition ripe with future Freudianism, Nietzsche speaks of the 'dangerousness with which the individual lives with himself.' Thus there is no question of an adventitious danger, not even of a menace bound to that person's history. The danger is the person himself, his interiority. It is the structure of absolute subjectivity insofar as that subjectivity is inexorably thrown into itself to experience what it experiences and to be what it is. The greatest danger is life.[59]

There is a traceable genealogy to this dire conception of the soul as a grave mystery to itself, a conception stemming, for Henry, from a long series of misunderstandings of Descartes.

As the very topography of the sensate self as a whole possesses its history, so does the topography of the speaking and the contemplative self; so here Henry views Nicolas Malebranche as an unfortunate captive of the notion of estrangement once, for him, the soul had become delivered over to night. It is true that our ideas of what comprises the interiority and the exteriority of the person are conspicuously historically mutable. If Descartes's persuasiveness indeed effectively displaced the seat of the passions away from the heart and towards the soul, then that shift from a pulsating fleshly inner towards an ethereal spiritual inner redrew the whole notion of the inside and thereby strongly revised that of the outside.[60] Indeed Malebranche's scepticism went further again, asking in effect, what *was* this externality, anyway? For he offered a seductive twist on his contemporaries' question about how we could be truly confident that souls exist, when he declared that it is surely only faith which could persuade us that there really are bodies.[61]

Today's imperative injunctions to self-knowledge, too, continue to reiterate the self as its own fascinating riddle. We have become phenomena to ourselves, in such a way that we're constantly invited to discover our truth through the foregone revelations of new categories of social being, new pedigrees and affiliations. The gamut of twentieth-century suppositions about our necessary alienation includes that of our self-estrangement within language. If we tacitly agree to conceive of ourselves, in a deathly manner, as standing outside ourselves, we may all too readily harness an idea of the necessary opacity of language to that very end. Do we need, though, to accept this conviction that we stand outside ourselves in a way that confirms language as a snare, confirms self-knowing as achieved through introspection, and self-reassembling by the light of retrieved memories? Against all such thinking, against any haunted and hermeneutic depths, Henry is emphatic that there's a fatal collusion between a depressive ekstasis and the memory of self which tacks together its own little shreds: 'Thus every thinking that confines Being to the gathering of memory is prey to contradiction. Memory joins with the juxtaposed and the dispersed through a sort of pre-established harmony. It is an "I think" that accompanies all our representations, that drags them one after another from the virtuality that is nothing, the unconscious, to confer being on them in phenomenological actuality.'[62] It follows that memory cannot do the critical work so regularly entrusted to it: 'To confide to memory the reassembly of our being, of all the morsels of ourselves scattered throughout the absurd exteriority of *ekstasis,* of all those so-called traumatic events that mark the course of our existence, to restitch infinitely the infinitely broken thread of all those little stories, is to forget the reassembly is always accomplished.'[63]

Like some earlier philosophers of mind, Henry insists that consciousness is always self-sensing, self-feeling, self-aware. A self *is* its affects. This is a thesis of immediacy. There is no unconscious affect, Henry argues – and in Freud himself there is this statement too. But here I'd want to add that language is itself an affect. Merleau-Ponty's conviction that we are outside from the start implies that we live in an ekstasis which should not be considered as alienated; far from trailing mournful veils, it shines with immediacy. Consonant with this approach, a conception of the affect of language can be used to reconsider ekstasis, but in a way now far removed from any creepily melancholic rendering of the self as a phenomenon to itself. To counter Henry's position, I'd suggest that there is one non-pathological, quite ordinary kind of ekstasis. And that is language.

Language's affect is immediate; overhearing ourselves, our awareness of our inner speech, is usually a harmless enough sensation, and congruent with what Henry describes as a self sensing itself, or original affectivity. Such an ekstasis arouses no second order brooding upon its excitable inhumanity. For language, as a non-alienated kind of self-distance, is a plain feature of being alive and hearing oneself. We need neither become bewitched by our capacity to study our own inner speech, nor settle into a stance of dispossessed melancholia over it. In practice we move through an endemic linguistic ekstasis without any miserable separation. Such 'alienation' as there is is just constitutive, a matter of mild interest rather than any cause for elegant despair. Here we end up, too, with some comical reversion: if ekstasis is intrinsic to inner speech, what is most 'inner' is actually outer. But this kind of reversal can be understood matter-of-factly and undramatically, whereas the popularised Lacanian renditions of 'lack' tend always to carry an air of ontological tragedy, as if psychological realism were forced into a solemn acceptance of a grievous shortage inherent in simply being alive.

Indeed, in other critical traditions, the fact of internal division actually furnishes the self with itself as its own companion in solitude, and is the precondition for reasoning. Hannah Arendt's striking elaboration of this argues that, if thinking consist of the dialogue of the two-in-one, when such a necessary inward flow of conversation is interrupted, an unhappy unity can be imposed on the thinker:

> Then, when he is called by his name back into the world of appearances, where he is always One, it is as though the two into which the thinking process had split him clapped him together again. Thinking, existentially speaking, is a solitary but not a lonely business; solitude is that human situation in which I keep myself company. Loneliness comes about when I am alone without being able to split up into the two-in-one, without being able to keep myself company, when, as Jaspers used to say, 'I am in default of myself' [*ich bleib mir aus*], or to put it differently, when I am one and without company.[64]

This silent dialogue with yourself, this self-scrutiny, lies on the side of the good, because it works against your risks of slipping into dissociation or incoherence, inclining you instead to live in critical harmony with yourself: 'Conscience is the anticipation of the fellow who awaits you if and when you come home.'[65]

The pertinence of all this to our topic of inner speech is this: if critiques, like Michel Henry's, of unhelpful and pessimistic ekstasis also swallow up all possibility for any useful ekstasis to exist, then too much is lost. For arguably there is in language a necessary impersonality – or if you like, an alienation, but only if that word is taken in a less dispirited manner. Then whether I imagine that though this impersonality the world drags me over towards it and out of myself, or whether I feel I apprehend the world through an exuberant spilling-over of myself, seems not to matter greatly for the outcome: a bearable ekstasis. But if once language, too, is supposed by the principled foes of ekstasis to incarnate self-distance as sheer threat – if, to avoid a debased post-Saussureanism as a mechanically cold and clanking sign system, words are instead treated as some reduction of the fuller possibilities of soul – then antagonism to post-structuralism has indeed won the day, although at the cost of great travesty. And then, too, any renewed interest in the phenomenon of inner speech would find that, after all, it had merely relearned some old and discouraging truisms about the opposition between words and feeling.

## 9   Ins and Outs

Still, there's quite another approach to considering the possibility of language, not as an unhealthy, but as an amiable ekstasis; which is to interrogate the usual topology here. How truly *inner* is our inner speech? From a neurological point of view, there's no uncertainty. Nor is there for the particular philosophical psychologies already mentioned, where confusion about the meaning of its innerness only arises if we suppose that the experienced inwardness of the voice in the head guarantees it an origin as a thought preceding words, in an inviolable secrecy. Yet what is hidden is not at all synonymous with what is innermost; and anyway, the innermost is not itself necessarily concealed. The very display of articulation can perfectly do the work of hiding.

Inner speech in its secretive commentary supplies us with endless opportunities for obscurantism. In this, it's the negation, oddly enough, of its other facet, conscience's still small voice. Is it partly our recognition that we can lie and dissimulate that sharpens our conviction about the deeply *hidden* nature of our inner speech? Yet to be a bad liar means that I am someone readily detected in untruths by my observed actions, my gestures, my blushing, my stammering – that is, not only by the implausible content of my lies. If I cannot carry off my own dissimulation, my failure is often due simply to my inept bodily behaviour. What I utter will lack conviction for others – not because they have no access to my inner meaning, but because of my own gestural shortcomings which show that I've failed to smoothly present some lie.

On such grounds, Wittgenstein set out his objections to a hermeneutics of mental processes. What is obscure should not be equated with what is internal: 'If I were to talk to myself out loud in a language not understood by those present, my thoughts would be hidden from them.'[66] The obverse of outwardness is not secretive concealment in an interior location. 'Silent "inner" speech is not a half hidden phenomenon which is as it were seen through a veil. It is not hidden *at all*, but the concept may easily confuse us, for it runs over a long stretch cheek by jowl with the concept of an "outward" process, and yet doesn't coincide with it.'[67] We can readily observe both feeling and the evidence of thinking in others. If inner processes have a literal invisibility, that still doesn't mean that they pose an unassailable mystery to us. There are signs and indications which demand no skilled translation or guesswork in order to be plainly intelligible. As Wittgenstein puts it: ' "What is internal is hidden from us." – The future is hidden from us. But does the astronomer think like this when he calculates an eclipse of the sun? If I see someone writhing in pain with evident cause I do not think: all the same, his feelings are hidden from me.'[68] It is because the machinations of inner speech are often displayed on it that we are able to read a face.[69] Even a state of scepticism possesses a legible physiognomy, and philosophical doubt has its bodily expressiveness, as do cynicism, fear and reserve. Then, I think, all this emphasis from Wittgenstein on the perfect intelligibility of gestures or facial expressions (which, to be understood, do not need to be retrieved by guesswork from some inaccessible innerness) coheres perfectly well with Volosinov's weighting on the sociable nature of the language of the outside. Both philosophers of language concur that to be able to understand something in someone else, we do not first have to read entrails.

In fact, if we turn from the debatable inscrutability of inner speech to inner musicality instead, then all this supposition of concealment drops away, and questions about the nature of inaudible singing are merely neural. As Baldwin commented on the relative scarcity of studies of musical deficiencies, as opposed to those in speech, 'The question of "internal song" is a newer one. What do we mean when we say that a "tune is running in our head"? What sort of images are really in consciousness then ?'[70] He decided that the matter could be resolved neurologically: 'Evidence goes to show that the internal tune is almost entirely auditory: that is, that the auditory centre is intrinsic to musical reproduction. It is probable, accordingly, that there is a brain-centre for tune memories' – something by no means uniform in its gifts since, while most people could mentally carry a tune they know, few owned 'the power of reproducing a note of any desired pitch absolutely from memory'.[71] In short, this question of inner musical pathologies was blessedly clear of the conceptual torments which had so haunted the cases of inner verbal pathologies, the aphasias. Then the difference was nothing to do with their innerness as such.

Yet concealment is anyway not a permanent feature of the concept of inner speech, one peculiarity of which is its mobility. Considered intuitively to be buried, indwelling, from other perspectives it can be volatile and expansive in its location, spilling from its containment as freely as any articulated sound. There is nothing fixedly *inner* about our inner speech; for the idea of its innerness, if pushed further, soon melts down the supposition that we live as an inner and outer speaking body whose division runs cleanly along a line. We could even say here that what, for its speakers, distinguishes outer speech is its reverberation and our efforts in projecting it, small movements of throat and lips. My inner or outer speech is not usually differentiated for me, its issuer, by whether it is sited inside or outside my head, but rather by the kind of its utterance, and its purposes. And this is another matter altogether from interiority versus exteriority.

To assert the frequent *outerness* of the intimate innerness of speech can seem a violent thought, even an inhumane violation of that inner voice which suggests privacy, profundity and the truth of conscience. Yet the trouble here is that it is the unspoken which is taken to protect the secret. As mentioned above, one of Wittgenstein's recurring arguments against this supposition is that the bodily manifestations of 'inner' states are *not* the explanatory companions, or the translations of, some feeling which is hidden from us and which we deduce only with difficulty. A similar immediacy can obtain with words, in that they are not, as is often supposed, the companions or the interpreters of otherwise concealed feeling. It's not that I'd claim there's always a transparency in language – rather, that its assumed *non*-transparency is misconceived. Its opacity tends to be assigned askew; credited to some inherent treachery, seduction or veiling. To pursue this train of thought, it's conceivable that the unconscious is better imagined not as a deep pouch of the self, but as something outside of it, and hanging between people.[72] This speculation alters the usual topographical metaphors we rely on. To reflect on the idea of inner speech will soon throw into crisis all the standard conceptions of inside and outside in their symmetry, and will result instead in an image of inner speech periodically turned, like the celebrated Moebius strip, inside out. But in any event, we can readily sense, without any dramatic topographical straining, that outer and inner speech do not run in parallel. Nor are they opposites, as we might at first glance assume. That there are strong differences between them doesn't mean that these differences must own the symmetries of a thoroughgoing opposition. To query the parallelism of inner and outer, we aren't forced to adopt a polemical preference for the surface, like this: 'Everything that happens and everything that is said happens or is said at the surface. The surface is *no less explorable and unknown* than depth and height which are non-sense ... The philosopher is no longer the being of the caves, not Plato's soul or bird, but rather the animal which is on a level with the surface – a tick or louse.'[73] Instead of shrinking to Deleuze's louse, engaging though that prospect is, it's quite enough to follow upright along the venerable nineteenth-century path of gentlemanly introspection and to reach an equally tangible collapse of the spatial certainties through asking, where in us do we feel that our inner speech *happens*? (And this isn't an enquiry about, for instance, what modern neurological imaging can reveal about hot areas of brain activity.) William James, a man always in ardent pursuit of the officially intangible, wrote emphatically about something far more ineffable than the inner voice, the nature of self-consciousness itself: 'in one person at least, the "Self of selves" when carefully examined, is found to consist mainly of the collection of these peculiar motions in the head or between the head and throat.'[74] If I try to follow James in pinning my inward voice down by isolating the spot where it lives, this is impossibly difficult; it is not quite 'somewhere in my head' and not at all in my mouth. But maybe it is whirring somewhere vaguely behind my eyes, the only location which offers itself, perhaps because, in trying to concentrate hard on the site of the voice, I inevitably close my eyes. There seems to be no precise spot in which this inner speech unwinds itself. The task is made worse because my entire impression of my interiority has no discernible margin, is not bounded by some clear edge at which I can sense the skin on my face giving way to the air. Often only a fog of something somewhere behind my forehead comprises my innerness, and then only if I tug this nebulous thing forward into my focus. Nevertheless even this indeterminacy keeps its own limits, and the skin of my ankle doesn't ever seriously propose itself as the roof of the dwelling place of my inner self.

Other and more literary topographies of language don't so much rearrange the territories to redistribute outer and inner, as cut out the inner. In Michel Foucault's bleakly lyrical depiction of the 'language of the past in the act of hollowing itself out', there is a vertigo of the void.[75] As it was for Blanchot 'They [words] do not speak, they are not inside; on the contrary, they lack all intimacy and lie entirely outside.'[76] This language is a splendidly inhuman thing in its rustling, 'the always undone form of the outside'.[77] Its invocation also lies close to a literary affection which has grown into something more impassioned, an allegiance whose origins may lie in the history of Foucault's aesthetic rather than political loyalties: 'Not reflection, but forgetting; not contradiction but a contestation that effaces; not reconciliation, but droning on and on; not mind in laborious conquest of its unity, but the endless erosion of the outside; not truth finally shedding light on itself, but the streaming and distress of a language that has always already begun.'[78] There is an intense love here for Blanchot's whiteness. And Foucault links the rising of an idea of language as a thing in itself to the decline of particular persuasions about the human: 'We are standing on the edge of an abyss that had long been invisible: the being of language only appears for itself with the disappearance of the subject.'[79] This 'subject' is, though, a very different kind of philosophical entity from the speaker or the listener to inner speech. This speaking listener is certainly stripped of authority and is de-dramatised by the ambiguous topography of her inner speech. But she is also both a condition of and a witness for the enacted materiality and historicity of language, rather than, like Foucault's fading subject, being in herself a disappearing act.

In fact, to dwell on the inner voice alerts us to the persistent tangibility of what, at first sight, would seem quintessentially evanescent. Meditating on inner speech, far from drifting towards verbal ectoplasm, throws us hard back on the materiality of words, including the aural quality of the *sotto voce*. Despite the Siren call that some philosophical writers have felt towards the whiteness of the beyond of language, one great teller of talking to oneself clings stoutly on to the this-sidedness of inward speech: 'It's not true, yes, it's true, it's true and it's not true, there is silence and there is not silence, there is more and there is someone, nothing prevents anything. And were the voice to cease quite at last, the old ceasing voice, it would not be true, as it is not true that it speaks, it can't speak, it can't cease.'[80] Samuel Beckett, surely the arch inscriber of inner speech on the page, is not remotely headed towards the lure of silence, or the impersonal streaming of language as the vanishing point of the speaker. His work keeps steadfast to the stubborn presence of language in its utterer, in all its monotony and attrition; and 'not by a burgeoning silence or aporia, but through a quiet dedication to itself'.[81] The voice without a mouth still stirs in the head.

## 10   Topographical Metaphor and Embodied Mind

'Semen, excreta, and words are communicative products.'[82] George Steiner might have added that menstrual blood, in its presence or its absence, is also dramatically informative. Words can, famously, also be ejections, hard pellets or other emissions. Not only in the celebrated instance of logorrhoea can speech resemble a bodily fluid. Or as Malebranche remarked of the fruits of the act of generation, 'They are the children of their parent's speech as much as of their flesh.'[83]

But while such vivid analogies of words with bodies are common enough (or analogies of money with the circulation of blood, as Marx wrote of capital) the question of some inbuilt bodily perspective inhering in duller spatial metaphor is more vexing. If the lived topography of inner speech arguably throws the inner versus outer distinction into uncertainty, some recent linguists and philosophers of metaphor have been far more captivated by the apparently stolid basis of figurative language in the body. Our physiological experience of boundedness, of being situated in the world, guarantees a rock-solid basis to our least exciting metaphors. Or rather, it does in some particular well-established quarters of conviction about language where, if we were to adopt this almost Kantian line dear to some linguists, we'd discover apparently universal schema being played out through the most ordinary spatial metaphor, so forming a radical linguistic organisation of perception. In this vein, Elizabeth Closs Traugott explains how some conventionally 'dead' metaphors of direction are actually 'linked to the superordinate cognitive organisation that concretizes and spatialises relations in terms of source, goal, path', so we will say, for example, that we convey, we get across, or we channel an argument.[84] Such fundamental spatial arrangements are what the linguists George Lakoff and Mark Johnson call orientational metaphors. They argue that the concepts through which we frame our whole understanding of the world arise from a human embodied point of view. In this respect, they suddenly recall I. A. Richards's formulation about metaphor, published in 1936: 'Our world is a projected world, shot through with characters lent to it from our own life.'[85] Mark Johnson renders this kind of intuition formulaic: 'The *inner–outer* pattern also supports the imposition of a *subject–object* orientation, in which our subjectivity is defined in terms of that which is inmost or central to our conscious being.'[86] This, he writes, relates to the self–other distinction as well. Such a claim at once and neatly solves the riddle of why we use so very many metaphors of depth and surface, of interiority and externality: it's because they stem from our grounding of perception in our own bodies, and pave our way in the world. And this concept of orientational metaphor could immediately explain, too, why our inner speech is indeed perceived as 'inner'.

Is that enough to make any question of inner speech's topology redundant, though? No. Even if we accept the initially persuasive thesis that many conceptual metaphors do have perspectival foundations drawn from the body's outlook, this can't guarantee a theory confidently founded in the flesh *tout court*. For any topography of the body also has its own history, as do the facts of its very isolation and its hypostatising. Certainly our impressions of our own interiority can seem to back the authority of a founding spatiality in thought, and our spoken words can feel as if they rise upward to our lips. Yet it's also a changeable schema; our ideas of the disposition of bodies in space are not timeless. So we could expect to find metaphors of the body which are, though not labile, nevertheless malleable and apt to be transformed over long periods. In this vein, we need only glance at the heart considered as the seat of the passions. Here one historian of the heart in thought, Milad Doueihi, has proposed that 'the heart rests at the intersection of the figurative and the literal, of the body and its passions, of food and speech.'[87] This intersection, though, is no constant. If one can indeed to this day be said to nurse secrets in one's heart, this assignation of mysteries to the heart is founded on a metaphor inside which very old understandings of the passions have mummified. While this observation would hardly confound the linguist philosophers of bodily metaphor, it does serve to modify as it historicises the conception of the body.

Even thoroughly modern metaphor need not be founded on some immutable physiological base, of course. For all the soberly realistic bodily metaphors to be found, many others can be adduced which are much less of derivations from bodies installed in the world, and more of enactments of a non-literal depiction. Or even of a surrealist visualisation of the body, such as 'I got there by the skin of my teeth.' But this isn't to claim that metaphor ought to be illustrative, or should be expected to be 'rational'. To do so would fly in the face of metaphor's nature. Nonetheless, body-based metaphors cannot always be taken as guarantors of the body-in-the-mind linguists' thesis about the physiological nature of language, since often they are by no means naturalistic. Some of the more floridly or spectacularly metaphorical language of the body turns out, on examination, to be counter-intuitive. 'On the tip of my tongue' is a decidedly strange metaphor for the business of almost retrieving a word; the fact that as an expression it 'feels right' surely has far more to do with its comfortable familiarity than with any oral sensation. Examine the tip of your tongue by holding it against your teeth and the roof of your mouth, and not only will you not find any barnacle clumps of all the lost words you never managed to find still stuck there, but that zone of the mouth itself is not even redolent of the possibility; it is stubbornly silent, awaiting quite other than verbal sensations. So 'on the tip of my tongue' isn't the place where introspection could really lead us to imagine that our mislaid word awaits us, or where our delayed utterance of this lost word trembles, poised for its articulation. No, if anything, the experience of looking for a word and then suddenly having it pop into the mind is more like a faint synaptic click, or a flick in the brain, as if some compartment of verbal memory had suddenly snapped open. Here we are plunged into different metaphorical sets. There is an account, for instance, by Steiner of searching for the mislaid word, and which he has couched in an electrician's metaphor: 'Introspectively, one draws pictures. Thus one describes oneself as "looking for" a word. Whenever it is baffled or momentarily vacuous, the search, the act of scanning, suggest circuitry. The relevant sensation, or, more cogently, the vulgarized images we make up of what are subliminal processes, leave one with a compelling notion of nervous probes "trying this or that connection", recoiling where the wire is blocked or broken and seeking alternate channels until the right contact is made.'[88] Earlier, William James's treatment of what absorbed him, here the experience of blindly seeking for a lost word, concentrated on elaborating his own sense of locating a slot:

> Suppose we try to recall a forgotten name. The state of our consciousness is peculiar. There is a gap therein; but no mere gap. It is a gap that is intensely active. A sort of wraith of the name is in it, beckoning us in a given direction, making us at moments tingle with the sense of our closeness, and then letting us sink back without the longed-for term. If wrong names are proposed to us, this singularly definite gap acts immediately so as to negate them.

They do not fit into its mould. And the gap of one word does not feel like the gap of another, all empty of content as both might seem necessarily to be when described as gaps. When I vainly try to recall the name of Spalding, my consciousness is far removed from what it is when I vainly try to recall the name of Bowles.[89]

The final piece of this description does seem open to question – still, as James continues persuasively, we just don't possess a refined enough diction for describing these finely-graded shades of difference. This terminological lack, though, is in itself no bar:

But namelessness is compatible with existence. There are innumerable consciousnesses of emptiness, no one of which taken in itself has a name, but all different from each other. The ordinary way is to assume that they are all emptinesses of consciousness, and so the same state. But the feeling of an absence is *toto coelo* other than the absence of a feeling. It is an intense feeling. The rhythm of a lost word may be there without a sound to clothe it; or the evanescent sense of something which is the initial vowel or consonant may mock us fitfully, without growing more distinct. Every one must know the tantalizing effect of the blank rhythm of some forgotten verse, relentlessly dancing in one's mind, striving to be filled out with words.[90]

In short, these commentaries all agree that the sensation of trying to locate a word has nothing really to do with the tongue, a fleshy sensuous organ laden with its taste buds and tactility. Then 'on the tip of my tongue' must have more to do with the history of metaphors of orality, than with any bodily based mirroring of oral sensation itself. Or as Wittgenstein argued, we're dealing with a convention of verbal behaviour rather than with a faithful account of introspection:

'The word is on the tip of my tongue'. What is going on in my consciousness? That is not the point at all. Whatever did go on was not what was meant by that expression. It is of more interest what went on in my behaviour. – 'The word is on the tip of my tongue' tells you: the word which belongs here has escaped me, but I hope to find it soon. For the rest the verbal expression does no more than certain wordless behaviour.[91]

James's earlier explorations of this territory had led him to conclude that there was an orientation of thought in speech: 'The truth is that large tracts of human speech are nothing but *signs of direction* in thought, of which direction we nevertheless have an acutely discriminative sense, though no definite sensorial image plays any part in it whatsoever.'[92] But does this observation in fact support the convictions of those linguists who are certain of the bodily basis of metaphor? For James's directedness is an orientation which does not clearly rely on the body. Here his reader Wittgenstein acknowledges the intuitive physical locating of a feeling of resolve: ' "In my heart I have determined on it." And one is even inclined to point to one's breast as one says it. Psychologically this way of speaking should be taken seriously. Why should it be taken less seriously than the assertion that belief is a state of mind? (Luther: "Faith is under the left nipple.")'[93] And Luther's nipple well illustrates this will to fix states of mind on the body. That is, there is more of a psychology of bodily metaphor, rather than an anchorage of metaphor in realism. Take the instance of the heart, an ancient metaphorical source. The heart lies much more centrally in the chest cavity than was traditionally realised; so, if we were to lead it in the direction of politics, we'd have to conclude that the modern electoral heart is actually less left-leaning and more social-democratic or centrist than communist in its inclinations (if the heart of Trotskyism might crouch under the left armpit). Contrary to the malleable naturalism just implied, 'by the skin of my teeth' is a picturesquely unnatural phrase. Again I don't mean that a successful metaphor should carry some literal application. What's striking about such expressions is not the fact that they hardly mirror the sensations of looking for a word, or of having a near escape, but that as clichéd metaphors they flourish so vigorously, despite their lack of anatomical basis. So the body itself is by no means the final court of appeal and explanation for the survival of apparently physiological metaphors; physical analogies are as often wild as they are prudently naturalistic, and to appeal to the foundational good sense of bodily metaphor can instead hurl us into absurdity. No new absurdity, this, though: in 1833 Thomas Carlyle savaged the concept of a fundamental bodily metaphor for style in his *Sartor Resartus*, a satirical if laboured exposition of an imagined German pedant's Philosophy of Clothes: 'Language is called the Garment of Thought: however, it should rather be, Language is the Flesh-Garment, the Body, of Thought.'[94] Except for 'some few primitive elements (of natural sound) ' continues Professor Teufelsdrockh, metaphor itself forms the muscles and tissues of language: 'An unmetaphorical style you shall in vain seek for: is not your very *Attention* a *Stretching-To*? The difference lies here: some styles are lean, adust, wiry, the muscle itself seems osseous; some are even quite pallid, hunger-bitten and dead-looking; while others glow in the flush of health and vigorous self-growth, some times [as in my own case] not without an apoplectic tendency.'[95]

All this speculation about ontological metaphor, so sardonically treated by Carlyle and dear to some poetics of today, impinges on the case of inner speech, where again the idea that our bodily situatedness proves the natural foundation of spatial metaphor only takes us so far. Rather, the non-symmetrical nature of our interiority and exteriority is something which actually *emerges through* the contemplated experience of inner speech. Doing so, it rebuts the belief that these rhetorical figures of inwardness and outerness are symmetrical oppositions which are soundly experiential, and bodily derived. This complication of what's really inner about inner speech has, I think, quite other resonances. Because I am also spoken from elsewhere, as authorship is arguably plagiarism, and speech is ventriloquy, so inner speech can be the site of autoventriloquy too. In its hope of starting to show how interpellative language might work in us, the sketch attempted here of the inner voice has inevitably bled into a characterisation of the outer voice too. So we have seen how Volosinov's meditation on inner speech pulled everything inside; and yet in the same blow, he made the interior of the head thoroughly washed through by the voices of outside, and turned back, inside-out like a glove. If the psyche is largely made by the raw word, the word is also social, public. But my very linguistic dispossession is also my securely innermost possession. I lose nothing in conceptually 'going public' through subscribing to the inner voice's societal nature – because that sociality is where, in all its idiosyncrasy and particularity, my linguistic self is founded and is to be found.

# 2
# Bad Words

## 1 Introduction

The worst words revivify themselves within us, vampirically. Injurious speech echoes relentlessly, years after the occasion of its utterance, in the mind of the one at whom it was aimed: the bad word, splinter-like, pierces to lodge. In its violently emotional materiality, the word is indeed made flesh and dwells amongst us – often long outstaying its welcome. Old word-scars embody a 'knowing it by heart', as if phrases had been hurled like darts into that thickly pulsating organ. But their resonances are not amorous. Where amnesia would help us, we cannot forget.

This sonorous and indwelling aspect of vindictive words might help to characterise how, say, racist speech works on and in its targets. But wouldn't such a speculation risk simply advocating a systematic cultivation of deafness on the part of those liable to get hurt – or worse, be a criticism of their linguistic vulnerability: 'They just shouldn't be so linguistically sensitive'? There is much to be said, certainly, in favour of studiously practising indifference. But the old playground chant of 'sticks and stones may break my bones, but words can never hurt me' was always notoriously untrue. The success of a tactics of indifference to harsh speech will also depend on the vicissitudes of those words' fate in the world, and that lies beyond my control. I change too. The thing upon which malevolent accusation falls, I am still malleable, while the words themselves will undergo their own alterations in time, and so their import for me will weaken or intensify accordingly. On occasion the impact of violent speech may even be recuperable through its own incantation; the repetition of abusive language may be occasionally saved through the irony of iteration, which may drain the venom out of the original insult, and neutralise it by displaying its idiocy.[1] Yet angry interpellation's very failure to always work as intended (since at particular historical moments, I may be able to parody, to weaken by adopting, to corrode its aim) is also exactly what, at other times, works for it. In any event, interpellation operates with a deep indifference as to where the side of the good may lie. And we cannot realistically build an optimistic theory of the eventual recuperability of linguistic harm. For here there is no guaranteed rational progress – nor, though, any inescapable irrationality. Repetition will breed its own confident mishearing,[2] but its volatile alterations lean neither towards automatic amelioration nor inevitable worsening.

This observation, though, leaves us with the still largely uninvestigated forensics of spoken injury. Pragmatic studies of swearing certainly exist, but swear words as such are not the topic I have in mind. Nor is 'righteous' anger. My preoccupation here is far darker, and restricted to the extreme: some sustained hostility of unremitting verbal violence, like the linguistic voodoo which can induce the fading away of its target, a phenomenon which cannot be dismissed as an archaism. The curse does work. Verbal attacks, in the moment they happen, resemble stoning. Then is it not too laboured to ask how they do damage: isn't the answer plain, that they hurt just as stones hurt? At the instant of their impact, so they do. Yet the peculiarity of violent words, as distinct from lumps of rock, is their power to resonate within their target for decades after the occasion on which they were weapons. Perhaps an urge to privacy about being so maliciously named may perpetuate the words' remorseless afterlife: I keep what I was told I was to myself, out of reserve, shame, a wish not to seem mawkish and other not too creditable reasons; yet even if I manage to relinquish my fatal stance of nursing my injury, it may well refuse to let go of me. Why, though, should even the most irrational of verbal onslaughts lodge in us as if it were the voice of justice; and why should it stubbornly resist ejection, and defy its own fading? For an accusation to inhere, must its human target already be burdened with her own pre-history of vulnerability, her psychic susceptibility; must it even depend on her anticipating readiness to accept, even embrace, the accusation that also horrifies her? Maybe, then, there is some fatal attraction from the aggression uttered in the present towards earlier established reverberations within us – so that to grasp its lure, we would have to leave a linguistic account to turn instead to a pre-linguistic psychic account. Yet here the standard contrast between the linguistic and the psychic, in which we are usually forced to plump for either the unconscious or language, is especially unhelpful. There is nothing beyond interpellation, if by that 'beyond' is meant a plunge into an ether of the psyche as soon as we topple off the ledge of the historical and linguistic. For refusing these thoroughly synthetic alternatives need not commit us to a belief in an instantaneous, ahistorical impact of the bad word – or to assume some primal word of injury which laid us open subsequently to verbal assault, as if the chronology of harm must always unfold in a straight line of descent.

The impact of violence in the present may indeed revive far older associations in its target. An accusation will always fall on to some kind of linguistic soil, be it fertile or poor; and here a well-prepared loam is no doubt commoner than a thin veneer on bare rock. Should we, though, necessarily call such a variation in anger's reception its 'psychic' dimension, in a tone which implies a clear separation from the domain of words? There has, undoubtedly, to be something very strong at work to explain why we cannot readily shake off some outworn verbal injury. The nature of this strong thing, though, might better be envisaged as a seepage or bleeding between the usual categorisations; it need not be allocated wholesale to an unconscious considered as lying beyond the verbal, or else to a sphere of language considered as narrowly functional.[3] For the deepest intimacy joins the supposedly 'linguistic' to the supposedly 'psychic'; these realms, distinct by discursive convention, are scarcely separable. Then instead of this distinction, an idea of affective words as they indwell might be more useful – and this is a broadly linguistic conception not contrasted to, or opposed to, the psychic. So, for instance, my amateur philology may be a quiet vengeance: my fury may be, precisely, an intense, untiring, scrupulous contemplation of those old bad words which have stuck under the skin.

The tendency of malignant speech is to ingrow like a toenail, embedding itself in its hearer until it's no longer felt to come 'from the outside'. The significance of its original emanation from another's hostility becomes lost to the recipient as a tinnitus of remembered attack buzzes in her inner ear. The bad word reverberates – so much so, that it holds the appeal of false etymology (it is easy to assume that 'to reverberate' derives from characteristically self-repeating verbal actions, whereas it meant striking or beating back). That it reverberates, rather than echoes, places it well beyond the possibilities of ironic recuperation that echo offers; reverberation will only resound, to its own limit. And rancorous phrases, matted in a wordy undergrowth, appear to be 'on the inside' as one fights them down while they perpetually spring up again. This is where it is crucial to recall that the accusations originally came from the outside, and the rage they echo was another's rage. But this half-consolation of the realist's recourse to history is not enough. We also need to de-dramatise the words as they continue their whirring, and to sedate their bitter resonances in the inner ear's present time. For however does anyone withstand this common experience of being etched and scored with harsh names? One art of survival, I'll suggest, is to concede that 'yes, this person really wanted me dead then'; yet in the same breath to see that the hostile wish is not identical with the excessive hostility of the lingering word, which has its own slow-burning temporality. The accuser's personal rage has a different duration from the resonances of the recalled inner word: to be able to separate and apportion these two will help. We would need to try out some art of seeing the denouncer as separate from the denunciation, while also at its mercy himself. Is there some stoical language practice to counter the property of accusation to continue its corrosive work, even though the accuser may have died years ago? How this might be attempted is ventured in the following discussion, where no kindly strategy of humanising and forgiving the pronouncer of the bad word or of grasping the special susceptibility of its human target is suggested, but a cooler tactic of enhancing the objectification of the word itself. It is the very thing-like nature of the bad word which may, in fact, enable its target to find release from its insistent echoes.

## 2  Accusation Often Lodges in the Accused

There was until recently in Paris, on rue Pavée in the quatrième, a decrepit-looking language school which displayed in its window, in English (on a dusty cloth banner, in fifties-style white on red lettering) this injunction: 'Don't let the English language beat you – Master it before it masters you.' A curious exhortation to have been chosen as a motto by any language school – since for the native speaker the onrush of language is unstoppable, yet the exhortation is also irrelevant for the non-native, who's never subject to joyous capture by a language not her first.

But what certainly threatens any comforting notion of our mastering language is the gripping power of predatory speech, which needs our best defensive efforts in the face of its threatened mastery of us. It's true enough, though, that not only imperious accusation is apt to indwell. So can lyric, gorgeous fragments, psalms and hymns; beautiful speech also comes to settle in its listeners. There is an unholy coincidence between beauty and cruelty in their verbal mannerisms; citation, reiteration, echo, quotation may work benignly, or as a poetics of abusive diction. If graceful speech is memorable, by what devices do violently ugly and lovely language both inhere; what does the internal strumming of metrical quotation have in common with the compulsions of aggressive speech? Yet perhaps the happily resonant indwelling of lyric may be explained in ways also fitting the unhappy experience of being mastered by hard words far better forgotten. Evidently there exists what we could call 'linguistic love', a love sparked and sustained by the appeal of another's spoken or written words – that is, by something in the loved person which is also not of her and which lies largely beyond her control – her language. But if there is a linguistic love which is drawn outward to listen, there's also linguistic hatred, felt by its object as drawn inward. A kind of extimacy prevails in both cases. Imagined speech hollows can resemble a linguistic nursing home, in which old fragments of once-voiced accusation or endearment may resentfully or soulfully lodge. Where verbal recurrences are distressed, they are carried as scabs, encrustations, calcification, cuts. If inner speech can sing, it can also tirelessly whisper, mutter, contemplate under its breath to itself, and obsessively reproach itself. It can angrily fondle those names it had once been called. If there is a habitual (if not inevitable) closeness between accusation and interpellation, there's also an echolalic, echoic aspect to interpellation itself. Persecutory interpellation's shadow falls well beyond the instant of its articulation. There are ghosts of the word which always haunt any present moment of enunciation, rendering that present already murmurous and thickly populated. Perhaps 'the psyche' *is* recalled voices as spirit voices manifesting themselves clothed in the flesh of words, and hallucinated accusation may underscore some factually heard accusation. There is in effect a verbal form of post-traumatic stress disorder, marked by unstoppable aural flashbacks. Here anamnesia, unforgetting, is a linguistic curse of a disability. We hear much about the therapeutics of retrieved memory. The inability to *forget*, too, has been classified as a neurological illness.[4]

If language spills to flood everywhere, if it has no describable 'beyond', such a broadly true claim cannot tell us exactly how it operates on its near side and why its apparent innerness is so ferocious. The reach of a malevolent word's reverberation is incalculable; it may buzz in the head of its hearer in a way that far exceeds any impact that its utterer had in mind. Yet its impress may be weak. Or it may feed melodramas of an apparent addiction to domestic-as-linguistic violence: imagine someone who habitually ends up in a position of pleading with those deaf to all her appeals to act humanely, when it was long clear that they would not do so, yet at those dark moments it seemed to her that her whole possibility of existence was at stake in extracting a humane word from them, although in the past this had always proved impossible. She compulsively redesigns a scenario in which her question 'Am I a bad person?' can be asked and answered in its own unhappy terms; for she cannot get her ancient interrogation taken seriously by someone who is not already her opponent; anyone else would rephrase her question, returning it to her to demonstrate its hopelessness. Only she can undo it. Meanwhile if she persists in posing it as it stands, it will only receive an affirmative answer. Then must the force of 'the psychic' be isolated here, if the unrelenting person to whom she presents her hopeless appeal is always rediscovered with a terrible reliability, if some damaging interlocutor conveniently appears and reappears for her – while she, the impassioned questioner, labours as if to discover grounds for believing, despite her own sound memories of actual events, that such cruelty could not really have happened?

To continue in this (fatally exhilarating) vein of psychologising speculation – the capacity of lacerating accusation to indwell may be such that, while its target is fearful that it may be true, she is also fearful that it may *not* be true, which would force the abandonment of her whole story. As if in order to 'justify' the decades of unhappiness that it has caused her, she almost needs the accusation to be correct – as much as in the same breath, she vehemently repudiates it. Perhaps she would rather take the blame on herself for the harm of the past, because it has already and irretrievably been visited upon her, than to admit it had happened arbitrarily in that she was then (as a child) truly helpless, an accidental object lying in the path of the assault. Perhaps the need for the accusation to be true, as well as to be simultaneously fought against, is in part her wish to have some rationale, and hence less of frightening contingency as the only explanation for the damage. Perhaps her pleadings for exoneration are also pleadings to have some logic underlying the blame laid bare, so that at last she can grasp and understand it. Hence her tendency to ask repeatedly 'But then why am I, as you tell me I am, an evil person?' There is an anxiety of interpellation, in which its subject ponders incessantly to herself 'Am I that name, am I really one of those?' Her query, while it interrogates the harsh attribution, stays under its rigid impress. She needs to find those to whom she can address it and have it taken seriously, despite its capacity to provoke their irritation; this is why recalcitrantly obdurate people will always prove her 'best' (that is, least malleable) addressees. She is reluctant to be emancipated from her distressing situation, only because that rescue would make retrospective nonsense out of a wrong that she was forced to live out as if it had a rationale. Her attachment to the apparent truth inherent in her damnation (even while she nervously denies it) is that in order to make sense of the misery it has caused, she must know it to have been deserved. To have that mimesis of logic taken away from her in retrospect, to be shorn of its 'necessity' in the name of her own emancipation is hard – despite the fact that she also profoundly disbelieved in it. For a long time she has struggled intently to convey intelligibility to the damage in the moment that she underwent it, as if there had to be a truth in it. This is a difficult point, and I'm not hinting at any masochistic notion of hers that her pain is deserved, is her own fault – I'm simply describing her wish for there to have been some necessity to it, in order to justify it in retrospect.

These last two paragraphs have mimicked a train of speculation as to why, for some purely imaginary heroine of pathos, another's bitter words might have come to be entertained gravely by her. Yet if we're enquiring what exists already that chimes within its target in order for lacerating interpellation to work, the pathology of that accusation itself might accompany our habitual attention to the weaknesses of the accused. An air of reason makes its fatal appearance whenever accusation insistently claims that it is speaking a purely rational cause and effect in its sentence 'You are this bad thing, because I say so.' The fantasy of formulaic interpellation is that it is only addressing the target which stands before it, whereas its own temporality is badly askew.[5] Then the distorting work of repeated echo may happen for the hearer too: 'I've heard this accusation before, so it must hold some truth.' Compelled to seek out any logic in the charges against her, she may desperately try to impose some sequence upon what is skewed. Perhaps her will to unearth some reason within cruelty will mean that she won't ever detect and register anything intelligible in whatever benign utterances might later come her way. But now we have slipped straight back on to the terrain of speculative psychology again. Next we might try turning it, not on to the target, but on to the utterer of the bad word.

## 3   Accusers Themselves are Forcibly Spoken

It is the cruel gift of the malignant word to linger and echo as if fully detached from its original occasion, whose authoritative hostility I might by now, having recognised it as such, have dethroned. For the word itself still retains its reverberating autonomy, despite my potential

overthrow of its speaker. This fact may offer one answer to the suspicion that accusation can retain me in its clutches only because I am
especially emotionally pliable in the face of the authority of the Other.
The word, instead, may be the real Other. The Other may be cut down
to size as words, and de-dramatised to lower-case.

A difficulty with theories of the capitalised Other is that they short-
circuit the complexity of influences, suggesting a narrowed dialectic,
since they function as descriptions of a fantasied mastery which operates within and on the singular figure of the self. But my 'I' also always
emerges from somewhere else, before the congealing of the Other, and
across some history of linguistic exchanges prior to my mastery of
words.[6] I am the residue of echoes which precede my cohering and
imbue my present being with a shadowiness. These aural shadows may
be dispelled, but they may thicken and assume deeper powers of obscurantism. This uncertainty also troubles my accuser equally – perhaps
worse. Which is not to deny that there is domination; but we could
remember that the big Other of theorised fantasy is also mapped on to
the mundane lower-case other in the daily world, those ordinary
human others who are also produced by the script of rage, driven
along by its theatrical auto-pilot. The accuser, too, is spoken.

Wittgenstein, a nervously driven questioner himself, brooded over
the psychology of compulsive philosophical doubt: 'Why should
anyone want to ask this question?'[7] The same musing could be turned
towards the accuser as a phenomenon: 'Why ever should anyone want
to speak with this violence?' But there's another thought which side-
lines such an interrogation of my accuser's motives: the reflection that
he is dispossessed of his own words in advance. The rhetoric of rage
speaks him mechanically and remorselessly. However much the
accuser feels himself to triumph in the moment of his pronouncement,
he is prey to echo. For, as Wallace Stevens neatly observed of the cav-
ernous grandeur of inner oratory, 'When the mind is like a hall in
which thought is like a voice speaking, the voice is always that of
someone else.'[8] The orator of violence is merely an instrument of dictation by tics and reflexes. There's nothing gratifyingly original about
the language of attack, in which old speech plays through the accuser;
it is the one who speaks the damage who becomes its sounding board.
(I'm not inching towards a sneaking sympathy for the utterer of hate:
that he himself is not remotely in possession of his language does
nothing whatsoever to soften his words as they streak through him to
crash on to their target.) Rage speaks monotonously. The righteousness
of wrathful diction's vocabulary sorely restricts it, the tirade marked by

that lack of reflection which alone lets the raging speaker run on and on. Once any awareness of his repetitiousness creeps over him, rather than feel vindicated by the tradition which is driving him, he's more likely to feel embarrassed enough to stop. His fury may be exaggerated by his helplessness at being mastered by his own language (whether or not he gives this description to his subjugation). For the language of anger is so dictatorial that it will not allow him to enjoy any conviction that he is voicing his own authenticity. Meanwhile, my very existence as the butt of his accusation is maddening to him, since under his onslaught, I'm apparently nothing for myself any longer but am turned into a mere thing-bearer of his passion. This is almost irrespective of my own passivity or my retaliation; it is because his utterance has, in its tenor, thrown me down. For the rage-speaker, I can have no life left in me, or rather none of that combative life that he needs to secure his own continuing linguistic existence for himself. Attacked, I'm rendered discursively limp, but no real relief can be afforded to my adversary by what he has produced as my rag doll quiescence. The more intense the anger, the less the sense of any agency its utterer possesses, until eventually he feels himself to be the 'true victim' in the affair. Hence that common combination of rage with self-pity: a lachrymose wrath. In the light of all this, the injunction to 'get in touch with your anger' is hardly the therapeutically liberating practice its proposers assume. Instead, the following variant on the Parisian language school's exhortation – 'master the language of anger before it masters you' – would prove more emancipating.

But what about being the bad speaker myself? There's an experience that could be described as a 'linguistic occasion', of being poised somewhere halfway between 'language speaks me' and 'I speak language'. It is the flashing across the mind of words which fly into the head as if they somehow must be said. A clump of phrases shape their own occasion, which swells towards articulation. But I can stop their translation into speech; when maxims are actually uttered aloud, then something else has already given these wordy impulses a currency and licensed their entry into a world of ordered fantasy. This 'something else' runs close to the question of somewhere else. Where is the place where language works? A doubtful contrast of inner and outer haunts the puzzle of whether I speak (from the inside outward) or whether I am spoken (from the outside in.) This old tension between speaking language and being spoken by it still stretches uncertainly; neither the topography of language's extrusion from the speaker's mouth like ectoplasm, nor its companion, the topography of linguistic entry from the outside, seem apt resolutions. The latter offers a vision of penetration through the ear, like that persuasive Byzantine myth of the annunciation and conception, in which a falling star has shot the ear of the patient Virgin Mary. Sometimes, in an attempt to resolve such puzzles of the place of speech, its polarities get folded together so that the conventionally outer traverses the conventionally inner. Here, for instance: 'This passion of the signifier now becomes a new dimension of the human condition in that it is not only man who speaks, but that in man and through man *it* speaks, that his nature is woven by effects in which is to be found the structure of language, of which he becomes the material, and that therefore there resounds in him, beyond what could be conceived of by a psychology of ideas, the relation of speech.'[9] How does such a resonance work in respect of bad words? If words themselves can neatly exemplify the concept of extimacy, in that they are good candidates to be that trace of externality, the foreign body lodged at the very heart of psychic life, nevertheless our impression of an unalloyed inwardness in the case of inner speech is still acute. Despite the attractions of conceiving language as lying out there and lunging in from the outside to speak the speaker, we still sense that we fish up our inner words, or dredge them up. But in the case of recalled damaging speech, it's less like a trawling expedition to plumb some depth, but more of its rising up unbidden, Kraken-like, to overwhelm and speak us. Yet at the same time we can also understand this unconscious to come from the outside, in the shape of the common and thoroughly external unconscious of unglamorous language. This mutates into what we experience as our profoundly inner speech. Or as Volosinov (who by the word 'ideological' appears to mean the whole world of signs and gestures[10]) tautly formulated it: 'Psychic experience is something inner that becomes outer, and the ideological sign, something outer that becomes inner. The psyche enjoys extraterritorial status in the organism. It is a social entity that penetrates inside the organism of the individual person.'[11] These shards of imported sociality as bad words remain as impersonal traces in me, in the way that swearing is impersonal; I have not thought them up, they are derivations, clichéd fragments of unoriginality which have lodged in my skull. Usually my verbal memory is not bland or kindly, or even discreet in its recall. Linguistic shrapnel can lie embedded for years yet still, as old soldiers from the First World War reportedly used to say, give me gyp in damp weather. Still, language is not exactly speaking me at these points – for, unlike the swear word that escapes me when I hammer my thumb, I retain some capacity to not utter it. A single speech event does not work in isolation, but darts into the waiting thickness of my inner speech to settle into its dense receptivity. It may become a furious dialogue where I'll plead with some imagined inward other; its script grows heavy with his antagonism, which it preserves in me. My subsequent distress is rehearsed intently and silently under my breath, in a darker version of Volosinov's more benevolent persuasion here:

> Therefore the semiotic material of the psyche is preeminently the word – inner speech. Inner speech, it is true, is intertwined with a mass of other motor reactions having semiotic value. But all the same, it is the word that constitutes the foundation, the skeleton of inner life. Were it to be deprived of the word, the psyche would shrink to an extreme degree: deprived of all other expressive activities, it would die out altogether.[12]

My swollen (because word-stuffed) psyche can, however, assume the most unbecoming shapes. Some graceless prose of the world has got me in its grip, and my word-susceptible faculty is seized and filled up by it. It is a neurolinguistic circus, this wild leaping to my tongue of banally correct responses, bad puns, retold jokes to bore my children, and undiscerning quotes. To this list could be added many other kinds of stock formulae, in the shape of racist utterance, idle sexism and other ready-mades. Inner language is not composed of graceful musing, but of disgracefully indiscriminate repetition, running on automatic pilot. Nevertheless, even if such reflections mean that I'm displaced as an original thinker, I'm not quite evacuated. Even if my tawdry inner language is thinking me (although 'thought' is too dignified a term for such gurglings) there's many a slip between inner thought and lip. It is certainly speaking *in* me; but I can subdue it before it fully speaks me, I can edit or inhibit the invading words. I am an enforced linguistic collaborator, but only in so far as a long parade of verbal possibilities marches across my horizons. Thought is made in the mouth, but it can also be halted before it passes the lips. And if it isn't, this is hardly an expression of my spontaneity, but rather of my consent to language's orders. Uttering bad words entails an especial passivity of allowing myself to be spoken by automated verbiage, by an 'it is speaking in me'. If I don't moderate my bad words, my supposedly authentic expression of my feeling consists merely in my obedience to the rising of what is ready-made to the tongue. I am not literally compelled to speak my love, my despair, or my cynicism. Uttered aggression happens when something in me has licensed the articulation of my linguistic impulses into more than flickers. An expression flashes over me and it will have its way, but only if I don't throw it out. That's the extent of the action of my linguistic will; it is no powerful author of its own speech. It comes puffing up in the wake of the inner linguistic event to deal with its violence, to assent to it or demur, or to ascribe some given sentiment or abrogate to myself that standard echoing opinion. What it takes for me, apropos being or not being a bad speaker myself, is not to be a beautiful soul with the hem of my skirts drawn aside from the mud of linguistic harm, but to elect whether to broadcast or to repress the inward yet still thoroughly worldly chattering of imported speech that fills me.

## 4  The Word as Thing

Gripped by visions of exuberance swelling into parsimony, Hegel writes: 'Speech and work are outer expressions in which the individual no longer keeps and possesses himself within himself, but lets the inner get completely outside of him, leaving it at the mercy of something other than himself. For that reason we can say with equal truth that these expressions express the inner too much, as that they do so too little.'[13] Such a reflection seems to lean towards an anti-expressivist stance, in which a notion of language's natural 'expressivity' becomes terribly misleading, either because my utterance is too immediately saturated with me, or is too radically separated from me and is under the sway of whatever carries my words away and out of the range of my intentions. It would be bad naming in particular, through its overblown immediacy, which 'does not therefore provide the expression which is sought'[14] and lacks that finally productive self-alienation which pertains (at least in the spasmodically softer focus of the 'Hegelian' view) to language proper. In this, Language or Word is Spirit. And if in addition we hold the word to be also historical and material, then the cruel word must also call us into social being, if of a deathly kind. As for the possibility of our resisting it, the language hangs there, supremely indifferent as to whether it is resisted or not. What is more critical for what we could roughly call the Hegelian word view is that to ignore language's sociality would go violently against the way of language in the world. Sociality, of course, is not sociability. On the aspect of making people up, one post-Hegelian has claimed:

What I seek in speech is the response of the other. What constitutes me as subject is my question. In order to be recognised by the other,

I utter what was only in view of what will be. In order to find him, I call him by a name that he must assume or refuse in order to reply to me ... But if I call the person to whom I am speaking by whatever name I choose to give him, I intimate to him the subjective function that he will take on again in order to reply to me, even if it is to repudiate this function.[15]

In this manner, Lacan continues to emphasise, I install him as a subject.

Yet we might demur here, in respect of bad words. For hatred aims, not at any animated exchange with a respondent, but at that person's annihilation. My defence against serious verbal onslaught, then, could well adopt an analogous tactic of impersonality, and espouse a principled *non*-engagement with the proffered scenario of (hostile) recognition. I could ignore the utterer, the better to dissect the utterance. To isolate the word as thing, to inspect it and refuse it, demands a confident capacity to act unnaturally towards language, which normally functions as an energetic means of exchange. Bad words' peculiarly seductive distraction incites me to slip towards self-scrutiny, because another's angry interpellation so readily slides into becoming my own self-interpellation, where a thousand inducements to self-description, self-subjectification and self-diagnosis are anyway waiting eagerly at its service.[16] But if I simply act 'naturally' towards these lures of the bad word, by treating it as any token of exchange and recognition between speakers, I'll be thrown down by it. Then how may I shield myself from its furious resonances? If I don't want to stay petrified by it, then instead *I* have to petrify *it* – and in the literal sense. That is, I'll assert its stony character.

Verbal aggression may seem, at first, to be only formally language, and scarcely that at all. It resembles a stone hurled without reflection, which the furious thrower has snatched up just because it lay to hand. The target cannot deflect the blow, but will be spared its after-effects because she realises the impersonal quality of the thing. The word considered as stone will shock but not break her. The denunciation hurts on impact but later it weakens, as its target sees there is only an accidental link between what was hurled and the will to hurl. She realises that the bad word is not properly 'expressive' of the speaker's impulse to aggressive speech (it cannot be, since 'there is always at once too much as too little'[17]) while the impulse needs to be understood in itself and independently of its instrument. So if I decide to embrace this defensive strategy, I can inform the malignant word that it is not really a word by the strenuous artifice of detaching it from the person who pronounced it (dispatching him, for the time being, to wander stripped of his tongue in the idiosyncratic shades of his own psychology). This is my opening gambit. Next I'll turn to contemplate the malevolent word, now separated from its speaker, and quivering furiously like an abandoned dart lost to the guiding authority of the hand that threw it. Now I have to aim at its death, in the same way that, as a spoken accusation, it had aimed at my death. I can kill it only by artificially abstracting it from the realm of language altogether (although I realise perfectly well that human utterance always bristles with such weapons). I have to let it go indifferently, as a thing to which I myself have become as indifferent as the bad word itself had really been, all along, to me. The *accuser* was not indifferent, then. But the after-life of malignant speech is vigorously spectral, quite independent of its emission at the instant of rage. The bad word flaps in its vampire's afterlife in the breast of its target, who can try to quell it, but 'cannot go the length of being altogether done with it to the point of annihilation: in other words, he only *works* on it'.[18] The spoken savagery hovers there still. However can its target 'work' on it? Stripping the speaker away from the word brings it into a loneliness, into its prominent isolation from the occasion of its utterance. This act of detaching it returns it to its impersonal communality, and into the dictionary of latent harm, while wrenching it away from its respectably bland and democratic-sounding claim to share in language's supposed intersubjectivity. And as suggested, I can also turn the phenomenology of cruel speaking against my accuser to characterise him as not having been the master of his own sadism, but of having been played like a pipe, swayed like a hapless reed. The words that rushed to his tongue were always an ersatz rhetoric. Meanwhile, I can also recognise his distance from me, his indifference – an indifference which, by now, is not only a spent feeling only coolly attentive to me, but of a psychology which has long since returned to itself, and now wanders about the world intent on its fresh preoccupations, far out of the range of my unhappy surveillance.

But may not this commentary have dealt in too cavalier or too sunnily optimistic a fashion with the hurtful word's curious duration? I've been implying that the intention to hurt can be treated by its target as almost irrelevant, and that there is an impersonality in hate speech which can be harnessed for protective and quasi-thera-peutic purposes. But the injured person may well feel that the aggressive speech was heavy with a plan to hurt her and was calculatedly aimed at the gaps in her armour; how, then, could her conviction of this deliberate intent to cause pain be at all eased by the thesis that bad words also enthral, in all senses, their own speaker? To which reasonable objection I'd reply that my speculations are indeed an exercise in mounting a defence, and they do sideline this question of recognising a pointed intention to destroy. But they also usefully detach the fact of an intent to hurt from any assumption that the angry speaker controls the repercussions of his words; for the targeted person might well assume his invincibility, and so credit the violent speaker with far more than he owns.

Yet there's still a further turn in the work that has to be done. Love's work[19] pales in comparison with Hate's work, in the sense of the legacy of being hated, which condemns its recipients to an iniquitous toil of elucidation. Having returned the bad word to its waiting niche in the stout dictionary of unkindness, I'll need not only to return the speaker to the accident of himself, but I have to attempt a further labour of emancipation for myself. I must recognise his indifference to my present tormented memories of his old utterances, and return him to an absolute indifference in which I abandon him, even in my speculations. I, too, need to 'have done with the thing altogether'.[20] But to succeed in having done with it demands a prior and ferocious dwelling on it, which first unsparingly remembers the reverberating word as word – yet only in order to restore its truly impersonal quality, to return it to the generality of utterance from whence it came, and to acknowledge its superb and sublimely indifferent capacity to take me or leave me. That is, I'll get rid of understanding myself as 'the suffering person'. And I shall manage to give up that unhappy and unproductive self-designation only at the same stroke in which I can fully grasp the impersonality of the bad word. This I will come to do as a consequence of registering its cruelty, letting it sink completely into me – that is, by going straight through the route of the profoundly personal. Only then, through entering its peculiar blackness unprotected, can I sever the word from its speaker in order to imaginatively return him to his true contingency and to his present cheerily amnesiac indifference to my continuing lacerations by his verbal attack, the occasion of which has doubtless long since escaped his mind.

By this stage, I've gradually and waveringly relinquished what is standardly taken to be a 'Hegelian' concept of language, because it would have been too optimistic, since too tranquilly intersubjective, for the task at hand. Now instead some of Hegel's own and less sunny descriptions of language as a 'stain', a 'contagion', and the ground of 'a universal infection' of selves may receive their testing-ground on the territory of damaging words.[21] (Admittedly there are pleasant kinds of stains, and perhaps even happy contagions; but Hegel's scattered metaphor of infection is harder to recuperate.) Let's follow its logic. To enable my release, my initial infection by the bad word with virulent fear and the most relentless self-doubt is necessary. A mild anxiety will not suffice. My entire self-conception must have tottered. 'If it has not experienced absolute fear, but only some lesser dread, the negative being has remained for it something external, its substance has not been infected by it through and through.'[22] With this apparently paradoxical association of language with infection, we're dealing, in short, with the true sociability of language – as contagion, as a mouth disease. To recover, as I must, from accusation's damaging impact on me, I cannot effectively stand lonely proof against it, but instead have to admit something that so far I have been reluctant to consider: that, *exactly as my injury*, it enjoys a fully language-like status. Now, in this moment, I have abandoned all my earlier humanist strategy of seeing the bad word as a hurled stone and therefore not as true language. Instead I've begun to understand that the bad word is an indifferently speaking stone. In sum, that harsh language evinces a sheer indifference both to me and also to my accuser, an ultimately sociable impersonality, and a sadism, that (uninterested in me though it is) has worked successfully on me while it also suffers its own corrosion and decay.

But if instead I overlook all these characteristics of language, and meditate solely 'psychologically', I'll examine only my own idiosyncratically undefended subjecthood by discovering some prior susceptibility within my depths, an early wound which is the key to my constant vulnerability – as if therein I could unearth some meaning to my haunting by the word and free myself. The trouble with this speculation is that the linguistic structure of my childhood verbal wounding was and is exactly the same as that which vexes me now; when I was two years old, there was no 'purely psychic' naming for me even then, but an interpellation which, always linguistic, was thereby always affective. Infancy's learning to speak is also entangled in parental emotions – the hostility, anxiety, lucidity, mildness. But this evident fact only reinforces my persuasion that the linguistic and the psychic are neither separable, nor to be subsumed one under another. If there is now the same scenario, an original injury which I relive, its endless reanimation in me is not surprising, given the paucity of my capacities for self-protection then. That is, there's not a chronology of depth of my early (psychic) injury which precedes, founds and accounts for some later and categorically different (linguistic) vulnerability – other than that vital history of my childish and necessary dependence on others' affective words.

All of these considerations which might help to deflate lacerating speech – considerations of the vatic nature of the language itself, and the transient emotion of its speaker driven by the rhetoric he deploys – might be equally applied to a recollected 'I love you'. The erratic love-speaker claims to have meant his declarations *then*, but that now he has changed his feelings and disavows everything. And he protects himself from the charge of fickleness by avowing the innocent contingency of his declaration, rather in the way that to protect oneself from the hate-speaker, one considers how the bite of his words might be eased through a recognition of their awful contingency. If we compare the aftermath of hearing 'I love you' with the aftermath of hearing 'I hate you', in both instances the hearer may fight to sever the utterance from its vanished utterer. With the former declaration, the struggle is to find compensation in the teeth of impermanence (those words were definitely said to me, so at least I can be sure that once I was loved even though their speaker has gone). And with the latter, to find protection from the risk of permanence (those words were directed at me, but it wasn't especially me who was hated, I just accidentally got in that speaker's way).

The stoic's route to consolation, however, cannot follow this path of detecting necessity in the instance of her being loved, but contingency in the case of her being hated. She is more prone to regard both love speech and hate speech alike as workings of that language which (to return to our Parisian language school's slogan) we have not the faintest hope of mastering before it masters us. Nonetheless, we can still elect to suffer our subjugation moodily and darkly, or we can treat it more lightly and indifferently, as a by-product of the disinterested machinations of language. To espouse such a notion of linguistic impartiality in this way is, I think, the sounder course. I could be more effectively freed from damaging words by first confronting and then conceding my own sheer contingency as a linguistic subject. I am a walker in language. It is only through my meanders and slow detours, perhaps across many decades, towards recognising language's powerful impersonality – which is always operating despite and within its air of a communicative 'intersubjectivity' – that I can 'become myself'. Yet I become myself only by way of fully accepting my own impersonality, too – as someone who is herself accidentally spoken, not only by violent language, but by any language whatsoever – and who, by means of her own relieved recognition of this very contingency, is in significant part released from the powers of the secretive and unspeakable workings of linguistic harm.

# Part II (Jean-Jacques Lecercle)

# 3
# A New Philosophy of Language

## 1 Point of Departure

Denise Riley begins her analysis of 'bad words' with the followings words:

> The worst words revivify themselves within us, vampirically. Injurious speech echoes relentlessly, years after the occasion of its utterance, in the mind of the one at whom it was aimed: the bad word, splinter-like, pierces to lodge. In its violently emotional materiality, the word is indeed made flesh and dwells amongst us – often long outstaying its welcome.

What exactly does it mean to begin the question of language and subjectivity, of subjectivation by language, of naming and identity, by considering insults or 'bad words'? More generally, can such an opening be of interest if our aim is to produce a philosophy of language, by which I mean a theory of language, subjectivation and interpellation? Is there any sense in beginning to look at language from the vantage point of 'bad words'?

The answer is yes. Bad words, of any type (insults, swear words, aggressive naming) have a certain number of advantages over the usual 'the man hit the ball' tame assertion, in the shape of a simple declarative sentence, evincing elementary linguistic structure. In a word, bad words give us an idea on how to bridge the gap, emphatically indicated in *The German Ideology*, between 'language' and 'the language of real life'.[1] For bad words are words, and yet they undeniably partake of 'the language of real life', in the shape of agonistic action, a form of *praxis*. In other words, they have the considerable advantage of inducing us to start the question of language from the point of view of the social situation of interlocution, not the abstract system we have learnt to call *langue*. At the cost of the construction of another philosophy of language, one that will be utterly unpalatable to mainstream linguistics and current philosophies of language (of the analytic kind, but not only those).

This shift, bad words allow because they have four striking characteristics:

(1) Bad words suggest that the primary function of language is not discourse, the (cooperative) exchange of information, but *naming*. What is known as *deixis*, verbal gesturing, pointing at, becomes (becomes *again*, if we believe those who claim that language finds its origin in gestures of indication, that is, if we read Tran Duc Thao, the Vietnamese Marxist, or Merleau-Ponty[2]) the original, if not the central, function of language.

(2) Bad words are a form of verbal action, not discourse as representation of states of affairs. This does not merely suggest that pragmatics (the performative function of utterances) is the centre of language (rather than mere syntax), but that language is concerned with subjectivation in the shape of the *interpellation* of subjects. This has been excellently analysed by Judith Butler in her *Excitable Speech*.[3] It tends to support the idea that if pragmatics is the core of language, it is because language is the archetypal human *praxis*, in the Marxist sense, and must be analysed as such.

(3) Bad words, as Riley forcefully demonstrates, are wounding words (a fact we have always already known, to our detriment). They inflict pain, of a quasi-physical nature. In that sense, when faced with bad words, we are all like Louis Wolfson, the schizophrenic who could not read or hear words in English, his mother tongue, as they caused him physical discomfort (more on him later). This points out the *materiality* of language, its capacity to act on bodies, to be inscribed on the human body as a trace, from the erotic and symptomatic tracing of the mother's words on the baby's body in Leclaire, to the effects on bodies of performative utterances, provided they are endowed with social felicity (the best example of this is the death sentence) – in other words, such materiality is not merely physical, but also social-institutional.[4] The body is captured by language and, as a lived body, at least in part constituted by language, as symptoms are not only affections of the body, but inscriptions of words or sentences on it; it also bears the

mark of the subjectivation of the subject by institutional discourses: the words of authority and power, and the words of the ideological struggle, contribute not merely to my general behaviour but to the very shape of my body. My stunted growth or athletic make-up are not merely natural or organic developments: they speak the language that is inscribed in them.

(4) Bad words are *disconnected*. This is perhaps where they most clearly enable us to leave mainstream linguistics and philosophy of language. By 'disconnected', I mean that they have either no syntax (aggressive naming or interpellation merely requires the single word without any need for connective placement, as in syntax: 'Idiot!'), elementary syntax, with hardly any structuring (as in 'You fool!'- compare with 'You are a fool!'), or a different form of syntax from the common and garden variety. Thus the grammar of insults (for instance the phrase 'that fool of a man', where the 'possessive' preposition hardly denotes possession) requires either its own syntax[5] or modifications to the standard structure, as when the Chomskyan linguist Ann Banfield feels compelled to add an extra node, the E, or emotive, node to the deep structure that determines the syntax of the canonical sentence.[6] And it is true that the graffito I often encounter in my Paris suburb (which shows that English is truly a world language, and which is a tribute to the effect of secondary education on French youth), 'Fuck you', perhaps now the best-known English utterance, has problematic syntax. It is sometimes called (by Banfield for instance) a 'quasi-imperative', a phrase which only means that linguists are baffled: 'fuck yourself!' would be a proper imperative, with erased second-person pronoun; 'let me fuck you!' only testifies to the absence of a first-person imperative; 'I fuck you' is hardly a performative, although it is closest to my initial utterance; as to 'fuck!', another favourite, it is difficult to decide if the word is a verb or a noun, or even whether the question is relevant.

The only conclusion is that the 'language of real life', as incarnated in bad words, has little to do with the language of linguistics, with *langue* as a system. The crux of the matter is the relationship between language and the psyche which linguistics and the mainstream philosophy of language carefully ignore, or simplify: is language to be considered as abstract system, or as practice? And is language a question of intersubjectivity or, as Riley suggests, of 'impersonality'? Which is the master, as Humpty-Dumpty said: language, or the subject?

There are, however, difficulties in this position, of which Riley is entirely aware, as she walks up the rue Pavée in Paris. The first difficulty is that hate speech 'is only formally language' (Riley, p. 58), even 'scarcely that at all' (ibid.). How can I hope to understand the workings of language from what is not even language (even if it is 'words')? Perhaps what we are looking at is some form of action, with only coincidental proximity to language.

The second difficulty is formulated by Riley in the conclusion to her text. The adopted point of view avoids intersubjectivity for impersonality: 'I am a walker in language. It is only through my meanders and slow detours, perhaps across many decades, towards recognising language's powerful impersonality – which is always operating despite and within its persuasive allure of "intersubjectivity" – that I can "become myself" ' (Riley, p. 62). The problem here is the status of this linguistic 'impersonality'. It seems to take us away from a form of linguistic philosophy which is found in the analytic tradition, with its methodological individualism of speakers' intentions of meaning and rational choice of co-operative communication (the reference here is, of course, to Habermas's 'universal pragmatics'[7]); or again, which is also found in the phenomenological tradition, as exemplified in so-called 'enunciation linguistics', with its insistence on utterance-as-process, a subjective individual process, as the speaker negotiates her 'situation of enunciation' through a series of 'operations' that locate her utterance-as-result both in relation to herself and to the external situation.[8] The question then is: does such 'impersonality' take us back to the system of *langue*, which, we suggested, cannot account for bad words as linguistic *praxis*? The answer is no, and compels us to look for another philosophy of language.

There are two reasons why the answer should be in the negative. The first is that systemic linguistics (the linguistics of Saussure, Chomsky or Halliday) is based on the sentence as predicative structure (the sentence is made up of Subject Verb Object, SVO, in that, the preferred order, or in any other), with the main function implicitly ascribed to language being the function of communication. The sentence is a statement; it embodies a proposition: it takes the form of a judgement communicated by an addresser to an addressee, which takes us back to intersubjectivity. The powerful impersonality of bad words, on the other hand, operates through utterances as events, as interventions, rather than through propositions and sentences.

The second reason is that this 'impersonality' is not the abstract ideality of the system. It is called 'powerful', a metaphor which must not be taken in the scientific sense in which a theory is 'powerful' in its capacity to generate results, but in a more material sense, in which it exerts force on the bodies of the agents involved. But again, such force must not be taken in the sense of the performative force of Anglo-Saxon pragmatics, where the analysis of forces leads to classification, but in a sort of abstract way, hardly fleshed out: once we have distinguished the speech-act that a promise consists of, we leave it at that, and the exact form of the force exerted by the promise, its exact strength and mode of operation on bodies and things is forgotten. Whereas the force that is implied in Riley's 'powerful impersonality' of hate speech is a material force; it directly affects bodies, it leaves traces, or inscriptions, on it. We are closer to the world of psychoanalysis than to that of Searle's speech-acts.

Which of course implies that we are leaving mainstream philosophy of language, as we have left mainstream linguistics. We do need another philosophy of language. The time has come to give that vague and portentous phrase some contents. And the exploration I am going to engage in may even yield vistas on the concept of the subject. I shall begin by carefully reading Riley's text.

## 2 Reading Denise Riley

This is how Riley describes the bodily effect of bad words:

> Where verbal recurrences are distressed, they are carried as scabs, encrustations, calcification, cuts. If inner speech can sing, it can also tirelessly whisper, mutter, contemplate under its breath to itself, and obsessively reproach itself. It can angrily fondle those names that it had once been called. If there is a habitual (if not inevitable) closeness between accusation and interpellation, there's also an echolalic, echoic aspect to interpellation itself. Persecutory interpellation's shadow falls well beyond the instant of its articulation. There are ghosts of the word which always haunt any present moment of enunciation, rendering that present already murmurous and populated. (Riley, p. 50)

Let us take this passage as a manifesto for a new philosophy of language, and comment on the 'key words', in the approved fashion, in the gleeful knowledge that a mainstream linguist would not recognise his favourite objects of study in this account.

The first significant word is 'distressed'. What does it mean for a segment of language, a 'verbal occurrence', to be 'distressed'? Simply that the utterance is not the linguistic incarnation of an abstract proposition, not a carrier of information but of affect. And we note that the distressing force affects not only the addressee, at whom it is directed, not merely the addresser, who, as Riley points out later, is himself interpellated by his own hate speech, but the verbal occurrence itself, which is thus turned into a suffering body. I suffer from bad words, and the words themselves are suffering bodies. Hence words like 'scabs', 'cuts', etc., words that describe the situation of bodies as they encounter one another and mix. We are in the world of the pan-somatism of the Stoics, from which Deleuze derived a theory of sense and language.[9] Language is incorporated because it is itself a material body. Or rather, since the ontological metaphor, or abstraction, which glibly (for the sake of unavoidable convenience) talks about 'language' in general, fails us in that it repeats the fetishism of positive science, words are bodies that freely (or on occasion painfully) mix with other bodies, first of all the bodies of the speakers that utter or receive them. What we need, therefore, is a philosophy of language that takes into account the materiality of incorporated language.

The second important word is contained in the phrase 'inner speech'. In spite of a long and venerable tradition in ancient and medieval philosophy,[10] the phrase has vanished from accounts of language, and Riley is one of the few who use it (the list includes Vygotsky, Volosinov and, more unexpectedly, George Steiner in *After Babel*).[11] Yet, if we wish to think the interface between language and the subject that utters it, but also the interface between the subject and the world of objects, an interface in which language is notoriously concerned, we ought to reflect upon the nature of inner speech, and its relation to thought: is inner speech an inner form of external language, or a separate form, called 'mentalese'? Is thought independent from language? And what is the role played by visual images? For inner speech 'sings', it 'tirelessly whispers, mutters' and 'reproaches itself': language is not merely articulated speech, propositional statements, there is a continuum, and continuity, between *phone* and *logos* (we remember the traditional role ascribed to the science of language, from Aristotle onwards, is to account for the passage from *phone* to *logos*). And this raises the problem of what lies beyond language, in silence or in other media, in what Deleuze and Guattari sometimes call 'visualities' or even 'audibilities' (*ritournelles*).[12]

The third important word is the word 'name': inner speech 'fondles those names it had once been called'. This suggests that there is more to language than mere denotation, that the relation between word and world is not merely one of correspondence. Searle was already aware that the 'direction of fit' between word and world worked both ways: sometimes, in assertive or descriptive language, the word fits the world, but in performatives it is the world that has to change in order to fit the word.[13] Naming, with its overtones of word-magic, points towards this situation: it points towards language as a historical cultural practice, even as a form – the archetypal form – of Marx's *social praxis*. So that it is no wonder that the next sentence in Riley's text evokes the link between accusation and interpellation. For naming is not the innocuous Adamic practice of giving animals their names, under the supervision of God who makes sure that the naming is right, that each animal receives its proper name, in other words that the direction of fit is indeed from the word, God's gift to Adam, to the world, God's creation, and that all is as it should be. Naming is an essential part of the process of (violent) subjectivation, in the shape of interpellation of the individual into a subject via the ascription of a name. We understand why mainstream philosophy of language cannot give a convincing account of the language practice, as it ignores such violence, and why Anglo-Saxon pragmatics, which recognises that language is a practice, ultimately fails, as it, too, ignores the violent imposition of the forces it describes, and their effect on the subject (I should say 'in constituting the interpellated individual into a subject'). We also understand why intersubjectivity gives way to impersonality: interpellation is always achieved impersonally, addressing the company at large, at the very moment when it interpellates a subject, as the basis for a 'personality'. We understand, finally, why in Deleuze and Guattari's reconstruction of linguistics,[14] the building brick of language is not the predicative sentence, the assertion, but the slogan, the *mot d'ordre*: the violence of interpellation is present from the very beginning, it is constitutive of language. Rather than an irenic account of the world through linguistic representation, we have the Althusserian chain of interpellation,[15] which goes from ideology to practice, from practice to ritual, and from ritual to speech-act: at the end of the chain appears the interpellated subject. Bad words are not an exception: they are at the core of language. Not that interpellation is always explicitly violent: it often takes the form of what Riley sometimes calls 'dulcet interpellation': such sweetness, however, must not be taken as an instance of *eirene*.

No wonder, this is the fourth important word in Riley's text, that 'there are ghosts of the word that haunt any present moment of enunciation, rendering the present already murmurous and populated' – the relevant word is of course 'ghost'. Do I perceive echoes of intertextuality or Derridean 'hauntology' here? What I do perceive is the temporality of language, which is certainly not captured by the usual dichotomy, 'synchrony vs diachrony'. The time of language is always out of joint, and language is the site for indefinite layers of sedimentation, so that the synchronic *coupe d'essence*, as Althusser calls it, can never do justice to the actual workings of language.

What emerges from Riley's text is indeed another picture of language. In the rest of her essay, it receives a number of determinations. Let us take them in order, and read other passages.

This is how Riley raises what, it seems to me, is the central question:

> Yet here the standard contrast between the linguistic and the psychic, in which we are usually forced to plump for either the unconscious or language, is especially unhelpful. (Riley, p. 47)

At the centre of the new picture of language lies the relationship between the linguistic and the psychic, which mainstream philosophy of language either factors out (the speaker in the structuralist account has no psyche; in the enunciation account, her psyche can hardly be called that, being reduced to the site for linguistic 'operations', sometimes dubbed 'psycho-grammatical'). Not that having recourse to the Freudian account (in spite of Freud's seminal analyses of parts of language, like jokes, which other accounts always failed to reach, or of the early Lacan's interest in the workings of language) really helps. The metaphor of depth that governs the depth psychology of the unconscious, and which finds its equivalent in the Chomskyan 'deep structure' for language, has limitations:[16] it buries language in the unknowable, outside the public environment of human practice. And Riley is right to query the opposition between the psychic and the linguistic (even in the early Lacan, if 'the unconscious is structured like a language', the 'like' implies a separation between the psychic and the linguistic: the unconscious is *not* language). The question is: how can we query this opposition, which appears to be supported by common sense (my psyche is not restricted to my language)?

We could do a number of things. We could *invert* the hierarchy implied in the dichotomy (the psyche comes first, language is one of its properties or characteristic): we could decide that language comes first and that the psyche, as the subject is interpellated by language, is an end-of-chain effect. We could *deconstruct* the dichotomy, like countless others, at the cost of keeping it under erasure. We could *abolish* it, and simply declare that the psychic *is* the linguistic. Or we could establish a *parallelism* between the two, in Spinozan fashion, as in Davidson's theory of the supervenience of the mental over the physical: thus the linguistic would be the psychic, but from a different point of view, as thought and matter are two attributes of the single substance, and therefore strictly parallel.

My suggestion is twofold. First, we may explore the idea that the linguistic and the psychic are so intermingled as be almost identical. There is a passage in Macherey,[17] where he suggests, *en passant*, that ideology is language. He does not take up the idea, no doubt because it is too simplistic. But I propose to develop the idea that the psychic is the linguistic under another name, to spell out the concept of *linguistic interpellation*, which is already present in Riley's analysis of bad words, and which provides a reasoned link between language and ideology. An interesting consequence of this is that the concept of subject will be replaced by the concept of subjectivation. Secondly, we might explore the intermingling of the psychic and the linguistic under the concept of *expression*, whereby the psychic is the expression of the linguistic. Shades of Spinoza, and of Deleuze's reading of him are evoked here.[18] Meanwhile, let us proceed with our reading of Riley's text:

> For the deepest intimacy joins the supposedly 'linguistic' to the supposedly 'psychic'; these realms, distinct by discursive convention, are scarcely separable. Then instead of this distinction, an idea of affective words as they indwell might be more useful – and this is a broadly linguistic conception, not contrasted to, or opposed to, the psychic. (Riley, p. 48)

This develops the formulations of the first text I have quoted in terms of (a) intimacy, (b) inseparability of 'realms', and (c) indwelling. The first two can be taken as characteristics of Spinozan expression. The last, 'affective words indwell', suggests an idea of inhabitation (in the sense of Heidegger: we inhabit language) as incorporation (words indwell in us: again, we have mixtures of bodies). The question here is whether this concept of linguistic affectivity has something to do with the concept of affect which Deleuze derives from Spinoza, or with theories of the crypt, such as can be found in the work of Nicolas Abraham and Maria Torok.[19] We cannot avoid an excursion into the philosophical treatment of affect, in its relation to language.

> But what certainly threatens any comforting notion of our mastering language is the gripping power of predatory speech, which needs our best defensive efforts in the face of its threatened mastery of us. (Riley, p. 49)

We understand the crucial importance of the encounter with the sign in rue Pavée, and the language-school slogan. It goes further than the Humpty-Dumpty question of who is master, language or I (I have developed this point in *The Violence of Language*,[20] under the contrast 'I speak language' vs 'Language speaks'): the question raised here is that of the sheer violence of the power thus exerted at my expense. This takes us further than the opposition between the ideality of the system and the materiality of the inscription of discourse, between the abstraction of meaning and the imposition of material force. In other words the centre of the study of language does go from syntax and grammar to a form of pragmatics, but not Anglo-Saxon pragmatics: a Marxist form of pragmatics, in terms of interlocution as *agôn* and *rapport de forces*, of contradiction, interpellation and fetishism. We shall have to consider, for instance, whether the idea that it is language that speaks is not an example of linguistic fetishism, but also whether the methodological individualism of Anglo-Saxon pragmatics is not the ultimate form of fetishism.

One of the essential questions for a philosophy of language is that of the choice of guiding metaphors. This is how Riley envisages the question of the 'workings' of language:

> Where is the place where language works? A doubtful contrast of inner and outer haunts the puzzle of whether I speak (from the inside outward) or whether I am spoken (from the outside in). (Riley, p. 54)

What is the type of spatial metaphor we must use in order to frame our concepts about language? As we saw, mainstream linguistics and philosophy of language tend to think in terms of the contrast between surface and depth, or inner and outer, a verticality they share with psychoanalysis. Such a system of metaphors conditions our thinking about language. Thus, according to the 'conduit metaphor', a chain of metaphors that seems to be almost unavoidable whenever we speak about words, we pack as much meaning as we can into our words, which we then send along the chain of transmission so that they are received and decoded by the addressee: it all starts inside, with the encoding machine of our brain; it reaches the surface, as the encoded words are produced as containers for the inner meaning; it eventually leaves the public surface to enter the depths of the addressee's mind and be decoded. So we think about language in terms of deep and surface structures (the semantic versus the syntactic, in one version of the contrast), of inner conception and outer expression of meaning. But can we imagine a site for language that is not 'inside' our psyche, as a faculty inscribed *in* the 'mind/brain' (as Chomsky terms it)? Can we imagine a language the structure of which would not be concealed from view, a black box (this is Chomsky's metaphor) the contents of which are unknown to us and have to be modelled by science? We remember the passage in Lévi-Strauss's *Tristes tropiques*, where he compares Marxism, psychoanalysis and geology: all three reconstruct hidden structures from the appearance of surface phenomena – linguistics as Chomsky envisages it can easily be added to the list.[21] The advantage of the geological metaphor is that it enables us to think language and the psyche together. The disadvantage is that it takes us back to the philosophy of language that fails bad words (and a host of other linguistic phenomena), or excludes them from consideration as irrelevant.

One solution to this quandary is a philosophy of reversal, which decides that the inside is in fact outside, that linguistic structure is there, on the surface, that the depths of human psyche are superficial and public. This would imply a philosophy of immanence, rejecting both the transcendence of Platonist ideas or of God as *nomothetes*, and the inverse transcendence of the depths of the unconscious or of deep structure. The Deleuzean concept of the plane of immanence may be of use here.[22]

We understand Riley's interest in inner speech ('Inner language is not composed of graceful musing, but of disgracefully indiscriminate repetition, Riley, p. 56), and her use of Volosinov.[23] For inner speech as Volosinov conceives it (by deciding that the old *logos endiathetos* is not some form of mentalese, but natural language interiorised) is the very image of the reversal just suggested. If we decide that inner speech *is* natural speech, then it is 'inner' (in my head) because it is first 'outer', in the public space of interlocution: inner speech is the dialogue the speaker constantly holds with herself. And inner speech, far from being a product of the psyche, is the constituent element of the psyche, as Volosinov, quoted by Riley on p. 55, suggests: 'Psychic experience is something inner that becomes outer, and the ideological sign, something outer that becomes inner. The psyche enjoys extraterritorial status in the organism. It is a social entity that penetrates inside the organism of the individual person.' Or again, 'it is the word that constitutes the foundation, the skeleton of inner life' (p. 56).

We can now return to our point of departure (is verbal aggression really language? Are bad words a suitable point of entry into the general question of interlocution and/or intersubjectivity?):

> [Verbal aggression] resembles a stone hurled without reflection, which the furious thrower has snatched up just because it lay to hand. The target cannot deflect the blow, but will be spared its after-effects because she realises the impersonal quality of the thing. The word considered as stone will shock but not break her. The denunciation hurts on impact but later it weakens, as its target sees there is only an accidental link between what was hurled and the will to hurl. She realises that the bad word is not properly 'expressive' of the speaker's impulse to aggressive speech ... while the impulse needs to be understood in itself and independently of its instrument. (Riley, p. 58)

This can be taken as the outline of a new pragmatics, constructed around another set of founding dichotomies: slogan vs proposition, *agôn* vs *eirene*, *rapport de forces* vs co-operation, interlocution vs intersubjectivity, force vs communication. The 'intersubjective' view of language is that adopted by Anglo-Saxon pragmatics, from Grice to Habermas. The other view, which the first half of the contrasts delineate, is best exemplified so far by the continental pragmatics of Deleuze and Guattari. Our task is to make the philosophy of language their critique of linguistics contains explicit. We shall start on that road by making an excursion into the world of *fous littéraires*.

## 3   Two Philosophies of Language, or: éloge des fous littéraires

Imagine a keen philologist who wants to demonstrate that the word 'eight' does not merely denote a number, but is the bearer of a more interesting, and so far concealed, meaning, namely the meaning of 'day' or 'light'. How does he set out to convince us? By the method of antonyms. Across a number of languages, he claims, if we add a negative prefix to the word 'eight', we obtain the word 'night'. This gives the following table:

> French ... huit *ne huit* nuit.
> Italian ... otto *ne otto* notte.
> Spanish ... ocho *ne ocho* noche.
> German ... acht *ne acht* nacht.

English ... eight *ne eight* night.
Swedish ... aetta *ne aetta* natta.[24]

There is something odd, to say the least, in this mode of reasoning, for our philologist deliberately ignores what should be the main tool of his trade, etymology: in the Romance languages, the origin of this phonic resemblance is in the Latin words *nox* and *octo*; in the Germanic languages in something like *nieht* and *ehta*. The surface resemblance, which seems too extraordinary to be a mere coincidence, conceals a common origin, the Indo-European roots *octo* and *nocto*, which closely resemble each other, but have no semantic link. But our philologist is not concerned with this, as he denies the existence of Latin, which for him is a mere jargon, imposed upon a gullible world by a mixture of Roman banditti and university professors.

This philologist, whose name was Jean-Pierre Brisset, is what is known as a *fou littéraire*. He wrote books with titles such as *The Science of God*, *The Origin of Man*, *Logical Grammar*, published at his own expense, in which he sought to prove that man does not descend from the banal ape, but from the frog. And he proved it, being obsessed with language, through philological means: a kind of extended punning, the constant reanalysis of words, as in the example I have quoted, which, by his standards, is relatively tame.

The question that immediately arises is: why waste our time with the ravings of a bunch of lunatics? And why entitle this section: 'in praise of "literary madmen" ', as if there was something to be learnt, for linguistics or the philosophy of language, from their ravings. My contention is precisely that there is something to be learnt from such texts, that they reach parts of language that mainstream linguistics or philosophy of language do not reach, that they encourage us to cast another look at the workings of language, not least the workings of language at their most complex and fascinating, in literary texts. In other words, they play the same role for me as bad words for Denise Riley, or hate speech for Judith Butler.

But let us go back to the beginning. The phrase *fou littéraire* was coined by the novelist and poet Raymond Queneau, one of the founders of Oulipo, a group of writers who specialise in games with language. He was also something of a philosopher: he edited Kojève's book on Hegel, which was so influential for French philosophers after the war. He collected instances of eccentricity, usually published at the author's expense, and meant to use this material for a thesis, which he never wrote, but which became one of his novels, *Les Enfants du limon*.

A *fou littéraire*, therefore, is an eccentric, animated by a fixed and demented idea, or system, who goes to print, usually via a vanity press. The objects of such cases of monomania are infinitely varied: we find circle squarers (for patronymic reasons, I have a certain tenderness for them), flat earthers, people who are convinced that Shakespeare was actually Francis Bacon, or a Frenchman, or an Arab (sheikh Speare, of course), so convinced indeed that they elaborate complex, if delirious, systems of proof. A very recent example in France is the case of the man who sold tens of thousands of copies of a book in which he claimed that 9/11 never occurred, that the Pentagon was never attacked, and that the whole thing is a dark plot by the American government, in the best style of the *X Files*. Such people are only rarely certified madmen (there is a difference between *fous littéraires* and what is usually known as 'the art of the insane'), they live normal petty-bourgeois lives, they have a job, a family and a bee in their bonnet. There lies the difference, if any, with you and me: they have a bright idea, a solution to an age-old problem, a system, or an analytic device, in which they firmly believe, even if, and especially if, it beggars belief.

What I like about Queneau's phrase is its paradoxical flavour. On the one hand, such people are more than slightly mad. On the other hand, they can be said to be 'literary': this is where they interest me, as I shall take the word to mean that, in the midst of their madness, they have intuitions about the way language works and literature is constituted. Before all this becomes too abstract, let us look at a few case histories.

## 4   Three *fous littéraires*

Not all *fous littéraires* are geniuses. I shall briefly present three, in growing order of interest, or genius.

In 1990, one Richard Wallace published a book called *The Agony of Lewis Carroll*.[25] His thesis is simple: Charles Dodgson was a secret gay, repressed by the moral and legal climate of Victorian Britain, and forced to express his sexuality in Aesopic language, in the shape of nonsense. He then proceeds, in order to prove his thesis, to give an interpretation of Carroll's work.

Several things must be noted about this.

1. Lewis Carroll must have been very repressed: there is no hint, either in his works, or his correspondence, or his contemporaries' accounts of him that suggests that he was gay. Such an argument, however, has little validity: 'Lewis Carroll' is what his texts allow us to construct.

2. The interpretation is not improbable in our conjuncture (indeed, one has the feeling that it would inevitably have been attempted some day): the development of gay and queer studies is part of our critical *doxa*.

3. The historical hypothesis is not lacking in verisimilitude: think of what happened to Oscar Wilde. No wonder Dodgson's sexual orientation remained strictly secret.

4. Nonsense is a good candidate for the Aesopic expression of a repressed sexuality. There is a passage in Freud where he claims that nonsense words are fragments of repressed sexual words. That there is an undercurrent of sexual energy in the *Alice* books is clear.

5. However, what the text of the *Alice* books induces us to construct for the figure of their author is not a homosexual position: it is the position of a heterosexual adult hopelessly in love with a little girl. A terrible spectre is raised here: the paedophile, the contemporary version of the Devil. This is why this interpretation, which is traditional and authoritative, is more difficult to sustain at present – but strongly present in the text it is, as in all sorts of peritexts (for instance Lewis Carroll's letters to his child-friends).

6. It is, however, when we get to the detail of Wallace's interpretation that things go radically wrong. He is an enthusiastic decipherer of riddles, and the instrument he uses is the same as Saussure: anagrams. I shall provide two examples. (i) The exact title of the second *Alice* tale is: *Through the Looking-Glass, and What Alice Found There*. This, you would hardly have guessed, is the anagram for: 'Look with a lens through the cute darling, he's a fag don.' (ii) In *The Hunting of the Snark*, there is a famous line that describes the method of navigation of the boat on which the heroes have embarked: 'Then the bowsprit got mixed with the rudder sometimes.' This is an anagram of (again, would you have guessed?) 'To Mother: Disturbed, I themed the worst pig-sex with men.' Wallace adds that 'theme' is a valid Victorian verb. May I risk two conclusions on this? Wallace's interpretation is more than bizarre (but it is typical of a *fou littéraire*). But his 'demented' interpretation is also, in a way, faithful to Carroll's own practice, since Carroll's works contain innumerable games played with language, including mirror-image readings, acrostics and indeed anagrams.

There is no doubt, however, that Wallace is mad. Not content with his extraordinary interpretation of Carroll, he published a second book (*fous littéraires* are usually afflicted with a compulsion of repetition), in which he 'demonstrated', through the usual means, that Lewis Carroll was ... Jack the Ripper.[26]

It is easy to see why Wallace, as an interpreter of texts, is dreadful. His interpretation is entirely predictable, a product of the *Zeitgeist*. The riddle of Jack the Ripper has always fascinated a gullible public, because no really convincing solution has ever been offered: how tempting to combine it with the riddle posed by nonsense texts that refuse to yield any meaning. And the instrument used, the search for anagrams, has the advantage that with a little ingenuity one can prove exactly what one wishes to prove: should I so wish, I could prove, using Wallace's method, that Carroll was a secret Leninist or a Corsican nationalist. Note, however, that Wallace is in good company, since Saussure did the same (he was sane enough to desist after a while, and never published his anagram notebooks).

Here is my second example: it concerns Lewis Carroll again. In 1966, an American Hassidic Jew, a medical doctor by profession, Abraham Ettleson, published an eighty-page pamphlet entitled '*Through the Looking-Glass' Decoded*. The text demonstrates that the tale is a cryptogram for the Talmud, that the subtext of Carroll's text is made up of references, not even allegorical but cryptic, in other words both literal and coded, to the Jewish ritual and what Ettleson calls 'the Jewish way'. Three examples will be enough to give you an idea of his method. Take the title of the poem 'Jabberwocky', he says, cut it into two ('Jabber' and 'Wocky'), and read the result in the mirror (which is, need I remind you, what Alice has to do when she comes upon the poem). The operation gives 'Rebbaj Ykcow', which, Ettleson triumphantly adds, is Rabbi Jacob, the name of the Bal Shem Tov, the founder of the Hassidic sect. Or take, in the same poem the coined word 'frumious', a portmanteau word (and we know that this is how Carroll coined his new words, and that he also invented the term 'portmanteau word' to describe what he did): it coalesces the words 'frum', meaning pious in Hebrew, and the English word 'pious'. Lastly, take the word 'Bandersnatch' ('Beware the Jubjub bird and shun / The frumious Bandersnatch'): it contains an anagram of 'Satan'.

Mirror-image reading, portmanteau words, anagrams: the least one can say is that Ettleson is faithful to the methods of interpretation practised in Carroll's own text: he is a sort of real life Humpty-Dumpty. And it is easy to see why he is no better than Wallace: he betrays the encyclopaedia (there is not the slightest hint that Dodgson was Jewish, or that he knew anything about Judaism), and he forces the text to say what he wants it to say (the word 'Bandersnatch' also contains an anagram of 'Barnes' – whether it be Julian, or William, the Dorset poet, I leave you to decide). But it is also easy to see why he is much better than Wallace, since what he does is nothing but what Carroll's text does to itself all the time. He is therefore faithful to Carroll after a fashion.

And we understand why both my *fous littéraires* are interested in nonsense: by refusing meaning, nonsense texts provoke interpretation, endless attempts to force meaning out of them or into them. Such forceful attempts develop intuitions about the workings of language, even as nonsense itself does. If Humpty-Dumpty is a philosopher of language, as I suggested in one of my books, so are Wallace and above all Ettleson.[27]

My third *fou littéraire* has a history as a mental patient. He suffers from a form of schizophrenia. The son of Russian Jews who emigrated to the United States in the first half of the twentieth century, Louis Wolfson has a problem with the English language, which is his maternal tongue, but not that of his parents (who started life speaking Russian and Yiddish): the sight or sound of a word in English is a source of quasi-physical pain in him. The feeling of exquisite unease that English words provoke in him cannot be explained away as mere intellectual distaste: it can only be compared to the (rare) feeling of horror that certain movies cause in us, as we leave the cinema with despising hearts but wobbly legs – it is not merely a case of intensity of affect (is this real fear, or only make-believe fear?[28]), it concerns an affect that becomes so unbearable as to produce physical unease. As a result, he takes all the precautions he can to avoid contact with the English language, which, as he lives in New York and his mother insists on speaking English to him, is not easy. His ears are plugged with the earphones of a Walkman tuned to a German channel, he keeps a Russian grammar open on his knees all the time, etc. Such tricks naturally sometimes fail, and this is where his device comes into play: he has got into the habit, whenever he is confronted with an utterance in English, of immediately translating it into words of other languages he knows (and he knows quite a few, being a keen student of languages), words which must have roughly the same sound and roughly the same meaning as their English equivalents. You understand how easy this can be, and how difficult. If the English word in question comes from the Romance stock of the English language, it will have an exact equivalent in French or Italian or Spanish (think, for instance, of 'interpretation'); but if it comes from the Saxon stock, it is not at all certain, the common origin being much more ancient, that such a word will be found (although sometimes it is, for instance, as we saw, 'night' and 'nacht').

Wolfson tells his story and explains his translation device in a book which he wrote, not in English of course, but in French, *Le Schizo et les langues*.[29] An example will explain how the device works. Wolfson is walking in the streets of New York, and he cannot help seeing a sign, which for us is innocuous enough, but for him the source of exquisite pain: 'Don't trip over the wire!' The only way he finds to escape the pain is immediately to translate the words, through the operation of his device, into the following sequence, 'Tu nicht trébucher über eth he Zwirn', a German sounding sequence, with borrowings from French ('trébucher') and Hebrew ('eth' and 'he' are the markers for the accusative case and the definite article respectively). You understand why I am reluctant to call this sequence of words a sentence: it mixes several languages in one sequence, which for the linguist is the ultimate sin (and, incidentally, whenever it occurs, the sign that we are reading a literary text). Indeed, a device similar to Wolfson's, called *traducson*, or translation according to sound, is a never-ending source of literary games.

A few provisional conclusions about my three *fous littéraires*. The first concerns the question of truth and belief. The problem is not so much that they are certain that what to us is blatantly false is true, it is that they have a two-fold relationship to truth. Take Wallace, for instance. He believes in his hypothesis, and this belief imposes itself upon him as an incontrovertible truth (I leave aside the possibility that Wallace is in fact a hoaxer). He also believes in the truth of his results, of what he found because he was looking for it. This redoubling of the truth of the investigation (truth of the hypothesis that inspires the interpretation, truth of the result that it yields) smacks of Freudian denial: the theory is false because of its excessive appeal to truth, whereby it betrays both the text and the encyclopaedia. The second concerns the question of respectability. What is seriously wrong with Wallace and Ettleson (but not Wolfson) is that they are profoundly respectable, in that they want to capture the canonical text of *Alice* for their respective ends: Alice, the archetypal Victorian child, is turned into an icon of gay or Jewish culture. The third, and most important, conclusion concerns the intuitions of *fous littéraires*. In Wolfson, less so in Ettleson, even less so in Wallace, a philosophy of language is involved, different from the common and garden variety, and I think more rewarding. Thus,

Wolfson is convinced that language is not the mere conveyor of meaning we usually take it to be, but the site for the deployment of material forces, that in language action is more important than meaning; thus also, we find in Ettleson and in Wallace another type of linguistic analysis than the usual parsing. The time has come to make this difference clear.

## 5 Two Philosophies of Language

The philosophy of language from which *fous littéraires*, in their intuitions, stray, is, of course, the philosophy of language that informs mainstream linguistics. I shall formulate it through a number of principles. They are usually found in the very first pages of treatises of linguistics, when the average linguist gets rid of the first principles in order to get to the detail of his linguistic theories quicker. All of my principles may not be found in every single linguistic theory, but all theories are united by a family resemblance.

The *first principle* is the principle of *immanence*. It is central to the structuralist version of linguistics. It states that the explanation of the workings of language must be sought in language itself, and not outside it. As a consequence, the philosophy of language on which structuralism is based deliberately ignores both the speaker and the context: it is concerned with the system of *langue* and the system only (the rest is excluded under the name of *parole*). The result is what is sometimes called an *internal* form of linguistics.

The *second principle* is the principle of *functionality*. Language has functions (Jakobson numbers six of them), revolving around one central function, which is the exchange of information. Language is first and foremost a means of communication. The consequence of this is that it is often conceived as an instrument, which the speaker has at her conscious disposal: I, the speaker, speak my language, I make it work according to my will.

The *third principle* is the principle of *transparency*. It is a consequence of the second. If language is an instrument of communication, it must make itself easily forgotten, it must not obtrude. Its function is to transmit meaning, and every single aspect of it is adapted to that function. Thus, in English, the distinction between the two deictic pronouns, 'this' and 'that', is neither idle nor arbitrary: it conveys an element of meaning (usually captured in the contrast between proximal and distal reference), but in such a way that it is forgotten by the native speakers who unerringly observe it.

The *fourth principle* is the principle of *ideality*. Language is divided between an abstract ideal system and its actualisation in speech or writing: the contrasts between *langue* and *parole*, or competence and performance, capture this (a point of comparison might be the abstract existence of the ideal sonata, its inscription on a manuscript, and its actual performance). As a system, language has no material existence, it belongs to the third world of ideas (neither the first world of objective reality, nor the second world of subjective thoughts – I am speaking the language of Karl Popper).

The *fifth principle* is the principle of *systematicity*. What is relevant in language is not *parole*, which is expelled from the consideration of science as too individual and too messy, but *langue*: the study of language is the study of a system. This, of course, reinforces the first principle, the principle of immanence.

The *sixth*, and last, *principle* is the principle of *synchrony*. The system, the true object of linguistic science, is achronic, not subject to time and history. Since language is obviously a historical entity, since actual languages have a long and complex history, a new concept is invented, the concept of synchrony: it denotes the abstract and ideal moment in time at which the system is described, *as if* it had no history. As a result of which, historical analyses of language are devalued, if not expelled, under the name of diachrony, a subordinate region of science.The doxic interpretation of Saussure's 'great revolution against philology,' which was, if not downright historical, at least evolutionist (think of the discovery of the genealogy of Indo-European languages) holds that it consisted in putting synchrony in the foreground and pushing diachrony into the background. Chomsky takes this position to its limit: his research programme is not merely synchronic, it is achronic: he is a fixist linguist, a linguist for creationists, as he believes the capacity for language is inscribed in the human genes, and therefore belongs to human nature.[30]

Against those six principles, our *fous littéraires*, even if they are in no way conscious of what they are doing (even Brisset, who is obsessed by language), suggest at least a sketch of another philosophy of language, in which language will have the converse characteristics. I shall spell them out by formulating the six converse principles.

The first is the *principle of non-immanence*. This states that it is impossible to separate language from the world in which it appears, in which it functions, and which it allows us to understand. Language is *of* the world and *in* the world. It is inseparable from human praxis, of which it is one of the main forms. Hence the necessity to develop not an internal but an external linguistics, in which there will be no radical separation between language and society, language and the body of its speakers, language and human actions. My *fous littéraires* may be mad, but they do treat language as form of action, as a means of intervention in and on the world.

The second is the *principle of dysfunctionality*. It suggests that language works on its own, not always, perhaps even not at all, at the speaker's bidding. This is what the language-school in the rue Pavée in Paris tells Denise Riley. So it is not certain that I speak language: there are moments when it is language, not me, that speaks, when language speaks through me, reducing me to the role of a mouthpiece (an obvious example is Freudian slips of the tongue). The consequence of this is that language is not necessarily, not even centrally, meant to allow the exchange of information. There are other possibilities, if we are looking for a central function of language: the expression of affect, the free play of language itself, not least the absence of a central function. My *fous littéraires*, of course are convinced, as their practice of language obviously shows, that this is the case.

The third is the *principle of opacity*. It states that transparency of meaning is an illusion. Language is never an instrument, wielded and forgotten when it has fulfilled its function. Language obtrudes, the speaker must always negotiate her meaning with her language: her meaning is always distorted and refashioned by language. This is a common enough experience: words mean more than I meant them to mean, in other words there is a constitutive gap between intention and expression. Literature, of course, can be said to be the systematic exploration of such a gap, and my *fous littéraires* literally *live* in such gaps.

The fourth is the *principle of materiality*. Language can never be separated from its performance (it consists in an exertion of force more than an exchange of information) because it is never separated from its material existence in bodies and institutions. Envisaged from this point of view, language is not an ideal system, it is a material body that is the bearer of affects. One of the consequences of this is that interlocution is a site for the contest of forces, not for the co-operative exchange of information. This is the *agonistic* view of language, which is essential for the understanding of bad words, and we must not forget that the adjective comes from the Greek word *agôn*, which means both struggle and dramatic production. Needless to say, my *fous littéraires* are entirely aware of the materiality of language, and of its agonistic character: in Brisset, language tells us a history of war and sex, which is inscribed in its very structure. And, as we have seen, for Wolfson language is at the same time the instrument of pain and the medicine that will, if not cure him, at least temporarily relieve the pain.

The fifth principle is the *principle of non-systematicity*. Language is only at best partly systematic (this is a deliberate contradiction in terms). The system is abstracted by the linguist from a messy collection of words, phrases, sentences or discourses, which are at best partly regular, never fully systematic. As a result, the generalisations that linguistics seeks to formulate, better known as 'rules of grammar', are not laws of nature, inscribed in our neurones or in our genes, but pragmatic maxims, of the type 'do this rather than that', or rather 'say this rather than that', which means that you can, if you so wish to express yourself, say that rather than this. Rules of grammar, all of them, even the syntactic rules of syntax that seem to be the most obligatory, are defeasible: they hold in general, in what computers call the default case, but you can ignore them if your expressive needs require it. And language itself, which, as we saw, speaks on its own, does ignore them: we call these exceptions, phonic coincidences, linguistic corruption, the work of metaphor, etc. Thus it is that the devices of *fous littéraires* provide a mirror of the workings of language: they are extremely strict and at the same time allow the most unashamed cheating (whenever language resists the *fous littéraire's* device, whenever it refuses to provide a proof of his mad idea, he changes the rule or forgets about it).

The sixth, and last, converse principle is the *principle of historicity*. It suggests that language is a messy object not because it is disorganised, or at best partly organised, but because it is made up of a sedimentation of meanings and rules. The synchronic value of a grammatical marker is never independent of its history. There is no point, for instance, in analysing the modal auxiliaries in contemporary English (that is words like 'may', 'must' and 'can') as a system without taking into account their long and complex history (thus, for instance, the homonymy of the auxiliary 'will' and of the noun, as in 'Let Your Will be done', is no coincidence). Or again, nothing in the core meaning of the reflexive pronouns ('myself', 'himself', etc.) could have predicted their use as pronouns of insistence (compare 'he killed himself' and 'he did it himself' or 'he himself did it'). And *fous littéraires* are natural historicists, where language is concerned: Brisset is only the most blatant case.

Because all this is threatening to become unbearably abstract, let us go back to the pleasant company of *fous littéraires*. We can note in passing that the reason for my praise of them is now clear: in their eccentric practice, they provide the elements of a new philosophy of language; they do not as yet construct its concepts, but they incite the philosopher of language, or at least *this* philosopher of language, to attempt such construction.

## 6  *Fous littéraires* as Practitioners of Another Philosophy of Language

Let us go back to Wallace, the least interesting of the three. The trouble with him is that he is too much spoken by the *doxa*, that he is not mad enough by far. He believes in a theory of interpretation that is commonsensical, and which I have called the tin-opener: when I have peeled off the layer of metal, I can tuck into the luscious sardines, or again, when I have solved the riddle of the text, its one and only meaning, so far concealed, appears in full light at last.[31] As a result of this, Wallace is only too predictable, and his books make boring reading. But one thing saves him: his device for opening the tin, the search for anagrams, is an excellent embodiment of the principle of opacity. What is decrypted is trivial, or plain stupid. The existence and the contents of a crypt, or code, is not in itself particularly interesting. But the systematic practice of anagrammatic rewriting of the text, with the *fuite en avant* it provokes, forces language to obtrude: language can no longer be said to be a transparent means of communication, as it has become a means to express a meaning, but one that is concealed and can only be perceived after the most harrowing work of deciphering. A consequence of this is that the principle of dysfunctionality also applies: the text is torn apart between two meanings, one apparent and one concealed, but also between the coherence of the ultimate meaning (Lewis Carroll was gay, he was Jack the Ripper) and the complexity of the encryptment (this purportedly public piece of language is in fact addressed to one reader, the first one capable of deciphering it).

Ettleson, like Wallace, and for the same reasons, implicitly posits principles of opacity and dysfunctionality. But he goes further. Because the encrypted meaning is neither personal nor necessarily intentional (since Carroll was in no way a Jew, we may imagine that it is God Himself who encrypted the Talmud into that apparently innocuous text), the principles of historicity and non-immanence are involved. What is encrypted is not a message, but a myth, an intertext which may, by special grace, have possessed the speaker unawares. Hence the peculiar quality of Ettleson's delirium (it makes his books much better reading than Wallace's): that it is historical. And we remember Deleuze and Guattari's theory of *délire*, expounded, for instance, in their book on Kafka:[32] delirium is always historical, its object is always the whole of human history, rather than the 'dirty little story' (this is what Deleuze calls it) of the individual subject. Hence also the interest of such delirium, the reason why it is more faithful to the original text than Wallace's, why it does to the text no more than the text does to itself. There is a whole sedimented encyclopaedia involved here, and Humpty-Dumpty (when he gives a close reading of the poem 'Jabberwocky') is, *like all literary critics*, the heir of countless generations of Talmudic commentators. We do not need to believe in Carroll's personal Jewishness (a guilty secret, as would be his being gay) for Ettleson's interpretation to work. All it needs is the operation of the principle of historicity, according to which contemporary language is sedimented bygone language, which it is the task of the interpreter to recover, or invent in the archaeological meaning of the term. And Ettleson's text, where text and commentary coexist on the same page, has the same structure as a commentary of the Talmud, or Derrida's *Glas*.

Wolfson, too, came from a Jewish background. He, too, had generations of Talmudic commentators behind him, and we understand his taste, and his gift, for foreign languages. In his delirium, all six of my counter-principles are, albeit unconsciously, put into operation ( you understand why his case is the climax of my list of *fous littéraires*: he is a better *fou littéraire* than Wallace, even as Jane Austen is a better novelist than Barbara Cartland).

The first is the principle of non-immanence. Language is definitely not a system for Wolfson, it is something to live with, or live by. What is necessary is not to engage in communication (he resists all attempts by his mother to talk to him – it is true that she insists on addressing him in English exclusively), but simply to live, often in spite of the presence of language (which also provides the means of the 'writing cure', when he writes his book). The separation of words and the world, which the principle of immanence postulates, does not exist for Wolfson, since words can cause him a form of pain that can only be described as bodily pain.

The principle of dysfunctionality is also practised by Wolfson, as his preoccupation is not to communicate, not to hear what his mother, who often shouts, is trying to tell him, not to read the road signs when he goes for a walk. So, for Wolfson, the question of who is master, language or the speaker, is highly debatable: he keeps trying to defuse, or conjure away a language that is trying to master him, and his life is one of linguistic struggle. And the enemy is not so much his mother, who could speak in gestures, or in another language, as the English language, which must be defeated and deconstructed through inter-linguistic *agôn*.

The principle of opacity is also at work. If Wolfson's point is to prevent language from transmitting a meaning immediately and straightforwardly, this can only be achieved by making utterances opaque, by literally working on the sounds of language, transforming the utterance into the simultaneous performance of several tongues, as a result of which the string of words is no longer an intelligible sentence but a linguistic monster, of which there can be no immediate understanding: it always needs a considerable effort of interpretation, which, for a single sentence, often takes dozens of pages of Wolfson's text.

This technique also involves, of course, the principle of materiality. For the problem with the English language is not that it expresses the wrong meanings (those are innocuous enough: it is difficult to interpret the phrase 'vegetable shortening', the object of a lengthy deconstruction by Wolfson, as a form of verbal aggression). The problem is that it causes the hearer quasi-physical pain. Thus Wolfson describes his mother literally 'bursting' into the room as he is listening to a Russian record and thinking about eating (always a complicated process for him) and 'in a triumphant tone' loudly uttering a sentence in English: the impression one gets from the description is one of physical struggle and defeat: the phrase he uses 'she made him suffer' is to be taken literally. So language has strong material effects: the sequence of words is also a string of sounds, capable of breaking crystal and of inflicting pain. We remember the pseudo-paradox of the Stoic philosopher Chrysippus, 'when I speak of a chariot, a chariot goes through my mouth': Wolfson takes this literally, and for him there is a correlation between speaking and eating, as Deleuze remarks in his celebrated introduction to Wolfson's book. Or again, we may remember Fonagy, the Hungarian phonetician of a psychoanalytic turn of mind, and his analysis of the iconic meaning of vocalic sounds, where the mouth and throat metaphorise other sphincters.[33] In Wolfson, as in Brisset, language carries with it a story of sex and pain. And it is not content with carrying it: it inflicts it on the hearer's suffering body.

Next comes the principle of non-systematicity. Wolfson's device is non-systematic at various levels. First, it confuses the levels and the sub-systems on which normal linguistic analysis rests. It analyses a single sentence more than once, even if it is not a case of syntactic ambiguity; it practises forbidden mixtures. The schizo is a lover (or hater) of languages, but not a trained linguist, and a professional linguist would indignantly reject Wolfson's idiosyncratic form of parsing. Secondly, Wolfson cheats: the device cannot keep its own systematicity. When English words, as they inevitably do, refuse to yield an instant translation into words of other languages with the same sounds and the same meanings, Wolfson, such is the urgency of the destruction of the English word, betrays his own device by loosening it, or invents other meanings. Thus, the word 'early' becomes the French words *'sur le champ'* ('on the spot', 'immediately'), *'de bonne heure'* ('early'), *'dévorer l'espace'* (literally, 'to devour space'), under the feeble pretext that, like 'early', they contain the sound 'r'. It is clear that the device, thus extended, can only end in delirium. The interesting point here is that the device, although delirious, is not entirely unfaithful to the workings of language. I coined the term 'wolfsonising' to describe certain aspects of the workings of natural language.[34]

Last comes the principle of historicity. The mixture of languages that Wolfson blithely practises also involves the sedimentation of various cultures. It is clear that Wolfson's delirium expresses his parents' history (the languages into which he translates English are the languages European Jews spoke before emigrating to the United States): he wants to revert from his mother's acquired tongue (and, with the fanaticism of the convert, she refuses to speak anything except English) to her (but not his) maternal tongue, and to his ancestors' maternal tongue (which was Yiddish). Wolfson's delirium allows him to travel in space and time, and language carries not only a story of sex and pain, but the whole history of a family lineage and of a people.

It appears, therefore that the interest of *fous littéraires* lies not in their engaging eccentricity, nor in the subtlety of their devices, nor in the breadth of their delirious imagination: in all of these, they can be utterly disappointing. It lies in their unconscious construction of another philosophy of language. The time has come to make a few suggestions

# 4
# The Concept of Language We Don't Need

## 1 A critique of Chomsky

The analysis of mainstream linguistics and philosophy of language, which I have presented in the form of six principles, as a background or foil against which to construct 'another philosophy of language', one that would enable me to understand both bad words and the productions of *fous littéraires*, suffers from one obvious defect: over-generalisation. I lump together schools of linguistics and philosophical positions between which there are serious, and sometimes unbridgeable, differences, and sharp polemics. The best I can claim for my six principles is that they are linked by Wittgenstein's family resemblance: all the various trends in mainstream linguistics and philosophy of language will resort to one or several of them, hardly any to the six of them. So, in order to make my critique more convincing, I must look in some detail at one subsidiary of this main stream, with its own coherence and limitations. I hope that this will make the necessity of the construction of another philosophy of language clearer.

There are three reasons why I have chosen the Chomskyan research programme as the object of this chapter. The first is trivial enough: it is by far the most important form of linguistic theory worldwide – in its case at least the terms 'mainstream' or 'dominant' are no exaggeration. The second is more interesting: in the work of Chomsky the philosophy of language that underpins all forms of linguistic theory is entirely explicit, which allows discussion and critique. The third reason is that Chomsky, because of the other, political half of his work, is highly aware of the violence of language that is inscribed in bad words and the texts of *fous littéraires*. Being the author of books entitled *Propaganda and the Public Mind* and *Necessary Illusions*,[1] he is aware of

91

the political violence exerted through language by the imperialist state and its media. But for him, such violence has nothing to do with linguistics. The following exchange with David Barsamian is typical:

> *Talk about the power of language to shape and control political discussion. For example, the IMF's much criticized 'structural adjustment programme' has now been renamed 'poverty reduction and growth facility.' The School of Americas, the notorious training facility for the Latin American military at Fort Benning, Georgia, is now called the Western Hemisphere Institute for Security Cooperation.*

> Let me just make clear, this has absolutely nothing to do with linguistics. There's no insight into this topic that comes from having studied language. This is all obvious on the face of it to anybody who looks. This is the topic that Orwell satirized, and of course it goes way back. If you have a war between two countries, they're both fighting in self-defense. Nobody is ever the aggressor. Furthermore, they're both fighting for exalted humanitarian objectives. To take some of Orwell's examples, if you're trying to control a population by violence and terror, it's 'pacification'.[2]

The question, of course, (apart from the interesting separation that Chomsky establishes between his scientific and his political activities), is: what is this 'language' that is not involved in what is obviously a political manipulation of words, the object of a rich tradition of analysis in terms of linguistic ideology, from Orwell to Althusser's first theory of ideology, where ideology works through systematic punning?

## 2  Chomsky's Language

The language that is the object of Chomsky's concern is altogether a strange object, which has little to do with what he calls the 'common sense' concept of language, although he claims it corresponds to at least some of its characteristics and therefore accounts for it (a claim I shall dispute). It is in fact an abstract object, a theoretical construct which Chomsky calls I-language, where the 'I' stands for 'internal, individual and intensional'. 'Internal' means that the study of language conforms to the structuralist principle of immanence, that linguistics is a natural science (what Milner calls a 'Galilean' science), closer to biology and physics than to psychology or sociology. 'Individual' means that the site for the production of language, and therefore for its scientific study, is the individual speaker, or rather the 'mind/brain' that is abstracted from it (the neuter pronoun is deliberate: this is a biological entity, but not a human body, no 'him' or 'her'). 'Intensional' means that the object of the theoretical construct is a generative grammar, a limited number of principles generating an infinity of occurrences (discrete infinity is for Chomsky a major characteristic of language).

In other words, the 'language' of which Chomskyan I-language is a model is a mental organ, the 'faculty of language', to use the outdated vocabulary of eighteenth century psychology of which Chomsky is exaggeratedly fond – in modern parlance, this becomes a species-specific 'biological endowment'. Such a faculty of language, being an 'organ', a biological system like the organ of vision, is not subject to historical development (its only time is the arrested time of evolution), and cannot be learned: the only part experience plays in language learning is the 'triggering' of the parameters that are always already there. In the child, language grows: you do not learn to grow arms, Chomsky claims, or to reach puberty. The language faculty involves the monad-like unfolding of a genetic programme. The only difference with the Leibnizian monad is that the language faculty has windows, since the learning process is granted a secondary and superficial role (it ensures that the child ends up speaking English rather than Japanese – a superficial difference according to Chomsky). The language faculty, therefore, being always under-determined by experience, is innate.

The concept of language thus constructed, it must be noted, is somewhat restricted but entirely coherent: there is nothing strange in a science abstracting its object from the phenomena and operating with a theoretical construct. Marx's concept of value is one such construct. Chomsky's philosophy is, to be sure, somewhat philosophically naïve. Thus, he repeatedly claims that his use of the terms 'mind' and 'language' bears 'no metaphysical weight' (and his rare allusions to post-structuralist philosophy are duly derogatory). He is in fact entirely dependent on contemporary American philosophy, and his natural opponents are Quine, Davidson, Searle and Putnam. There is a sense in which, philosophically, Chomsky emigrated from Europe shortly after the death of Hume: Descartes and Locke are his preferred European interlocutors.

Since I-language is a coherent and perfectly respectable theoretical construct, perhaps we should simply ignore it, and be content with noting that it is something entirely different from what *we* mean by language, different to the point of being the exact converse of the concept of language we need in order to account for bad words. We are interested in the pragmatics of verbal *agon*, in the relation between language and ideology, language and subjectivity, or subjectification, in the practice of literature as a specific experience of language, in the linguistic underpinnings of identity. This incites us to show an interest in the workings of grammar, not Chomsky's 'Universal Grammar', but the grammars of specific national languages, which are also their speakers' maternal tongues. And we are consequently incited to study the histories of such languages, of their syntax and of their semantics. All of this (*all* of this) is excluded by Chomsky as irrelevant to I-language, and (with the natural terrorism of the positivistic scientist) he discards it as 'folk linguistics', 'ethnoscience' and mere 'common sense'.

There lies the rub. At the very moment when he constructs a highly abstract, and restricted, concept of language, which excludes most of what we know and experience as language, Chomsky makes an implicit (and sometimes explicit) claim to account for language pure and simple, the whole of language (or, if not quite all, at least all that is of any relevance or interest). Thus, his contribution to the *Oxford Companion to the Mind*[3] is modestly entitled 'Language: Chomsky's Theory'. There are other entries entitled 'Language', but they all deal with partial areas of the field, such as 'Language: Learning Word Meanings', or 'Language: Areas in the Brain'. The very title of the main entry paradoxically suggests that what is expounded is only *a* theory of language, Chomsky's, but also all there is to say about language, as no other theory is mentioned.

This concept of language entails consequences, not least the consequence that all human languages are basically the same, and their differences are only superficial, which means that for the purposes of a theory of language, English (or Japanese) does not exist as an independent entity. Here is a typical passage:

> In the last twenty years or so, there has been a huge explosion of research which has dealt with typologically quite varied languages. We can suspect, and more or less know in advance, that they're all going to be more or less alike. Otherwise you couldn't learn any of them. The basic structure of them, including the meanings of words and the nature of sentences, just has to come from inside. You don't have enough information to have all that richness of knowledge.[4]

You have no doubt noted the danger words ('[we] more or less know in advance', 'just has to come from inside') and the one empirical argument, endlessly repeated, that linguistic knowledge is under-determined by experience and learning – an argument strongly reminiscent of the cosmological argument for the existence of God: the universe is too complex not to have been designed by a holy engineer. No wonder Chomsky is sometimes called a linguist for creationists.

But the passage quoted above shows why we cannot simply ignore the concept of language he constructs: simply because it tends to occupy the whole of the field, at the very moment when it excludes most of the phenomena. When Chomsky claims that 'the meanings of words and the nature of sentences' are determined by our inner biological endowment, and thus not subject to history, he is saying something that contaminates his conception of language and makes it thoroughly unacceptable.

The problem is the point where the line is drawn. For everybody will accept that our capacity to speak is, to some extent, determined by our biological make-up and therefore 'innate' (we may balk at the importation of idealist metaphysics that, in spite of Chomsky's disclaimers, the concept implies). The basic fact is that we speak and chimpanzees do not (when we go into the details of primate communication, the picture becomes somewhat blurred: remember the old joke that if dogs do not speak, it is because they are too wise to do so, since if they did, they would be made to fetch and carry – communication between chimps is adapted to their way of life). And everybody, even Chomsky, will accept that some of language must be learned. For the basic fact is that Japanese babies do not speak English, and that wolf-children (or Caspar Hauser) do not speak at all. Chomsky gets rid of that (to him) unwelcome fact through the metaphor of triggering. So what we have is a gradient, which can be represented thus:

| - innate | | | + innate |
|----------|---|---|----------|
| +acquired     I | | I     -acquired | |
| chimps don't | | Japanese babies don't | |
| speak | | speak English | |
| 1 | | 2 | |

A thoroughgoing empiricist will draw the line at position one, conceding that the general capacity to learn to speak is innate (she may dispute the idea that there is a specific capacity to *speak*, as opposed to a general capacity to learn): all the rest is acquired through experience, through a learning process which is dependent on the practice of inter-locution. Chomsky will concede that some superficial elements of lan-guage (such as the difference between English and Japanese) are acquired, and the rest is innate: he will draw the line at position two.

The Marxist that I am, who wishes to analyse language as a social and historical practice, sympathises with the empiricist. The question is: on which side of the divide are semantic configurations and gram-matical structures such as reciprocal or reflexive pronouns? For us, they are specific to certain languages or families of languages. For Chomsky, they are innate: this is where his concept of language cannot be ignored, where it must be criticised. I shall do this by looking at Chomsky's own examples.

## 3   Chomsky's Own Examples

The critique will achieve its goal if it establishes that Chomsky's account of his own examples fails actually to explain the phenomena, or that there is another, simpler, explanation. We shall see that Chomsky fails on both counts.

The first example deals with semantics. Chomsky observes that in the sentence:

(1)  He painted the house brown,

we understand that what he painted is the outside, not the inside, of the house. And he concludes:

> The fact that a brown house has a brown exterior, not interior, appears to be a language universal, holding of 'container' words of a broad category, including ones we might invent: *box*, *airplane*, *igloo*, *lean-to*, etc. To paint a spherical cube brown is to give it a brown exterior. The fact that *house* is distinguished from *home* is a particu-lar feature of the I-language. In English, I return to my home after work; in Hebrew, I return to my house.[5]

This is part of a more general claim that 'concepts are fixed',[6] that is, they belong to the innate universal grammar of I-language. The argu-ment offered in support of this is the usual one: 'It is hard to imagine otherwise, given the rate of lexical acquisition, which is about a word an hour from ages two to eight, with lexical items typically acquired on a single exposure, in highly ambiguous circumstances, but understood in delicate and extraordinary complexity, that goes vastly beyond what is recorded in the most comprehensive dictionary.'[7]

But are concepts 'fixed'? Even if we restrict ourselves to the names of physical objects and events (as opposed to philosophical concepts, like 'subject' or 'surplus-value', or abstract words like 'serendipity' – and then, we should have to offer an account of this division in our lexicon), we shall find it hard to believe that the concept 'house' is fixed in Chomsky's sense, that is, innate. Of course, Chomsky will immediately claim that what is fixed is not the concept 'house' itself, but a more abstract concept of 'a broad category of container words', adding, to make the vagueness of 'a broad category' more precise, that the container in question is typically seen from the outside, as shown by the contrast between our initial sentence and the following one:

(2) He painted his cave in red ochre.

But this a perceptual, or experiential, not a linguistic, contrast: certain container objects are typically perceived from the outside, certain others from the inside. The choice is determined by the position of the speaker's body in relation to the object: I usually apprehend the house as a unitary object before I enter it, and the converse is true of the cave, or flat. What Chomsky analyses as a linguistic universal is an experiential feature, which primarily involves the orientation of my body in the world –this is what is inscribed and represented in language. As a result of this, Lakoff and Johnson's theory of metaphor[8] provides a simpler and altogether more convincing account of the phenomena – with the added advantage that it also provides an account of the metaphorical process of reduction that goes from 'a broad category of container' to 'house'. If there is anything universal here, it is the bodily experience of orientation, perhaps even its transcription within language as the metaphorical drift involved in what Lakoff and Johnson call 'structural metaphors' (of the type 'a HOUSE is a CONTAINER (of a certain type)'), which are themselves based on 'orientational metaphors'. What is species-specific is a certain capacity of association, which is perceptual before it is linguistic: accounting for it does not require the complex machinery of an I-language where all concepts are always-already present, and not learned but remembered in the approved Platonist manner. So phenomenological accounts, such as Lakoff and Johnson's (or Merleau-Ponty's concept of the word as verbal gesture) fare better than Chomsky's.

Chomsky's account is not only uselessly complex. It is also altogether off the mark, in that it fails to account for the detail of the linguistic phenomena. Let us consider the two following sentences:

(3)  He painted the entire house brown.
(4)  He painted the house off-white.

In those sentences, the perceptual salience of the exterior of the house becomes less affirmed, and reference to experience, in the form of the encyclopaedia, is necessary to understand the sentence. Sentence (3) may of course mean that he painted the exterior of the house. But since it is not customary to paint the exterior of the house in alternate stripes of black and white so that it looks like a Newcastle United football shirt, why mention that the *whole* of the house is painted brown? A simple computation of implicatures (which are certainly not innate) will make me suppose that the inside of the house is concerned. The same is true of sentence (4), as 'off-white' is a colour for interior, not exterior, decoration. What this suggests is that the concept 'house' is not 'fixed', but culturally determined by an encyclopaedia and a historical conjuncture; that, like all concepts, it bears the mark of sedimented history and various types of social practice.

The second example concerns syntax. It comes at the end of Chomsky's contribution to the *Oxford Companion to the Mind*, when he moves from the abstract description of I-language to empirical justification through exemplification.

He starts with a brief description of the reciprocal construction in English, the construction that uses the complex pronouns 'each other' and 'one another'. The rule of grammar that governs such constructions is that the pronouns must have an antecedent in the plural. The problem is to find the antecedent. In typical cases, it is present in the same clause as the reciprocal pronoun, preferentially in the position of subject, as in:

(5)  The men recognized each other.

But there are complications, as the antecedent is not always in the same clause, and we must account for the fact that (6) and (7) are grammatical, but (8) and (9) are not (I am using Chomsky's examples):

(6)  The candidates wanted each other to win.
(7)  The candidates believed each other to be dishonest.

(8)  \*The candidates believed each other were dishonest.
(9)  \*The candidates wanted me to vote for each other.

In those four sentences, the antecedent is outside the subordinate clause that contains 'each other', but the relation of antecedence does not always hold across the clause boundary. A complex grammatical rule seems to be at work here, which native speakers of English unerringly apply, but which they would be at a loss to formulate. This state of affairs inspires Chomsky with the following conclusions:

> Such facts as these are known to all speakers of English, and analogues appear to hold in other languages. The facts are known without experience, let alone training. The child must learn that 'each other' is a reciprocal expression, but nothing more, so it seems. No pedagogic grammar would mention such facts as those described above; the student can be expected to know them without instruction. The principles that determine selection of an antecedent, it seems reasonable to assume, belong to 'universal grammar', that is, to the biological endowment that determines the general structure of the language faculty. From another point of view, these principles form part of a deductive, explanatory theory of human language.[9]

Every single sentence in this text is problematic, not least in the systematic use of hedges ('it seems to me ...'). And the main problem is that if native speakers unerringly abide by such rules, my French students are apt to make mistakes, and not to distinguish between (6) and (7) on the one hand, and (8) and (9) on the other. Perhaps this is due to the fact that they were exposed to English only after puberty, at a time when all the triggering that can be done has been done. But this explanation cannot hold: the French language, too, has reciprocal pronouns ('l'un l'autre', 'les uns les autres'), and if all the learner has to learn is that x is a reciprocal expression, the triggering has occurred in the French child in the same way as in her English colleague.

There is, however, another, simpler, explanation for my students' mistakes: the grammar of reciprocal pronouns is different in English and French, and the rules that Chomsky ascribes to the biological endowment of the species are in fact language-specific. In French, reciprocal pronouns are never subjects, always objects (or complements of a preposition). As a result of this, what the speaker has to ascertain in her parsing is not only which is the antecedent of the pronoun, but which syntactic slot the pronoun is inserted in:

(10)  Les candidats croyaient s'être vus l'un l'autre.
(11)  *Les candidats croyaient l'un l'autre se voir.

Ironically, Chomsky could eliminate this discrepancy by having recourse to an older model of his, in which raising transformations were allowed. He could argue that, in English too, the reciprocal pronoun is always in the object, never in the subject position. Thus, examples (8) and (9) are agrammatical because the reciprocal pronoun is the subject of the subordinate clause, whereas (6) and (7) are grammatical because the subject of the infinitive clause has been raised to object of the main clause (and here we may remember that in Latin the subject of the infinitive clause is in the accusative). But Chomsky has abandoned the early transformational model for a more abstract minimalist one, and he is no longer willing to make this move. And what he could not account for on any of his models is the changing nature of the reciprocal pronoun in French which is being assimilated to an adverb, so that sentences (12) and (13) are felt to be structurally similar:

(12)      Ils se félicitèrent l'un l'autre.
(13)      Ils se félicitèrent mutuellement.

What I am suggesting here is that 'l'un l'autre' is now perceived, and treated as a block, and no longer as the combination of two pronouns, which could, as is the case in English, be separated ('each girl trusted the others': this syntactic possibility is not mentioned by Chomsky, as it complicates the 'innate rules' for reciprocals).

So let us go back to Chomsky's conclusion, the vagueness of whose language I have noted, beyond the necessities of a short encyclopaedia article. Thus, when he states that 'analogues appear to hold in other languages', we can only wonder how many languages are concerned, and to what extent the analogies hold, that is, which is the aspect of the reciprocal construction that is supposed to be innate (the example of French, a language close to English, shows that Chomsky's rules are not part of this universal feature). And claims that 'such facts are known to all speakers of English' and 'known without experience, let alone training' must be resisted, or at least seriously qualified. Thus, the reciprocal construction, so my corpus grammar tells me, is extremely rare. There are fewer than sixty occurrences of the reciprocal pronouns per million words (compare with demonstrative pronouns, of which there are more than 25 000).[10] On the face of it, this should provide an argument in support of Chomsky's thesis: in the case of reciprocals, competence does appear to be under-determined by experience. But qualifications need to be made. First, the occurrences are low in conversation and news, that is in oral English, and higher in fiction and academic discourse, registers in which the speaker has been exposed to more linguistic and metalinguistic training, so the reciprocal competence is acquired through teaching to a far more considerable extent than Chomsky is prepared to admit (there are twice as many reciprocals in academic discourse as in ordinary conversation, three times as many in fiction). Secondly, the very rarity of the construction, combined with the elevated registers in which it occurs, may explain the grammatical correctness of the occurrences and their stability over dialect and register, so that reciprocal competence need not be innate: it is part of the grammar of English one learns through exposure, in the family and later at school, even if most 'pedagogic' grammars do not go into as fine details as the linguist. The rarity and fixity of the construction makes for easy learning, even with minimal exposure. In fact, the average explanation in a pedagogic grammar, 'a reciprocal pronoun has an antecedent in the plural that is usually the subject of the same clause', is sufficiently general to produce apt competence. Chomsky's examples, such as 'the candidates wanted each other to be successful', is hardly the sort of sentence you hear in ordinary conversation: such supposedly universal constructions are register bound, and a narrow register at that.

Because the reciprocal construction is rare, and therefore fixed, the arguments pro and contra Chomsky may remain inconclusive. So let us look at a similar construction, with far more numerous occurrences, the reflexive construction (involving pronouns such as 'himself', 'myself', etc.). There are 500 occurrences of such pronouns per million words in my grammar's corpus. And the syntactic question they beg is the same: how do we ascertain which word is the pronoun's antecedent? And we find similar syntactic contrasts:

(16)  He wanted himself to win.
(17)  *He wished (that) himself wouldn't have to do it.

There is one difference with the reciprocal pronouns: there must be agreement in person as well as in number between the pronoun and its antecedent. This is what ought to be innate, not subject to learning or change, together with the syntactic rules for selection of antecedent. There are, of course, apparent counterexamples, such as:

(18)  This section was written by Chomsky and myself.

It would appear that for a considerable number of speakers this sentence is blamelessly grammatical, and yet there is no antecedent for the reflexive pronoun, neither in the same clause, nor anywhere else (since the sentence has no co-text).[11] But it has a context, and the antecedent of 'myself' is, of course, the unexpressed speaker. If we want this *sujet de l'énonciation* to reappear as *sujet de l'énoncé*, all we have to do is postulate a deep structure superordinate sentence, 'I state that (18)', which provides an antecedent for 'myself' but, as it conveys no relevant information, is erased from the surface structure. This is Ross's solution, which he called the 'performative hypothesis' or 'analysis'.[12] It is (again: of course) a solution that Chomsky would not accept, but it does dispose of the apparent exception. We merely note that the dependency between antecedent and pronoun jumps across a clause boundary (here, the boundary of the 'that-clause'), and that it is not strictly confined to syntax, since situational or enunciative dependency is sufficient to account for the use of the reflexive (compare: (19) This section was written by Chomsky and me).

But here is a more tricky, and fully attested (it comes from a detective novel) counter-example. The irate customer is complaining to the station-master that the porter has insulted him: 'and this porter of yours runs into me and then has the cheek to tell me that I ran into him. With a heart like mine, the sudden shock might well have been very bad for me.'[13] This is the station-master's soothing answer (which I shall duly number, like a linguistic example):

(20)  If you've got a bad heart, I should calm yourself, Sir.

Here, there is no question of saving the rule by crossing clause boundaries or plunging into the enunciative situation. For the antecedent of 'yourself' can only be, and yet cannot be, 'I', as appears if we produce the following 'correct' sentences:

(21)  If you've got a bad heart, you should calm yourself, Sir.
(22)  If I had a bad heart, I should calm myself, Sir.

Our attested sentence is not unintelligible in any way: it makes perfect, and easy to grasp, sense.

And we cannot save Chomsky's account, not even by recourse to an older version of the model (of which there are many, as Chomsky completely overhauls his theory every five years – hardly the time for significant change in the evolution of our biological endowment). So either we add extra rules in order to account for the occurrence, at the cost of making the 'innate' machinery uselessly complex and hardly universal (this is a typically English construction, with no 'analogue' in French), or we seriously question the concept of rule, which for Chomsky is a law of nature, being inscribed in the biological endowment of the species, and treat it as a pragmatic maxim, of the type 'say this, if that really is what you wish to say', a maxim that is, therefore, defeasible for expressive purposes. Our sentence (20), in this case, is a totally apt sentence, a portmanteau construction combining (21) and (22), and allowing the station-master to make a diplomatic answer, not giving in to the irate customer while preserving his conversational face. But such an account has nothing to do with Chomsky's I-language: the interest is that it has everything to do with the concept of language, as historical and social praxis, that we need.

To come back to our counter-example, one move that is not possible is to discard it as a mere exception, a syntactic *hapax legomenon*. For, once we are aware that the 'normal' rules do not always apply, counter-examples will crop up everywhere. Here is a brief selection:

(23) 'We had complaints of a man prying on women like yourself,' said Liz. 'He claimed to be from the Water Board.'[14]
(24) 'Miss St Clair,' began Markham, in a tone of polite severity, 'the murder of Mr Alvine Benson has intimately involved yourself.'[15]
(25) [An old man is musing about his daughter-in-law] Marget would have spilt the kettle over the fender and one of the brats, and in the midst of the hissing and howling would have blamed himself.[16]

We might interpret those examples as 'enunciation' reflexives, albeit ones without easy syntactic transcription, as in the performative hypothesis. In (23) and (24) the 'antecedent' of the reflexive pronoun is not the *sujet* but the *objet de l'énonciation*, the interlocutor. In (25), an example of free indirect speech, we might reintroduce an introductory clause, of the type 'he thought that ...', to account for the reflexive, although the distance between antecedent and pronoun would be such as to make havoc of the usual neat syntactic rules.

There is, however, an alternative, simpler explanation, one that is in principle excluded by Chomsky's theory: syntactic constructions such as the reciprocal and reflexive pronouns, far from being innate traits of human nature, are caught in the history of the languages in which they occur. They evolve, not in the quasi-immobile time of species evolution, but in the much faster time of human history. In the case of the English reflexives, we might distinguish three synchronic uses of the construction, which are the sedimented image of three stages in the linguistic history of the construction.

First comes the *reflexive* construction proper (this is what Chomsky-type syntactic rules capture: it is not, as such, innate, but both arbitrary, that is language-specific, and dynamic, that is subject to historical change). It is found in sentences of the type:

(26)  I said to myself ...

In such sentences, the syntax conforms to rules of reflexive antecedence, and the semantics of the construction are homogeneous with its syntax – this reflexive construction has reflexive meaning.

Second comes the *emphatic* use of the reflexive, where the syntactic constraints are (roughly) the same, but the meaning is no longer reflexive, but intensive: syntax and semantics are dissociated. We can perceive this in the contrast between (26) and the two following sentences:

(27)  I myself said it.
(28)  Although I say it myself.

Last comes the *honorific* use of the reflexive, sometimes called 'semi-emphatic', where neither the syntax not the semantics of the construction are reflexive, although it does involve reflexive pronouns. Thus, a more polite (or more servile, or more affected) way of saying (29) is to say (30) instead:

(29)  Is it for you?
(30)  Is it for yourself?

What is at work here is another syntax (there is no antecedent in the co-text) and a pragmatic maxim of politeness, of the type: 'maximise the conversational interests of your interlocutor' (for not all words are bad words, some are kindness itself). And there is a certain logic in envisaging the passage from one form of the construction to another as a historical evolution, whereby the syntactic drifting (analogous to the metaphorical drifting in the meaning of words, or the process diachronic linguists know as 'grammaticalisation') takes the reflexive pronoun further and further away from its original construction, and changes its Saussurean 'value'.

## 4   A Spontaneous Philosophy for Scientists

It is not enough to discard Chomsky's theory as not the philosophy of language we need (as we saw, I-language excludes all the linguistic phenomena we wish to understand). It is not enough to say that the emperor is naked, that Chomsky's theory fails to account for what, in his own terms, are relevant phenomena. It is not enough to praise it, and use it, as a counterfoil, against which we shall construct the concept of language we need. We must also account for its existence and influence. Here Althusser's Course of Philosophy for Scientists will be of help.[17] In it, he analyses the philosophy of Jacques Monod, the Nobel prize-winner in biology, as a 'spontaneous philosophy for scientists', a mixture of gross materialism and arrant idealism. Come to think of it, this description fits Chomsky's philosophy of language perfectly.

In spite of his repeated denials (for him, 'materialism' is a term without much meaning – it is true his main reference is Friedrich Lange's history of materialist philosophy),[18] and his original position on the mind and body problem (for him, what is problematic is not the concept of the mental, as is usually thought, but the concept of the physical), Chomsky's 'naturalism', for that is the term he uses, is more than the indication of a striving towards scientificity (on the model of the hard, natural sciences). He claims that in his favourite phrase, the 'mind/brain', the slash does not indicate that the mind will ultimately be reduced to the brain, but the current state of the art, where relationship there is, but we do not yet know what it is. The ultimate goal, therefore, is not reduction of one term to the other, but unification, as the sciences of the mind and the brain converge or perhaps even merge. So the language faculty cannot be reduced to a certain configuration of neurones. But his very favourite phrase, and the individualism of his approach (the faculty of language is situated within each speaker, and since, as he quite rightly notes, we do not think with our feet, the brain is involved), does suggest a strong physical basis for language, but not in the erotic or phenomenological body: in the biological body (language is part of our 'biological endowment'), if not directly in the brain, its language areas and its neurones, at least in the genetic code that each of us inherits. As a result of this, linguistics is at best an ancillary, at worst a temporary science. It is temporary if we decide that one day it will be made useless, as an independent science, by the development of biology and genetics (and we may be sure that in the coming years, claims to the discovery of 'language genes' will regularly be made); it is ancillary if it survives as an independent science, but one that translates in a language closer to the phenomena as experienced by us the cryptic code of our genetic make-up. A form of reductionism is inevitable in the Chomskyan programme, because of its methodological individualism and its denial of history – because it ignores, or treats as irrelevant, the fact that language is a social-historical *practice*.

This appears clearly in the point where Chomsky places grammatical constructions, which we have seen are historical, and duly subject to historical change, on the innateness gradient:

| - innate | | + innate |
|---|---|---|
| +acquired | I | –acquired |
| | reciprocal and reflexive | |
| | constructions | |

An empiricist, and a Marxist for that matter, will place such phenomena at the opposite end of the gradient: the constructions are mostly acquired, they are not universal but language-specific, the non-acquired element being ascribed to general cognitive capacity, a specifically human talent for learning that goes far beyond the learning of language. One can read on this point Geoffrey Sampson's comprehensive critique of Chomsky.[19]

So reductive materialism there is in Chomsky. But it is inextricably mixed with rank idealism. This is apparent in the philosophical lexicon he resorts to, which goes back to the seventeenth century. Nowhere is it more obvious than in his theory of knowledge which, as we have seen, is Platonist: the child exposed to language remembers it, as the slave in *Meno* remembers mathematical truths. Cognition of language is always recognition.

We are now clear about the four characteristics we do not want in such a concept of language. (Such characteristics are by no means restricted to the Chomskyan research programme: a similar critique could be levelled at the spontaneous philosophy of Anglo-Saxon pragmatic linguistics, or continental 'enunciation' theories – although the detail of the critique would of course be different).

The first is *methodological individualism*, the idea that the site of language competence is in the individual speaker (this is, we remember, one of the meanings of 'I' in the name 'I-language'). Philosophically, this is a retreat from Saussure's or the structuralists' concept of *langue* as a system with a form of existence in society outside the individual speaker, even if every occurrence of *parole* must be attributed to an individual speaker. In this, Chomsky is to Saussure what analytical Marxists (Elster *et al.*[20]) are to the bearded prophet. Against this, we must defend a view of language not as a biological endowment of the human species, but as a social practice, giving rise to effects of intersubjectivity through interlocution, creating subjects and identity through interpellation. Chomsky takes this *asocial* concept of language to the point where he denies that communication is the function/source of language (he is not entirely wrong in this, communication is by no means the only function of language). The limitations of this asocial concept will be easily understood through an analogy. If language has its site in the mind/brain, economic production has its site in the mind/hand. Yet economics as a discipline is not solely concerned, not even mainly concerned with the (fascinating, and crucially important) development of the human hand, not even with the development of the human mind which has given us science and technology: economic structures (forces of production) and relations (relations of production) have their autonomous efficacy as well as their social existence.

The second characteristic is *reification*, which reduces what is essentially a practice to a series of 'things': a Universal Grammar, a Language Acquisition Device, situated (the spatial metaphor is highly relevant) in the mind/brain. Here the reduction is from practice to mechanism and the governing metaphor goes from human to artificial intelligence. But computers, beside being dumb, do not engage in social relationships, let alone class struggles, and the analogy with human language soon breaks down. And such reductionism through reification has two unwelcome consequences, the last two characteristics of this philosophy of language.

The third characteristic is *ahistoricism*. There is no history or development of language, only a phylogenetic development, in the aeons of evolution, and an ontological development of each speaker, a growth of her organ of language, which may be arrested (as in the case of wolf-children) or impaired, as various areas of the brain are damaged. This does not mean, of course, that Chomsky denies the empirical fact of language filiation and language change, simply that he totally ignores it: parameters do not only vary, from language to language, they also shift, as languages evolve. But the language faculty remains immobile. And why they shift is never considered, as it does not concern the biological endowment of the species. What this deliberately misses is simply that language is a cultural phenomenon, that it is spoken not merely by individual speakers but by *communities* of speakers. We are back to the asocial character of this concept of language. Chomsky's ahistoricism implies a denial of the relevance of culture and society.

But this is coherent with the fourth characteristic, that is the *naturalism* of Chomsky's concept. This implies two things: a misguided belief in human nature and its fixity (the 'biological endowment' again: we understand why Chomsky has been called a linguist for creationists), and the idea that the rules of language are laws of nature rather than defeasible pragmatic maxims. If the rules that govern the syntax of reciprocal or reflexive pronouns are innate, they belong to the same type of laws as the laws of physics. As we have seen, empirical evidence suggests that they do not: they are indeed defeasible, subject to variation and change. And Chomsky takes this naturalism very far, to the point where he denies the existence of natural languages. There is no such thing, at least for the science of language, as 'English': parameters are switched on and off, and we pass from one 'language' to another in a continuum, and the basic fabric of language is always the same. So that, as we have seen, 'English' is only superficially different from Japanese or Quechua.

As this is a crucial point, I shall briefly develop it. In a sense, Chomsky is right. There is no such thing as 'English', only a variety of dialects and registers. 'Standard English' is an ideological construction and a political imposition. The existence of mixtures of languages, such as Pidgins and Creoles, shows that boundaries of language can only be fixed through arbitrary decision, and the very rhythm of change works against the fixity of the referent of what is merely an ontological metaphor: the vast variety of 'New Englishes' is evolving fast, and moving away from the parent language. But this kind of argument is not open to Chomsky, who denies the relevance of history and society for the study of language: what I am describing is a historical, political and sociological process of language development, diversification and mixture. And from this point of view, it is equally necessary to argue that 'English' does not exist, and that there is such a thing as English, that the ontological metaphor must have a referent, that it is historically and politically necessary. We do indeed have a political history of English, the history of its conquests through invasion and imposition (on marginal communities like the Welsh), the history of its teaching (which involves a history of 'correctness', of which 'Standard English' is the embodiment, duly transmitted in school grammars and the industry of English as a second language), but also the history of what goes under the name of 'English literature' (which is of course not the same thing as 'literature in English') – the history of a special way of inhabiting language, or, to change the metaphor and go from Heidegger to Gramsci, of a specific conception of the world, elaborated through language and inscribed in it. All of this is (sorely) missing in Chomsky's concept of language. It is captured by other concepts, for instance in the continental pragmatics of Deleuze and Guattari, through the concepts of minority, of collective assemblage of enunciation, etc.[21]

That Chomsky's theory, because of those unwelcome characteristics, must be criticised is now clear. But I also suggested it must be explained: why such spontaneous philosophy, and why does it take this form? Chomsky's errors are only interesting if we understand their origin and appreciate their necessity. The explanation is to be found in the central Marxian concept of fetishism.

## 5  Fetishism

I have already hinted that, as far as language is concerned, there are two types of fetishism. One is the positive fetishism, hardly worth that pejorative name, of scientific abstraction, which produces the ontological metaphors, 'language', or 'the English language'. Such metaphors are not only a linguistic (we need such names to speak of objects, and they must have a certain generality) but also a philosophical necessity: a concept is an ontological metaphor for which justification is offered, for instance in the shape of a system of concepts in which it is inserted. But why not include 'I-language', a fine figure of a scientific abstraction, in the glorious list? Because there is another form of fetishism, the object of the Marxian critique, of which Chomsky's concept of language is an example: the fetishism that involves the atomisation, naturalisation and individualisation of a social-historical practice. And here I find myself speaking the language of Lukács.

Lukács's *History and Class Consciousness*[22] does not merely expound Marx's theory of commodity fetishism, it develops it in ways that are relevant to us. Commodity fetishism, as we know, turns human relationships (the economic relations of production and exchange) into 'things' that become independent from their human producers and oppress them. Lukács observes that under capitalism fetishism rules the relationships between (human) subject and object in the shape of *forms of objectivity* within which the world is perceived, theorised and acted upon. And what such reification achieves is the obfuscation of the point of view of totality which alone offers purchase on social understanding and action: the only advantage of the proletariat over the bourgeoisie (which has all the trump cards in its hands) is that its very position in the social structure allows it to grasp society from the point of view of totality (this, of course, is straight out of Hegel). The consequence of fetishism, therefore, is the atomisation of totality into a multitude of reified objects and facts.

Such fetishism has three consequences, all of which are relevant to the theory of language – they make such a theory an instance of bad scientific fetishism, and they are all three undoubtedly present in Chomsky's theory. The first is that fetishism is a source of *abstractions* (of the wrong kind), as it transforms processes (the phenomena are dynamic) into 'facts' (which, in order to become graspable, are the static and frozen images of real processes). This concerns not only the individual concepts of a single science (I-language is to language what a fetishised fact is to a series of processes), but the science itself, in that it abstracts and reifies part of the phenomena to the exclusion of the rest (this is the explicit programme of all forms of 'internal' linguistics, embodied in the structuralist 'principle of immanence'). Thus, 'scientific' linguistics, since its very inception in the work of Saussure, has been famously characterised by its refusal to consider language in its totality, that is by a refusal to consider language in its immersion in the totality of phenomena that constitute the world (a challenge taken up by 'external' linguistics). The exclusion of most or part of the phenomena has never ceased to return to haunt the science like Hamlet's father, as first diachrony, then syntax, socio-linguistics and finally pragmatics have sought to reintegrate part of the excluded phenomena into the language science deigns to consider. In his extreme scientific asceticism, Chomsky is faithful to the foundational move of Saussure, which he tends, however, to caricature. The price he has to pay for this is high. His theory, coherent as it is, has of course nothing to say about the innumerable linguistic phenomena it excludes, but also precious little to say about those it seeks to include (as we saw in the case of the reflexive and reciprocal pronouns).

This reification of processes into facts is made possible (this is the second consequence of fetishism) by the *naturalisation of history* that fetishism implies. We remember Barthes's definition of myth as that which transforms culture and history into nature.[23] The rationale for such mythical operation in the age of capitalism is fetishism: it turns the historically determined laws of capitalist society (this includes the scientific laws produced by the superstructures) into eternal laws of nature. Chomsky, who turns a social-historical practice (the archetype of all social practices) into part of the biological endowment of the species, into quasi eternal human nature (in the quasi immobile time of evolution: the 150 000 years of human language have not altered its fundamental structure), offers a strong version of this. Against it, we must remember Lukács's provocative thesis that 'nature is a social category'.[24]

For Lukács, fetishism has a third consequence. It does not concern only the object, it transforms the subject as well: it atomises it as much as it does the object. In other words, fetishism turns collective dynamic processes into individual facts perceived/theorised/acted upon by individual subjects. Chomsky's methodological individualism is coherent with his denial of history and reification of processes into facts. But we also understand why our discussion of language has to be disentangled from questions of identity and intersubjectivity, to the point that the dominant concept of the individual subject must be overturned, perhaps at the cost of discarding the concept altogether. The narcissism of the subject, the obsession with identity that characterise much contemporary thinking about society and about literature (not least in the overbearing interest in ethics) are effects of fetishistic modes of dealing with the subject; even as positivist 'objectivity' is a fetishistic mode of dealing with the object. To come back to Chomsky, we note, not without glee, that Lukács even singles out the concept of 'faculty' (of the human mind) as an example of this individualisation through fetishism: not only is the individual subject separated from the collective, but his mind is split into atomic 'faculties'.

We understand why Chomsky's theory of I-language has the four characteristics that I deplored, and we understand their coherence, which accounts for both the strength and the weakness of the theory. They provide us with an *a contrario* sketch of what a non-fetishistic theory of language might be: a theory that adopts the points of view of history, of social totality, of the dynamism of processes. That is the theory of language that we seek.

# 5
# The Concept of Language We Need

## 1 Introduction

So far, I have provided only a negative account of such a concept. I have criticised a specific concept of I-language as the concept we absolutely do not need. For Chomsky's philosophy of language has a number of advantages for us. Not only is it entirely explicit (and outdated), but it offers the *converse* of the concept of language we need. His theory is a photographic negative of the right concept – this should make our task easy: all we have to do is to say 'black' whenever he says 'white'. This is, however, unduly optimistic: such simple conversion is not enough, as it is obviously still dependent on the concept of language that has been criticised. Hence the second negative account I have provided, when I suggested, as the *inverse* of mainstream philosophy of language, a series of six counter-principles, which go far beyond Chomsky's theory of I-language, as they also involve a critique of Anglo-Saxon pragmatic linguistics and of phenomenological theories of language such as enunciation theories. The very names of those six principles (non-immanence; dysfunctionality; opacity; materiality; non-systematicity; historicity) smack of negative theology. Even the apparently positive names, 'opacity', 'materiality' and 'historicity' receive negative, or reactive, interpretations. Thus, 'opacity' is non-transparency, it is second to the transparency that is one of the tenets of mainstream philosophy of language; 'materiality' is abstract non-ideality, the reference to 'matter' and 'materialism' being at this stage only a philosophical gesture; 'historicity' in this context is mostly the antonym of 'naturalism', the name of the thesis that, as far as language is concerned, the very slow time of evolution is not fast enough to be relevant (this is what I have called, again and again, in deliberate exaggeration, the 'non-time' of evolution: Greek *aion* in its traditional, not its Deleuzean, sense as opposed to *chronos*). I am, of course, aware of the importance of the work of the negative, and therefore of the ultimate Hegelian positivity of my negative detour, a necessary moment in the dialectic. But I must move on to the moment of explicit positivity. I must operate a change in point of view, and I must propose a series of positive theses.

## 2   Changing the Point of View

Let us start with the *main positive thesis*, of which the theses that will follow are developments: *language is a form of praxis*.

Portentous words, and entirely vague. Let us spell out what they imply.

The *first implication* is the adoption of the *point of view of process*, not 'thing' or 'fact'. In other words, the thesis implies a non-fetishistic view of language, where language fetishism (in both its wrong and its unavoidable types) receives an explanation in terms of the dynamic processes that underlie the 'things' that words and sentences are, and the 'facts' that utterances and rules of grammar constitute. For this concerns the individual word (no longer a static thing but a series of variations, with their phonetic, morphological and semantic histories), the utterance (defined not in terms of the linguistic inscription of an ideal proposition but in terms of what Volosinov calls its 'pluriaccentuality') and the whole language itself (where 'English' is no longer an ideal type variously realised in token utterances, but a shifting array of dialects, registers and styles). In other words, language is no longer a 'treasury' of words and rules (as it was for Saussure and is, in a more modern theoretical language, for Chomsky), but a *system of variations* (the phrase, which is not paradoxical, is borrowed from the new pragmatics of Deleuze and Guattari – variations need not be random and chaotic, but they forbid the fixist treatment implied in the concept of synchronic *langue*). This is Vygotsky, the Soviet psychologist, on word meanings (we have already gone a long way away from Chomsky, or, to be more precise, *before* Chomsky):

> The discovery that word meanings evolve leads the study of thought and speech out of a blind alley. Word meanings are dynamic rather than static formations. They change as the child develops; they change also with various ways in which thought functions.[1]

And he immediately adds: 'The relation of thought to word is not a thing but a process, a continual movement back and forth from thought to word and from word to thought.'[2] The first quotation has an aspect of obvious common sense about it: we all know that word meanings change all the time, and we are all experts at tracing such intricate histories in the course of our lifetimes as speakers for the benefit of a younger generation, who do not care. But the second quotation tells us what we are up against: a positivist concept of language bent on fixing and isolating facts, the better to make them graspable through rules (there is a rich array of Lakovian metaphors at work here, and as usual they are highly relevant). Substituting processes for facts means accepting that the science of language is no longer dealing with natural laws but with sets of pragmatic maxims, of the type 'don't say this, but that', or 'if you say this, then ...', where it is obvious that issues of power, *rapports de force*, are involved, and where it is equally obvious that the maxims, unlike laws of nature, are defeasible, so that deviations from the norm, far from being exceptions to be reduced and resolved, are exploitations of the maxim in an unending process of semantic and pragmatic struggle. The passage, as it were, from the first to the second Kantian critique, substituting the language of 'maxims' for that of laws ('say this rather than that', not 'it is a law of nature that a sentence is made up of a subject and a predicate') is far from innocent. It avoids the pitfalls of naturalism, and the fetishism of scientific abstraction through exclusion.

What this means is that language is not a neutral instrument of communication and that our point of view must shift away from the usual one (Chomsky, Habermas, *même combat*): we must move away from the point of view that gives in to fetishism, in four ways.

First, we must adopt *the point of view of social interaction*, not individual subjects. The greatest fallacy of mainstream philosophy of language is that language is situated in the individual speaker (in her mind/brain, or in her (sub)consciousness as the site of psycho-grammatical, or enunciation, 'operations') – even as creativity is, for idealist aesthetics, firmly situated in the individual artist. By which I do not seek to deny that you and I speak, and I am constantly amazed at the deep originality of my own speech and writing: I am suggesting that such individuality is not an origin but an effect of language, which is constitutively collective. In political science and in economics, methodological individualism characterises what may broadly be called a liberal position (this is, of course, gross over-simplification): Ockham's razor is resorted to in order to rid political thought of collective entities such as class, or to make those

that one cannot dispense with, such as the state, the result of a combination of individual wills and rational choices. A cynical view of this
position suggests that it is the intellectual equivalent of the nineteenth-
century combination laws, which outlawed trade unions, but not
associations of employers or cartels. Methodological individualism has
never prevented corporate business from operating corporately, and not
as the democratic combination of individual decisions.

It will be argued that I am putting forward a political position
(I happen to believe in the class struggle and the reality of class) which
is debatable. I am prepared to grant this, *but not in the field of language.*
We may deny the very existence of classes, and claim that they are an
invention of the social theorist, but no one would dream of denying
that there is such a thing as language in general, and the English language in particular. For there are such things (and we note that, in that
set phrase, reification is inscribed in the very fabric of our common
parlance, and therefore of our thought). But those 'things' are not
things, but processes, and processes of social interaction, closely linked
to processes of learning and other social practices, like work. Because
language is a social process, involved in social praxis, the subject
becomes a speaker by being captured within the ambit of a language
that precedes her and is exterior to her (and on which, through praxis,
she will leave her mark, perhaps even a definitive one, through linguistic or literary creation). So the speaker appropriates her language as she
is appropriated by it: possession works both ways, as the very ambiguity of the term aptly notes. Hence the phrase 'language speaks', as
opposed to 'I speak language', is not a gross instance of language
fetishism (I hypostatise my language, make it a 'thing' that in turn
oppresses me), but rather the expression of the dynamic process of subjectivation (both subjection and the creation of active subjectivity) that
my interaction with language accomplishes – Denise Riley's analysis of
inner speech provides an excellent illustration of this. And the ontological metaphor, 'language', unavoidably fixes the process of appropri-
ation of and by individual subjects. The apparent fetishism of the term
expresses the fact that language, a social process, is manifestly not the
result of a combination of individual choices and decisions. We do feel
that we 'use' language as an instrument of communication and expression, but it is a dialectical case of the hammer wielding the hand that
wields it. This is why we 'use' language within strict constraints, and
why our power deliberately to alter it, while not null (if we manage to
combine and acquire political–linguistic, that is social, clout) is rather
limited. The history of the attempts by some feminists to invent and

impose an epicene pronoun in English (one that would avoid the masculinist use of 'he' to refer to a generic human being – 'thon' was one
of the suggestions), of their miserable failure, but also of the resounding success, at least in Anglo-Saxon countries, in the banishment of
that very masculinist 'he' (at the cost of periphrasis, 'he or she', or
innovative grammar, where 'they' is the anaphor of a singular noun),
is a good example of the ups and downs of what is clearly a *political*
struggle. Similar attempts by French ministers of culture to prevent
*franglais* from sullying the purity of the French language have repeatedly ended up in farce (which suggests that naked state power, in the
field of language, is not enough). One of the interests of Chomsky's
theory of language is that he is, in a way, aware of all this. He is aware
of it politically: he fully recognises that there is a politics of language.
And as a linguist he travesties the situation in the shape of the
fetishism of the individual speaker (a true instance of fetishism this
time): that the speaker is clearly not in full control of her language is
translated into the innateness of I-language, which has the great
advantage of preserving the individual speaker as bearer of a
mind/brain, and therefore the site, or owner, of linguistic competence
and the only origin, or source, of performance. The 'mind/brain', that
linguistic monster, is here a fetishised substitute for the process of
social interaction that language is.

The second point of view we must adopt is *the point of view of historicity*. We understand Chomsky's insistence on naturalism, in spite of
the manifest importance of linguistic change: leaving the time of
history for the aeons of evolution, the temporality of society for the
temporality of nature, enables him to take language not only out of
the time of human life (his one and only argument is that there is *not
enough time* for the child to learn all that she has to learn, and therefore
that there can be no process of learning language, no entering language through social interaction), but also out of the time of social life
(where language is the *monument* of the life of society: it inscribes it in
its words, phrases and grammatical markers; it fixes it in memory; it is
the repository, as Gramsci claims, of conceptions of the world). A historical, not a natural, concept of language will state that language does
not grow in the mind/brain according to an innate genetic
programme, but develops, as society develops, in historical time. We
certainly do not need the quasi-eternity of innateness; nor do we need,
however, the subaltern temporality of diachrony, through which
traditional linguistics, having established synchrony as the site for the
proper study of language, consigns the phenomena of language

change, which it cannot entirely ignore, to the margins, if not the dustbins of oblivion. For there is no immanent history of language, that is no mere history of the phonemes, morphemes and rules of syntax that make up a specific language. The history of a language is the history of a global social process, which must be envisaged from the point of view of the social totality: it is the history of a culture, of social classes in their struggles, as inscribed in common sense (which, too, has a history) – in clichés, in metaphors, in turns of phrase, in processes of grammaticalisation. In other words, the history of language can only be the history of a form of total praxis. From this, the point of view of history, we understand what is wrong with synchrony. What Althusser calls *coupe d'essence* fetishises language; it turns a series of processes into things and facts; it arbitrarily arrests the development and variation of the various strands that make up a language (which it kills the better to observe it and grasp its workings); it confuses the various temporalities of its diverse constituents (each has its own time, like the various constituents of Althusser's social structure): it substitutes the infinitely static image of a pyramid of levels (phonology, morphology, syntax – the pyramid crumbles when we reach semantics, not to mention pragmatics, as we do not quite know where to place them in the noble pile) for the dynamics of the sliding, commingling and rhizomatic dispersion of various strands or shoots of language (when phonology invades syntax, where iconicity disrupts the imposing ordinance of levels in the pyramid, based on the arbitrariness of double articulation). And we note, not without glee, that this model, or unacknowledged metaphor, reproduces the most determinist aspects of the base/superstructure model dear to dogmatic Marxism.

The third point of view we must adopt is, as has just been hinted, *the point of view of totality*. This is, as we know, Lukács's main point in his critique of fetishism. In mainstream philosophy of language, this fetishism through reduction takes the form of the separation of language from the world (in order to claim a specific object for the science of linguistics), and especially of the separation and double reification of *object* (language as system or structure) and *subject* (the speaker as the owner of her language, which she uses as an instrument). This is marked in the metaphors of instrumentality and possession (with the return of the repressed in the other sense of 'possession'), and in the separation of competence (*in* the speaker as in a container, that is, alienated from her) and performance (where the practical aspects of the speaker's linguistic activity are dismissed as irrelevant). This fetishism has the usual consequences: a tradition of mistrust of language, as betraying the speaker's meaning, as forcing her to say what she does not know she is saying and might not have said had she known: such a tradition is unable to understand one of the main aspects of the workings of language, the sheer violence of the interaction between subject and object, speaker and language. We understand the undeservedly bad name given to clichés as the incarnation of this reified language: dead metaphors kill meaning. At least, we think so till we realise, with Lakoff and Johnson, that, being the ones adopted by the community and therefore the most successful and long-lasting, dead metaphors are the only ones that can be said to be truly alive. But in order to see this, we must change our point of view, and adopt the point of view of totality. We must, in other words, go back to the non-fetishistic dialectics of subject and object, look for a subject subjectified by the language that interpellates her into a subject, and contributing to the process of language change, to its development and variations, through her linguistic practice, which amounts to a process of counter-interpellation. I counter-interpellate the language that interpellates me into what I am: I play with it, I exploit its virtualities of meaning, I reclaim the names by which it pins me down or excludes me, I send the bad words back to their original speaker who, as Denise Riley points out, is as interpellated by his language as I am. For the fact that language is a collective praxis does not mean that the subject is powerless: she acts on and in language by enacting it; every speech-act, however conventional, being an act of *parole*, moves *langue* a tiny fraction along its historical path, even if *langue* as a whole is beyond the reach of deliberate or even collective enterprise. What the point of view of totality means is substituting the dialectics of *parole* and *langue* (what Deleuze and Guattari describe under the phrase 'a system of variations') for their separation and the consequent reification of *langue* into an object of science and expulsion of *parole* beyond the pale. Such a substitution is nothing less than a sea-change: it means throwing overboard not only the Chomskyan bathwater, but the Saussurean infant, that is, the whole history of linguistics since its foundation as a science (which does not mean, of course, giving up the vast amount of scientific work that has been done since in the field of language).

I come to the fourth, and last, change of point of view involved in my main thesis. We must adopt *the point of view of rapport de forces*, or, to express it in another language, the point of view of *agon*, rather than the customary point of view, best exemplified in Habermas's general pragmatics, of *eirene*, of linguistic co-operation and exchange of information.

This change of point of view is no surprise: it is a natural consequence of the three that have preceded it. Even if, according to the
most plausible myth of origins, human language is a product of the
need for communication, when, in the the process of communal work,
thoughts need to be communicated as denotations of objects and not
mere expression of affect, this cannot be the sole origin of language.
For affect, precisely, will also be heard out, with the commands that
turn the expressive outcry into articulated language, with the rhythmic
ejaculations that accompany communal work and find artistic expression in dance. And I am fully aware of the unfortunate innuendo that
my use of an archaic word in the last sentence has introduced. Indeed,
among the theories of the origin of language, one will not only find
the 'bow-wow' theory (language as imitative of natural sounds), the
'yo-he-ho' theory, which I favour (language originates in communal
work), the 'ding-dong' theory (language is the offspring of musical
rhythmic 'ejaculations'), but also the 'come hither' theory, where language comes to humankind as a preliminary to sexual congress. Any of
those picturesque mythical theories is more interesting, and no less
plausible, that the usually unformulated, 'please could you pass me the
mammoth steak', theory that informs mainstream philosophy of
language. In all but the 'bow-wow' theory, which postulates a contemplative ancestor, language answers the need not so much for individual
expression, or irenic co-operative exchange, as for communal interaction, with the consequence that one of its main functions is the
establishment of a system of places, the emergence of a division of
labour, the verbalisation and attempted fixation of a pecking order, the
interpellation of individuals into subjects, in other words the establishment of *rapports de force*. We understand why bad words are not
marginal or exceptional utterances.

Such multiple change in point of view means that we have moved
from *internal* to *external* linguistics. For only external linguistics can
deal with the range of phenomena involved. The pyramid I have
evoked is not merely a *coupe d'essence*. It is also, with the addition of
pragmatics as a complementary 'module', a menu, listing the official
linguistic fare, and from which the potential linguistic *bon vivant* is not
allowed to deviate. The addition of the specific menu of traditional
philosophy of language, problems of meaning and reference, may
make the viands more wholesome, but hardly more palatable. In the
gastronomic world, bangers and mash are not all that counts. All we
have to do in order to realise this is compare this menu to what is on
offer in a form of external linguistics we have already encountered, the

embodied cognitive linguistics of Lakoff and Johnson. This is what they do when they list the favourite topics of what they call 'second generation cognitive science':

> There was ... a commitment to make sense of a vast range of phenomena that included polysemy (systematically related linguistic forms), inference, historical change, psychological experiments, poetic extensions of everyday language, gesture, language acquisition, grammar, and iconicity in signed languages.[3]

This is a great advance on the Chomskyan or structuralist agenda (not least in that it appears to be seriously concerned with 'grammar', without separating it from poetics and metaphor). But it is not enough for us, as it still ignores bad words and the productions of *fous littéraires*. Polysemy and iconicity are fine, but they still leave out *délire*. And verbal aggression is still not a subject for concern; Lakoff and Johnson's 'embodied reason' does treat words as they emerge from the human body: language for them is *in* and *of* the world, but this world still fails (in spite of the occasional token gesture) to include the social world. We still need a concept of language that allows for a sociology of language, a politics of language, an erotics of language, as well as a rhetoric and a pragmatics. We understand why the most interesting linguists are often not the professional ones: witness Freud on jokes and parapraxes, or Lenin on slogans. Witness Pasolini and his 'poetical notes for a Marxist philosophy of language'.

My account of language as a form of praxis naturally raises a number of questions. What is, for instance, the relation of this to other forms of praxis, productive or superstructural? We risk being caught up in the chicken and egg paradox: you need to have language for economic relations to emerge, and yet the most plausible of the myths of origin tells of the emergence of language in communal work, the primitive form of economic relations. Two points have to be made here. The first is that, unlike immanentist linguistics (which was famously founded on the exclusion of the question of the origin of language), external linguistics must envisage the problem of origins. The second is that the problem can only be resolved speculatively, that is not resolved at all, but illustrated in the form of myth (but a Marxist will not be shy of recognising the power, even the necessity, of myth, that is if she has the least inkling of a theory of ideology). For only myth can escape the vicious circle of paradox and think, *with the help of the concept of praxis*, the co-occurrent emergence of language and economic relations in the process of communal action, that is in tool-making, collective hunting, agricultural work, the sexual division of labour, etc. We can find a vivid, if outdated, illustration of the myth in the work of the Vietnamese Marxist Tran Duc Thao, published in French under the title *Recherches sur l'origine du langage et de la conscience*.[4]

Tran Duc Thao was one of the exceptions the supporters of empire were fond of mentioning in justification of colonial oppression: he managed to climb to the summits of the French educational system by being admitted to the Ecole Normale Supérieure in Paris, and successfully taking the *agrégation* exam in philosophy. In Paris, he moved from phenomenology to Marxism and communism (his first book was a Marxist critique of phenomenology).[5] At the end of the war of independence, he went home to North Vietnam. There, under the civilising influence of American bombs, and with no access to contemporary research except outdated Soviet articles on anthropology, he produced a Marxist theory of the origins of language, in which his first love for phenomenology is still apparent.

Tran Duc Thao's starting point is the nineteenth-century thesis, usually attributed to Haeckel, but quoted by him from Engels, that ontogeny recapitulates phylogeny: the origin of language may therefore indirectly be observed in the child's awakening to language. This is combined with a phenomenological thesis, that consciousness is consciousness of objects before it is self-consciousness (you will have recognised a version of the Husserlian thesis of intentionality), and with the Marxian thesis that consciousness has its source in language, a source that is material (in 'real life', in praxis), collective (the primitive group of hunters) and social (not only communal hunting, but the beginnings of communal work, with its division of labour).

The central thesis of the theory is that what distinguishes the incipient man from the ape is his capacity to point at objects, the use of *gestures of indication*: from such gestures both language and consciousness emerge (this is already a modification of the Marxian starting point).

From this a number of theses on the origin of consciousness derive. (1) The immediate reality of consciousness is language (both verbal language and gestures). (2) Conscious perception is that perception which is directed towards the external object *qua* external (this is a materialist thesis: it recognises the externality of the object in relation to the subject, and its precedence). (3) The pointing gesture appears as a call to work, and its primary function is social-collective (the allegory of Freedom in Delacroix's famous picture makes exactly that gesture). (4) This gesture is then reversed by the subject, who points at himself (command becomes self-command: thus, the isolated hunter, separated from the rest of the group, exhorts himself; at this stage consciousness is still contingent and sporadic). (5) The dialectics of internalisation of the external sign constitutes consciousness as relationship to self. (6) Consciousness then becomes not only consciousness of the external object, but permanent self-consciousness. (7) When the gesture of indication thus interiorised by the individual is interiorised by the whole group, it becomes available to denote not only the self, but any object in its absence: it becomes a sign. (8) The generalisation of signs among the group in turn produces individual subjects.

Thus, the emergence of consciousness, *la prise de conscience*, has three moments: the sporadic use of gestures of indication for self-reference, and the first appearance of a form of self-consciousness; the generalisation of this self-consciousness through the appearance of signs, into group consciousness, the consciousness of belonging to the community; the dialectical return to the self through the mediation of the group, and the transformation of sporadic self-consciousness into the stable self-consciousness that turns the member of the group into an individual subject. All this occurs in a story strongly reminiscent of Althusserian interpellation (of which Tran Duc Thao was blissfully ignorant) through the inversion towards self of the gesture of pointing at external objects, and the internalisation of this gesture into consciousness.

But what about the birth of language? Well, it is co-occurrent with the birth of consciouness, and finds its origin in the pointing gestures that accompany the Ur-economic activity of communal hunting. True to his starting point, Tran Duc Thao analyses the emergence in the child of what he calls 'syncretic language', the transformation of pointing gestures into *mots-phrases* (holophrases: each word is a whole utterance unto itself). The first *mots-phrases* accompany gestures, for instance the gesture of waving good-bye. Such *mots-phrases*, few in numbers, are variously polysemic. This is the crucial moment: not only when the verbal gesture is used to refer to a variety of objects, but when it does *in the absence of any object*, thus, in the passage from presentation to representation, becoming a sign. This passage to representation involves the moment of subjectivity: by producing signs even when they are alone, the primitive hunters recognise themselves, *provided such signs become public*; thus also, their descendent, today's child, becomes a person.

This is a fine figure of a myth. But a myth it is. No doubt recent developments in anthropology, genetics and primatology will forbid us from taking this picture of the origins of language and consciousness as factually correct. But a myth does not have to be 'true' to be powerful, witness the Freudian myth of the *fort-da*: it is enough that it should be relevant to our philosophical concerns, and to as large an extent as is possible, just. This myth has the advantage of letting us catch a glimpse of what can never be seen, making explicit what mainstream linguistics keeps implicit, probably out of sheer embarrassment: for the Chomskyan research programme, too, implies a myth of origins that it never clearly considers, and which is, on the whole, rather less plausible than this, not being able to go beyond the divine surprise of the inscription of the language faculty in our genetic make-up – a genetic version of the Adamic myth of the origin of language in *Genesis*.

Let us, therefore, in Hegelian fashion, treat Tran Duc Thao's myth as an anticipation of the truths that may come. And let us seek partial corroborations in theories not of the origin of language, but of the close link between language and social practice. A number of theorists, who may be said to make up the Marxist tradition in the philosophy of language, do precisely this.

The briefest references will have to do. We might look, for instance at Vygotsky and his theory of the relations between language and thought, in which he sees two distinct genetic functions. Unlike Tran Duc Thao, he is not concerned with the genesis of language as such, being more preoccupied by the developmental psychology of the child. He offers a theory of the appearance, in the development of the child, of inner speech, as the internalisation of public interactive speech, through the intermediate stage of egocentric language: like Tran Duc Thao, he starts from the point of view of the collective, the public, the interlocutory aspect of language; like him, he offers a *historical* view of the relations of thought and language and the development of human consciousness. The following is a typical passage: 'We found no specific interdependence between the genetic roots of thought and of word. It becomes plain that the inner relationship we were looking for was not a prerequisite for, but rather a product of, the historical development of consciousness.'[6]

All this is coherent with the central role of fetishism in capitalist societies. The myth is a projection on to the origins of language of the actual workings of language and society under capitalism, whereas the various metaphors of money, market and commodity, as applied to language, show that language offers both a special and an archetypal instance of fetishism, as it is both a special and an archetypal form of praxis. This accounts for its specific duality (we cannot do without some form of linguistic fetishism, call it abstraction, or ontological metaphors; and we must struggle to construct a defetishised concept of language). We understand why *fous littéraires* are both completely oppressed by language (in the case of Wolfson, such oppression has physical consequences), and intuitively aware of aspects of its workings that official linguists, steeped as they are in a worse form of language fetishism, altogether miss. And we understand why language *qua* praxis is both archetypal and specific: it is in fact a *prototypical* form of praxis, because it reaches the core of human praxis in the process of subjectivation.

## 3  Praxis

Perhaps the time has come to reflect on the exact sense in which the concept of *praxis* is used here. More precisely, what is its exact relation with the more common term, in Marxist circles, of 'practice'? For the question, 'can language be a form of practice?' does not accept an immediate and unambiguous answer.

There is a famous definition of practice in Althusser's *Pour Marx*:

> By *practice* in general, we mean any process of *transformation* of given determinate raw material into a determinate *product*, a transformation that is effected by determinate human labour, using determinate means (of 'production'). In any practice so conceived the *determinant* moment (or element) is neither the raw material nor the product, but the practice in the strict sense: the moment of the *work of transformation*, which within a specific structure organises human labour, means of production and a form of technique.[7]

The problem with this definition is that if this is practice, or praxis, then language cannot count as a token of this type, a species of that genus. Unless we are prepared to say that language transforms 'ideas' into 'words' or 'utterances', thus going back to a fundamentally idealist conception of the relations between language and thought, where language is merely an *instrument* (a 'means of production', a form of 'technique') of communication of thought, and thought is the raw material that pre-exists its transformation by language. The problem, of course, is not in the work of transformation (language is not transparent, a mere conduit for the expression of thought: it actively works on thought), it lies in the pre-existence and therefore hierarchical dominance of thought over language. The whole drift of my argument so far has gone against such pre-existence and hierarchical dominance: in the wake of Volosinov, I have sought to *invert* it, to show that thought is interiorised language, not that language is the instrument of exteriorisation of thought.

Althusser's definition may (or may not) be adequate to the needs of a Marxist concept of practice. But it is certainly not true to its origin in Aristotle. For Aristotle does not simply contrast theory and practice, *theoria* and *praxis*: he uses a three-term contrast, where *theoria* is distinguished from *praxis* but also from *poiesis*. And Althusser's definition of practice could be the definition of Aristotelian *poiesis*: *poiesis* it is that transforms raw material into finished product, that *makes* things. Whereas the distinguishing characteristic of *praxis* is not fabrication but communal action, the archetype of which is politics. And here we are reminded that in the opening of his *Politics* Aristotle defines man as a political animal *in so far as he is a speaking animal*.

In this original sense, language can be treated as a form of *praxis*, as it is the medium in which political action takes place (in the form of programmes, slogans, pamphlets, laws and statutes, but also, in the classic characterisation of democracy, debates). Language it is that causes ideas to acquire material force when they capture the masses, but only because such ideas find their only materiality in the words that do not so much translate or express them as constitute them.

The Italian philosopher, Paolo Virno, seeks to historicise this and make it a characteristic of late capitalism in what he calls its 'post-Fordist' stage. At that stage, he claims, language ceases to be a mere instrument, a collection of signs that are verbal tools for communication (monkeys can use such signs when they communally go in search of food). Language at the post-Fordist stage is irreversibly mixed with or in the labour process. The worker at that stage is also, *qua* worker, a speaker, and an important part of his work consists in communication (with the complex machines, with the whole structure of the production process). As a result of this, the worker's contribution is no longer mere *poiesis* but *praxis*: the labour process becomes an open, public process of interlocution, the analogon for which is political action. In a word, Virno says, the post-Fordist worker is no longer a mere producer, but something of a *virtuoso*, one whose 'production' is an 'interpretation' in the musical sense. And Virno does suggest we should reread the *Nicomachean Ethics*, where the contrast between *poeisis* and *praxis* is explicit. He even goes as far as suggesting that such contrast should be read in the light of Saussure's concepts of *langue* and *parole*, and Benveniste's concept of *énonciation* as marking a shift from result (the utterance as product) to process (the utterance as public practice of interlocution). Language in this conception is indeed a form of *praxis*, and the best account of it will consequently be a form of pragmatics.

Virno's analysis is based on a passage from the *Grundrisse* which he calls the 'fragment on machines', where Marx develops the notion of 'general intellect'. One can entertain doubts about his account of the post-Fordist labour process (similar analyses can be found in Marazzi, the Swiss economist much praised by Negri[8]). But it does have the advantage of accounting for language in terms of *praxis* rather than *poiesis*.

Can we find a corroboration of all this in Marx's few and cryptic pronouncements on language, mostly in *The German Ideology*? Let us look at a well known text:

> Only now, after having considered four moments, four aspects of the primary historical relationships, do we find that man also possesses 'consciousness'; but, even so, not inherent, not 'pure' consciousness. From the start, the 'spirit' is afflicted with the curse of being 'burdened' with matter, which here makes its appearance in the form of agitated layers of air, sounds, in short, of language. Language is as old as consciousness: language is practical consciousness that exists also for other men, and for that reason alone it really exists for me personally as well; language, like consciousness, only arises from the need, the necessity of intercourse with other men.* Where there exists a relationship, it exists for me: the animal does not enter into 'relations' with anything, it does not enter into relations at all. For the animal, its relation to others does not exist as a relation. Consciousness is, therefore, from the very beginning a social product, and remains so as long as men exist at all.[9]

The asterisk corresponds to a footnote, which recovers a few words crossed out in the manuscript (words that cannot be indifferent to us): 'My relationship with my surroundings is my consciousness.'

This text is probably unfair to animals, until, that is, we understand that 'relations' here are conscious relations because they are linguistic relations, and that such linguistic relations, being a form of praxis, are social-economic relations, relations of work and exchange. And animals do not speak and have therefore no praxis (a recent piece in *The Guardian*, has the story of a crow capable of making a hook out of a straight piece of wire: it is said, even if it does not speak, to be 'very clever'). In the equation of language and consciousness, we finally understand why language is the *archetypal* form of practice. If all relations are conscious relations, in so far as my consciousness is the sum of my relations with my surroundings, and if language is nothing but the materialisation of consciousness, *practical* consciousness, then it is involved in every form of praxis (which is not so obvious as it sounds: does my capacity, or incapacity, to hammer a nail involve some form of linguistic practice, except the expletives that are heard when I squash my thumb? The famous scene in *Three Men in a Boat*, which turns this everyday occurrence into a ritual, does suggest just this). More important still, language is the very structure of praxis, as it is the obligatory accompaniment, if not the guide and prime mover, of the relationships in which praxis consists: there is no such thing as solitary praxis.

So language is inextricably mixed up with the world, by being *of* the world (those layers of air, or scratches on a flat surface: there is no *logos* without *phone* or *graphe*), but also by being *in* the world, by being present whenever men get together and consciousness arises, by being the medium in which this togetherness becomes consciousness. We understand why the question of the origin of language can only be answered through myth: the way out of the paradox of the chicken and egg cannot be found in genesis, but only through a dialectics, whereby language and consciousness can only emerge, and exist, concomitantly. This is what Marx, in another famous text, captures in the implicit antimetabole (a trope of which he was notoriously fond): 'the real life of language is the language of real life'. Hence the recurrent use, in *The German Ideology*, of this curious phrase, as in the marginal note: 'Language is the language of reality.'[10] What exactly does he mean by this 'language of real life'?

First, this is a *materialist* thesis: 'the production of ideas, of conceptions, of consciousness, is at first directly interwoven with the material activity and the material intercourse of men, the language of real life'.[11] So material practice comes first, intellectual conceptions second, as *manifestations* of the material life. But where exactly is language in this, since the term appears in both halves of the antimetabole? The crucial importance of it is that it belongs to both realms and mediates between them as the Kantian schemes of the imagination mediate between intuition and understanding. On the one hand, 'neither thoughts nor language in themselves form a realm of their own ... they are only *manifestations* of real life'.[12] On the other hand, 'language is the immediate actuality of thought,'[13] and as such, as practical consciousness, it can be said to be 'the language of real life'. So the materialist thesis is not one of simple determination (language as one of the superstructures): it contains a supplementary thesis, not of the autonomy or independence of language (to be found in Stalin's commonsensical, and as such idealist, concept of a 'neutral' language, an instrument of communication available for the whole community), but of the *efficacy* of language, of its capacity to turn the primarily material, the objective, into the intellectual, the conscious, the subjective. Language is the archetypal form of praxis because it embodies the dialectics of object and subject: in and through language, the world becomes subject and the very clever ape becomes man. We understand why a theory of language must be both an external theory and a theory of subjectivation through interpellation.

So the link between 'language' and 'the language of real life' is not simply metaphorical (we know full well that real life is not a language, nor does it speak) but theoretical. What theory constructs is the concept of a *language of real (social) life*, with three main characteristics:

(a)  Such language is embodied/ inscribed in praxis.
(b)  In this language the literal is always dominated by the lateral. Here I am using terms dear to the Marxist philosopher Henri Lefebvre, in his book on language:[14] what he means is that in such language denotation is always less important than connotation, semantics than pragmatics, and downright signification is always surrounded by an aura of sense.
(c)  This language's main operation is the operation of fetishism, in its deep ambivalence (the necessity of abstraction, the oppression of reified words, separated into things from the processes that make up living language).

In a word, this language of real life is the language Marx describes in *Capital* as *the language of commodities*. This implies, as we have seen, not only a strong hypothesis on the genesis of language (in productive praxis), but it also allows us to understand the system of metaphors about language embedded (embodied) in our common parlance. It provides us with another explanation for the origin of the structural metaphors we live by, which Lakoff and Johnson so aptly chart (communication as exchange, words as coins, the fetishism of abstraction). And it confirms our intuition that pragmatics lies at the centre of language, that language is as much, if not more, about action as it is about reflection and communication.

## 4  First Positive Thesis

The main thesis of our concept of language, language is a form of praxis, is developed in *four positive theses*: (1) Language is a historical phenomenon. (2) Language is a social phenomenon. (3) Language is a material phenomenon. (4) Language is a political phenomenon. The main drift of those theses is clear from what has already been suggested. It will be the object of the rest of this chapter to supply the details.

*Thesis 1: Language is a historical phenomenon.* This thesis has two aspects: language *has* a history (which a theory of language cannot ignore or treat as marginal), and language *is* history.

The history of language, grasped through the history of languages, is not the even-flowing course, the *fleuve tranquille* that positivist history envisages, as languages develop, expand, merge and corrupt, recede and change into other languages. The temporality of change in a given language is complex and uneven, various strands evolve at various speeds.

Thus, the *semantics* of a language, as inscribed in the *lexicon*, will change fast, year after year, generation after generation: I do not use the same common name for 'cigarette' as my father used in his youth, neither does the next generation use what is still for me the common name; and this generational usage, or common sense, is the result of a competition between a host of alternative words, some witty, others dull, most of which can only be called the flavour of the month. And imagine the bewilderment of the eager foreigner first confronted, in the summer of 2002, with the new meanings of the word 'anorak' or the phrase 'white van man'. Yet the core of the lexicon (names of natural kinds, household names, etc.) hardly ever changes.

Then, there is the much slower time of *grammatical markers*, a time which, however, *pace* Chomsky, is not the immobile time of evolution, but a form of historical time: the time of grammaticalisation (the process whereby a form of the English gerund, 'he was on doing', meaning 'he was engaged in the process or activity of doing', became the progressive aspect, 'he was doing', with an intermediate stage that survives only in the archaic speech of ballads, 'he was a-doing') takes longer than it takes for a lexical fashion to emerge, gain acceptance, and vanish: but still such changes can be charted in history.

There is the equally slow time of *syntax*, which linguists usually treat as *aere perennius*, but which is not immune to change, witness the history of the 'unattached' or 'dangling' participle (as in sentences of

the type: 'when writing, the paper must be kept flat'). An utterly intelligible construction, its use was so widespread in the eighteenth
century as to be entirely normal. The appearance of firmer rules, hardly
more than grammatical prejudice, governing the relationship between
subject and predicate in the sentence (of the type: 'you can only elide
the subject of a subordinate clause if it is the same as the subject of the
main clause') has condemned the construction to the limbo of sole-
cism, at least in educated dialects, especially when written, but not, of
course, in everyday usage, where it still flourishes, increasing the gap
between 'actual' and 'grammatical' language. This is a good example:
the story is not linear (it is not a story of grammatical progress) and it
is rife with political and institutional interference, in the shape of the
school grammars that banned the unattached participle. Such condem-
nation, incidentally, is still current, and purists like me still reprove
what is generally described as the 'dangling adjunct' ('At 53, everybody
still admired Marlene Dietrich' – note that here the disapproval is more
easily justified, as risks of misunderstanding through ambiguity are
greater).[15]

Lastly, there is the temporality of a whole language, as the very name
('English') that makes a unique object of it is a historical and political
construct, a process of unification, which does not merely take place
within language, as a process of naming, but out there, in the political
history of the nation. 'English' is carved out of the forced union of
divergent dialects and registers (this does not concern only semantics
and the lexicon, but also phonetics and syntax: witness the importance
of class and regional accents in British English, and the rise, for
instance, of 'Estuary English', as not only a regional, but a generational
phenomenon). The historical process is here, as always, rather
complex. It involves divergence (the dialects and registers have a tendency to drift apart), convergence (the political imposition of a
national language: witness the Prayer Book rebellion, and the hege-
mony of the same instituted by the State Ideological Apparatuses of the
school) and divergence again (as English, a global language, diverges
through pidginisation, creolisation, and gradual separation of new
Englishes from the main stem). Being the language of contemporary
imperialism, English exerts its imperial dominance over other languages, to the point of being responsible for the death of a number of
them (there is hardly any language today that does not have the equivalent of *franglais*), but this imperial extension weakens it in that it
makes its minorisation easier (in the course of time, Singapore English,
which has limited divergence from 'standard' English, such as the cute

inversion of the main terms in the proverbial phrase 'to have one's cake and eat it', will be an entirely separate language, like Tok Pisin, the best known of the Pidgins – did you realise it means 'Talk Pidgin'?).

So history does impinge on the development of a language. A language does not unfold monadically, in natural growth, nor does it only, or even perhaps principally, develop by following its own, internally determined, lines of flight. Let us take an example, the influence of a series of historical events, whose importance is not in doubt, the First World War, on the English language. It has been carefully charted by Paul Fussell, in his remarkable account of First World War literature in English.[16]

The first thing he notes is a change of public language. Before the war began the experience of wars, real (the Boer War) or imaginary, could only be expressed in the 'high diction' that made a friend a 'comrade', a horse a 'steed' or 'charger', the enemy 'the foe', danger 'peril' – a language in which one showed one's 'valour' by being 'gallant', 'plucky' or 'staunch', and the blood of young men was 'the red / Sweet wine of youth (R. Brooke)': the list given by Fussell (pp. 21–2), in two columns, makes sorry, if gleeful, reading. This language, made up of the clichés of successful colonial conquest, was badly shaken in 'the collision between events and the public language used over a century to celebrate ideas of progress' (p. 169). A collision that did not take the immediate form of the intrusion of crude realistic language, corresponding to the horror of the real events (the English language, Fussell points out, did possess the requisite words, 'shit', 'murder', 'legs blown off', 'intestines gushing out over his hands', etc.), but it took the form of more indirect modifications, for instance the vanishing of the innocence of pre-war language, when one could talk, without innuendo, of 'intercourse', 'erection' and 'ejaculation', when 'Henry James could innocently use the word "tool" and Robert Browning indulge in artless misapprehensions about the word *twat*' (p. 23).

The old language did of course resist. It resisted in the persistence, in personal accounts of the clichés of the *Boy's Own Paper* ('Ah! The exultation of the roar of the bombardment veritable! Hour on hour's ceaseless rolling reverberation' –thus a sergeant trying to describe what the din was like, p. 170). It resisted in the form of *euphemism*, with regards both to taboo words ('going under', 'going West') and to the sillier forms of patriotism (thus allied Servia was renamed Serbia, a name that has stuck, because allies could not be slaves; thus German shepherd dogs became Alsatians, pp. 175–6). It resisted in the form of *officialese* and the effects of *censorship* that prevented the soldier in the trenches, had he wanted to, from conveying the full horror of his experience. Thus, readers of official communiqués eventually learned to interpret the adjectives 'brisk' and 'sharp', as in 'brisk fighting' and 'sharp retaliation', as meaning that about 50 per cent of the troops involved were dead or wounded (p. 176).

One of the interests of Fussell's analysis is that it shows that the lexicon was not the only aspect of language to be affected by the historical events. Thus, he analyses the use of the *euphemistic passive* (an important tool of official hypocrisy ever since) – euphemism being resorted to not only by the authorities, 'to keep the truth from others', but by the troops, 'to soften the truth for themselves'(p. 177):

> The troops became masters of that use of the passive voice common among the culturally insecure as a form of gentility ('A very odd sight was seen here'); only they used it to avoid designating themselves as agents of nasty or shameful acts. For example: 'We were given small bags to collect what remains could be found of the bodies, but only small portions were recovered.' (p.177)

Fussell quotes the memoirs of one Lt. Col. Graham Seton Hutchinson, who during the German offensive of March 1918, which broke the British line and nearly won the war for the German army, found a group of forty soldiers ready to surrender to the Germans and had thirty-eight of them shot (no doubt to put some stamina back into the remaining two – a somewhat wasteful solution, as Fussell wryly comments). When telling the tale, the Lt. Col. 'craftily deploys the passive voice':

> Such an action as this will in a short time spread like dry rot through the army ... If there does not exist on the spot a leader of sufficient courage and initiative to check it by a word, it must be necessary to check it by shooting. This was done. Of a party of forty men who held up their hands, thirty-eight were shot down with the result that this never occurred again. (p. 178)

It is fair to say that none of those thirty-eight ever became a second offender. But we perceive a macabre twist to the linguistic concept of the performative (or, when the word fails, shoot) and to Deleuze and Guattari's idea that grammatical markers are markers of power.

So far, however, I have mainly illustrated the resistance of the old language to the new, imposed by the stark encounter with the Real of history. But change the language did, and Fussell also charts such change. It takes the form of a development of the vernacular, often accompanied with grim wit, as when French place names were anglicised. Thus, Etaples, the site of the main training-camp, became 'eatables' or 'Eat-apples' (p. 179); Ypres, still remembered for its salient, 'Wipers'. The language acquired an all-purpose intensifier, which it has not only kept, but exported world-wide, 'fuckin'', with elided final 'g', 'and one exhibited one's quasi-poetic talents by treating it with the greatest possible originality as a moveable "internal" modifier and placing it well inside the word to be modified, as in "I can't stand no more of that Mac-bloody-fuckin'-Conochie" ' (p. 179). 'Maconochie' was the brand name of a meat-and-vegetable paste, the British answer to corned beef. In the same vein, Fussell notes the generalisation of the adjective 'old' to denote not age, but affectionate familiarity ('It's hanging on the old barbed wire. I've seen 'em' –'it' of course denotes the whole battalion, p. 179).

The change also implied the ironic (and in most cases temporary) *détournement* of bucolic common names to denote instruments of war. Thus, the *Wiper Times*, a satirical broadsheet produced in the trenches, had a parodic 'In the garden' column, where advice like the following could be found: 'It must be remembered that the planting of Toffee-apples on the border of your neighbour's allotment will seriously interfere with the ripening of his gooseberries'(p. 238). We need a footnote to remind us that 'gooseberries' were balls of barbed wire, and 'Toffee-apples' mortar shells. But not all such *détournements* were temporary. Some have remained in the language to this day, as monuments to the now long-gone historical conjuncture. The lexicon of a language is made up of such layers, whereby historical meaning is sedimented, that is both preserved and travestied. Thus, Fussell notes that our still current use of the adjectives 'lousy' and 'crummy' (originally, 'itchy because lousy') originated in the infestation of lice that plagued life in the trenches. Not to mention the replacement of 'keepsake' with 'souvenir', and the drift from 'Burberry' to 'trench-coat' (p. 189) – the interesting point here is that, with the disappearance of the last veterans, 'trench-coat' has faded and 'Burberry' would make a come-back, if the development of capitalism had not substituted it with 'Goretex', 'Polar', or similar novelties.

How can historical events affect language change so directly, although to a different extent in the matter of semantics, phonetics and syntax? Because of a universal feature of human semantics, a reflection of the nature of language as process and praxis: the tendency to *metaphorical drifting* that affects the meanings of words. Language being a never ceasing ongoing process in historical time, steeped in the conjunctures that succeed one another, metaphor and the semantic drifting it involves are fundamental characteristics of its workings. We have learned from Lakoff and Johnson the importance of metaphorical thought, which lies at the heart of their embodied reason. And we remember Nietzsche's scandalous definition of truth as successful metaphor (a definition that a Marxist should not lightly dismiss). The problem with Lakoff and Johnson is that their metaphors, although embodied and realised in language, are not linguistically incarnated: metaphors are concepts realised in a host of phrases and utterances, the governing metaphor itself (for example, ARGUMENT IS WAR) being situated at the level of abstract thought and its linguistic actualisations being as diverse as they are plentiful (for instance, 'he pounded my defences', where neither the word 'argument' nor the word 'war' are used). But linguistically incarnated those metaphors we live by are: words increase and change their meaning through metaphorical drifting, and that is how history affects language. The metaphorical drifting that extends the meaning of the word 'gooseberry' operates through catachresis, and not through the application of the previous metaphor-in-thought INSTRUMENTS OF WAR ARE VEGETABLE (or edibles, which would include 'Toffee-apples'). The linguistic wit comes first; the abstract generalisation, whereby the catachresis becomes productive, a token of a type, comes afterwards. The linguist, intent on fetishism as ever, simply inverts the order of events in the process of the phenomena. And if we turn to a historicist Marxist, we shall discover that Marxists have long known that language was metaphoric because it is historical. As early as the early 1930s, Gramsci stated in his *Prison Notebooks* that 'it is the whole of language that is a ceaseless metaphorical process, and the history of semantics is an aspect of the history of culture: language is both a living organism and a museum that exhibits the fossils of life and civilisation.'[17] Later in the same note, he adds 'language is always metaphorical',[18] a statement that is firmly historicised, as the metaphorical relation holds between the present signification of the word and its aura of sedimented sense that inscribes 'the ideological contents the word has had in previous periods of culture'. Thus, he claims, my using the word 'disaster' does not commit me to a belief in astrology, nor does my exclamation, '*per Bacco!*' prevent me from being a good Catholic.

Vygotsky gives an account of concept formation in the child that amounts to a description of such metaphoric drifting. It all starts with what he calls 'complexes', associations between objects in the child's sensory experience ('In a complex, individual objects are united in the child's mind not only by his subjective impressions but also by *bonds actually existing between these objects*').[19] These associations tend to form chains, where there is not a nucleus, from which all the associations derive, but a drifting from element to element, the chain cohering in a kind of Wittgensteinian family resemblance: a chain complex is 'a dynamic, consecutive joining of individual links into a single chain, with meaning carried from one link to the next'.[20] This is where the experiential association between objects becomes linguistic, an association between a word, with its meaning, and not a *single* object, but a chain complex. And this is not left to the spontaneous decision of the child, but guided by her interaction with adults, in an elementary form of social praxis: 'In real life complexes corresponding to word meanings are not spontaneously developed by the child. The lines along which a complex develops are predetermined by the meaning a given word already has in the language of adults'.[21] Vygotsky goes on to explain the gradual passage from pseudo-concepts associated with chain complexes and word meanings to complexes proper. But what interests us here is that this account ascribes a metaphorical nature to language from the very start. And not only this, but this metaphorical nature is grasped as a *process* of metaphorical *drifting*, not a discontinuous passage from reified meaning to reified meaning:

> What are the laws governing the formation of word families? More often than not, new phenomena or objects are named after unessential attributes, so that the name does not truly express the nature of the thing named. Because a name is never a concept when it first emerges, it is usually both too narrow and too broad. For instance, the Russian word for cow originally meant 'horned', and the word for mouse, 'thief'. But there is much more to cows than horns, or to a mouse than pilfering; thus their names are too narrow. On the other hand, they are too broad, since the same epithets may be applied – and actually are applied in some other languages – to a number of other creatures. The result is a ceaseless struggle within the developing language between conceptual thought and the heritage of primitive thinking in complexes.[22]

The interest of this genetic approach is that it reverses the usual relationship (on which mainstream philosophy of language is largely based) between the literal and the metaphorical, denotation and connotation. The literal (the concept) is the result of a process of literalisation (of narrowing and broadening of what is originally too broad or too narrow) of the metaphorical (the complex, the verbal meaning, the pseudo-concept). So *metaphor* in the strict sense can be said to be the historical motor of meaning, as meaning drifts along a paradigm of words, as *metonymy* in the strict sense is the syntagmatic, or synchronic motor of meaning, when the quilting point (*point de capiton*) fixes meaning retroactively along a verbal chain that has progressed according to Markovian processes.

I announced a second sub-thesis to the current thesis, that language is a historical phenomenon: language does not merely *have* a history, it *is* history. If we accept Gramsci's claim that every language contains a 'conception of the world' ('Even in the most modest manifestation of any intellectual activity, language for instance, there lies a definite conception of the world'[23]), we shall draw the conclusion that language *is* potted, or sedimented, history. This concept of language as monument to sedimented historical time informs the work of Owen Barfield (who was not a Marxist, but who deserves to be revived and properly appreciated[24]). It also informs the work of Raymond Williams.

Raymond Williams devotes one of the chapters of his book, *Marxism and Literature*,[25] to language (one of his 'basic concepts'). After deploring the small contribution Marxism has made to thinking about language, he proceeds to construct a Marxist concept of language, largely inspired by Volosinov. The two following quotations illustrate his starting point and his conclusions respectively:

> The key moments which should be of interest to Marxism, in the development of thinking about language, are, first, the emphasis on language as *activity* and, second, the emphasis on the *history* of language. (p. 21)

> We can add to the necessary definition of the biological faculty of language as *constitutive* an equally necessary definition of language development – at once individual and social, as socially and historically *constituting*. What we can then define is a dialectical process: *the changing practical consciousness of human beings*, in which both the evolutionary and the historical processes can be given full weight, but also within which they can be distinguished. (pp. 43–4)

The first passage simply shows that my own thinking about language does not come out of the blue, that it is inserted in a tradition, starting with Marx's few but weighty formulations about language. The second has, to me, an unwelcome flavour of compromise. By making a gesture towards the concept of 'biological faculty', Williams gives in to mainstream linguistics, showing the literary critic's dismissive respect for positive science. But since I do not wish to deny the phenomena, in this case the 'innate to acquired' gradient, I am prepared to accept the contrast between language as *constitutive* (chimps do not speak) and as *constituting* (interpellating individuals into subjects), provided that we also accept that it is *constituted* (in social-historical practice).

The interest of Williams's approach, however, is not that he merely theorised the historical constitution of language, but that he practised what his theory preached – in fact the practice (for instance in *Culture and Society*[26]) predates by far the Marxist theory just evoked. This practice culminates in *Keywords*,[27] a dictionary with a difference, as it is not so much concerned with the synchronic meanings of the words it lists, not even with the historical elements to be found in ordinary dictionaries, but with the historical constitution and drifting of the words' meanings in their various historical conjunctures, and in the arguments in which they were used and defined in action. What he analyses is not words, or fixed meanings, but *formations of meaning*. It all started as a glossary to *Culture and Society*, which got out of hand: 'every word which I have included has at some time, in the course of some argument, virtually forced itself on my attention because the problems of its meanings seemed to me inextricably bound up with the problem it was being used to discuss' (p. 13). And in order to understand such formations of meaning, we must go beyond dictionaries, even historical ones, or even essays in historical semantics. We must go 'beyond the range of "proper meaning" '. There we find

a history and a complexity of meanings; conscious change, or consciously different use; innovation, obsolescence, specialization, extension, overlap, transfer; or changes which are masked by nominal continuity so that words which seem to have been there for centuries, with continuous general meanings, have come to express radically different or radically variable, yet sometimes hardly noticed, meanings and implications of meaning. (p. 15)

Such words are not of course the homely names of natural kinds, 'gold' or 'cat' (and even in those cases, the purity and primacy of words denoting 'natural' objects, on which analytic theories of naming, from Kripke to Putnam, are based, is somewhat dubious: connotation is lurking in the wings), but the words we live by (in our social life), words like 'family', 'culture', 'industry', 'class' or 'subject'.

The result is the sketch of what could have become a specifically Marxist form of linguistics, a version of *historical semantics*:

> The kind of semantics to which these notes and essays belong is one of the tendencies within *historical semantics*, where the theoretical problems are indeed acute but where even more fundamental theoretical problems must be seen at issue. The emphasis on history, as a way of understanding contemporary problems of meaning and structures of meaning, is a basic choice from a position of historical materialism rather than from the now more powerful positions of objective idealism or non-historical (synchronic) structuralism. (pp. 20–1)

'Objective idealism' is the language of Volosinov attacking Saussure. And needless to say, the Marxist historical semantics here called for never went beyond this, the introduction to *Keywords* and the dictionary entries that make up the book. The task is still before us.

But Williams gives us an excellent idea of what we need: we need a concept of *linguistic conjuncture* to replace the outdated concepts of synchrony and diachrony. The linguistic conjuncture is the context in which meanings take shape in the social practice of speakers (first sense of 'meaning formation'), in which they are reified into formations of meaning (second sense of 'meaning formations'), as a multiplicity of forces or points of force in a field of meaning. The operation of fetishism tends to make such formations permanent, or at least stable – to isolate them from the processes in which they are active, or alive. But such freezing of sense, which turns language into a graveyard of obsolete, or even forgotten meanings, cannot halt the very processes that make up language. The arrest of meaning, of which the linguistic concept of synchrony is merely an image, is only valid for a moment. We also need, therefore, a concept (obviously of Hegelian origin) of the *moment* in the conjuncture, which must be analysed as Lenin analysed the moment in the political-historical conjuncture (a political moment in which, as we know, language is involved in the form of slogans). The linguistic moment stresses the fact that language is a series of processes, in a state of continuous variation.

The naming of the moment, the fixation of its temporal limits (the exact moment when the slogan 'All power to the Soviets' ceased to be the order of the day) is by no means arbitrary. It depends on the situation of the theorist that analyses it – and here 'theory' must lose its etymological meaning of contemplation, of mere observation, to take on a more active meaning of intervention in the conjuncture: the theoretical statement does not emanate from a subject separated from the object and observing it from a distance, but from an activist immersed in the object, of which she herself is a part; as a result the utterances of theory are not so much statements as performatives, speech-acts that contribute to the constitution and ultimate existence of their 'referent'. And because situations are various and multiple, so will be the various and multiple moments of a linguistic conjuncture. The moment of literature is not the moment of political intervention (they do not have the same *momentum*), nor is it the moment of peer-group language and social *milieu*. A result of this is that the analysis of an always complex linguistic conjuncture will be an analysis of *rapport de forces*. It will take in not only the place and role of institutions (as collective emitters of utterances), their explicitly formulated policies (language is not a neutral object for the contemplation of science, it is a field of forces and a site for struggle: not only linguistic policies but language politics), the balance of power between various apparatuses (schools and colleges, the media, the state), the role of economic and technical development driving linguistic change (the latest example is the language of text messages on mobile phones and its influence on language in general), the role of globalisation (not only the dominance and diversification of English as imperial language, but the influence of the imperial version of English on other versions, for instance in the form of the adoption of American slang by British teenagers). What we need is not only a sociolinguistics (a branch of the science that has already grown to respectable size), not merely a historical semantics of the Raymond Williams type, but also a *political linguistics*, centred on the concepts of *linguistic conjuncture, moments* in the conjuncture and linguistic *rapports de forces*.

## 5  Second Positive Thesis

My second positive thesis is that *language is a social phenomenon*. And I hope to show that this is not merely a resounding triviality (the argument against private language is well known in analytic philosophy). We have already encountered the myth of the origin of language that Marxists prefer, the yo-he-ho theory, so 'social' is not an entirely vague word, as language is grounded in work, production and the division of labour. Language is not the consequence of the needs of *intersubjectivity*, of the communication between constituted individual subjects; on the contrary, it is the *interlocution* that interpellates, in the course of communal work, the members of the horde or tribe into subjective workers and speakers. But this means that the concept of language we need cannot rely, as its core determination, on the concept of individual speaker on which linguistics is based. Whether it be the Chomskyan speaker, bearer of a mind/brain, the site of the actualisation of the competence the species is biologically endowed with, the phenomenological speaker of enunciation linguistics, the site of the operations that produce utterances, or the embodied speaker of Lakoff and Johnson, all three versions insist on the individuality of the speaker as source of utterances and owner of competence. All three, therefore, presuppose fully constituted individual subjects to whom language is granted as a faculty. We now know that we do not want this.

The question that follows is: with what do we replace the central concept of the speaker?

The obvious answer is *language itself*, as in 'language speaks', or 'it is language that speaks'. This concept of language speaking, notoriously to be found in Heidegger (*die Sprache spricht*), informs my theory of the violence of language, with its central concept of *remainder*.[28] And resorting to the entity 'language', and to the ontological metaphor of which it is the trace, is no mere instance of language fetishism. This language is not a creation of man turned into an oppressive 'thing', it is the mark of the reintroduction of the point of view of totality, as a totality of processes. It marks the reintroduction of the human subject in the totality of praxis: it is praxis, an always linguistic praxis, that subjectifies the individual into a subject, that makes a man of her. The same applies to the concept of class, which is an instance of abstraction, but not of fetishism: since classes only exist in so far as they oppose one another in the class-struggle, the point of view of class must be the point of view of the social totality. In the same vein, individual speakers only exist as they engage in interlocution, as they are spoken by the totality of language, of which they are offshoots.

But there is a second answer, to be found in the continental pragmatics of Deleuze and Guattari. The central concept of linguistics, the source of utterances, the entity constituted by language as it speaks is not the individual speaker but the *collective assemblage of enunciation*. The main interest of this concept for our concept of language is that, far from separating language from the rest of the world into a reified system, it involves *ontological mixture*: a collective assemblage of enunciation connects bodies (of speakers and addressees), institutions (as collectives sources of utterances), utterances (conversations, speeches and books). Thus, Deleuze and Guattari's canonical example, the feudal assemblage of utterance, involves the bodies of knights and ladies, of peasants, but also the horses and armour, cattle and ploughs and spinning wheels, etc.; and it involves the institutions of feudalism, both in their material aspect (the organisation of the castle, the feudal courts of justice) and their ideal aspect (the laws edicted in those courts), and it also involves a vast number of diverse utterances, including the poems of courtly love. What such a concept is based upon is the concept of social praxis, as action in and on the world, producing subjects and objects, in their places, out of the totality. So that language is both part of that social praxis (in feudal tournaments, as in today's tennis matches, you grunt more than you speak), and the medium that links together those various aspects, at various ontological levels, into a collective *assemblage* that orders them into *arrangements* ( the French word '*agencement*' bears both meanings).

And the concept has crucial consequences for us. We can no longer found our linguistics or philosophy of language on the basis of the proposition or judgement, embodied in the assertive utterance. Primitive utterances in Deleuze and Guattari's pragmatics are slogans, not propositions: commands rather than judgements, the performative prior to the constative. Or, to say the same thing in slightly different terms, interpellation prior to the subject. Another obvious consequence is that the ideality of the system, which lies at the heart of the mainstream concept of language (with the exception of Lakoff and Johnson's embodied language) is superseded by the materiality of the utterance and of the assemblage (this is the subject of the next thesis). The same applies to the centrality of the subject, another dogma of the mainstream conception: the reflexive return of the individual subject upon herself now appears as that form of fetishism which is expressed in the myth of Narcissus.

But perhaps the main consequence is the closeness, even the inseparability, of language and ideology. As we saw, in a passage of his *Pour une théorie de la production littéraire*,[29] Macherey suggested, *en passant*, that language *is* ideology, a thought he does not pursue, probably because of its sweeping nature. Let us see whether we can make more precise sense of it, in its two converse forms, that ideology is linguistic, and language ideological.

That ideology is linguistic has occurred to many thinkers, from Orwell (and Chomsky alluding to him, as we saw earlier), to the first theory of ideology proposed by Althusser,[30] where ideology works through punning. Examples abound in the history of imperialism and colonialism, from the French operations of 'pacification' which made war against Algerian peasants, to the French 'humanitarian' intervention in Rwanda, to protect the authors of a genocide, taking in our stride the war waged by the Israeli army in Lebanon under the name 'Peace in Galilee' (not to mention more recent examples). The main terms of our political vocabulary, words like 'freedom ' and 'democracy' are, as everyone knows, prime sites for the operations of ideology, a process that is one of the main sources for disaffection with electoral politics in the democratic West. We can understand why a philosopher like Alain Badiou can claim that 'democracy', is the great fetish on our political scene.[31]

But we can go further than this, which is clear enough, by going to Althusser's second theory of ideology, as expressed in the 'Ideological State Apparatuses' essay, with the linguistic slant that I give it in my *Interpretation as Pragmatics*,[32] in the shape of the linguistic chain of interpellation: institution/ritual/practice/speech-act. The end-of-chain product is the interpellated subject: not merely interpellated into a subject by ideology, as Althusser famously claims, but produced as a subject by the language that speaks her. And each stage of the chain is concerned with ideology as it is with language, with both aspects together, indissolubly.

Thus, we start from the massive materiality of *institutions* as producers of discourse: they are material in the sense that their apparatus relies on a number of bodies (the bodies of functionaries, the buildings in which they function, etc.); they are material in a wider sense in that they produce impersonal laws and decrees that place the subjects the apparatuses produce; and they are material-linguistic in that they secrete ready-made utterances which their subjects endlessly repeat and through which they recognise themselves: the public metaphors and clichés we live by, alive only in so far as they are dead, and the common sense within which our minds operate, which is always threatening to freeze into the good sense that attests we are the right subjects in the right places.

I have spoken of subjects as if they were directly interpellated by the institutions that give them their identity. But they are not. The subject is an end-of-chain product, and her interpellation first goes through the stage of *ritual*, where, precisely, individuals receive an identity by being ascribed a role in collective organised action or behaviour. This is the glorious moment of the performative (before infelicity sets in), the hanging judge donning his black cap, the vice-chancellor holding out a scroll in his left hand and holding out his right for students to touch, and thereby to graduate, etc. We are all, each at our level, concerned with such rituals, even if they lie in our distant past, because they determine the position from which we speak. Had I not (metaphorically speaking) touched the vice-chancellor's hand, you would not pay the same attention to what I am writing (in the sense that I would not have found a publisher). Note that the subject that tentatively emerges at this point is a *collective*, not an individual, subject: the vice-chancellor's hand being endowed with five fingers, five students can touch it at the same time, to save time. The question is, at which point does this collective subject separate into individuals? And the answer is: when the ritual becomes practice.

A *practice*, therefore, is the transformation of the solemnity of the collective ritual into the triviality of everyday individual life – the humdrum existence of the married couple, after the ceremony and back from the honeymoon. This is where collective ideology, with its attendant set phrases, clichés and systematic metaphors, is distributed, or dispersed, as everybody attends to their own business. This is where individual action appears, where, in Bourdieu's terms, the constraints of the field are met (that is accommodated, resisted, bent) by individual strategies, where the actor-subject emerges from the merely subjected subject. Such individuality, of course, has its limits: there is no such thing as solitary practice, and any form of practice involves contact (in pre-Great War parlance, I could have said 'intercourse') with others. Hence the crucial role, in their reversibility, of clichés: they are produced by the institutionalised rituals, and as such constrain the free expression of the speaker, but they also enable her to conduct the everyday intercourse that will make an individual subject out of her. And at this stage we should not indulge in a thoroughly pessimistic concept of linguistic interpellation. For in her practice the emerging subject is not only interpellated by ideology, she counter-interpellates the ideology that interpellates her. This is what Denise Riley analyses in her account of inner speech in terms of the 'middle voice' of inner speech (where the ritual is gone through 'in the interest of the speaker') and its 'autoventriloquy' (see the section on 'Autoventriloquy and interpellation'). We note that this does not imply the free creativeness of an unconstrained subject endowed with consciousness and in possession of her language, merely the multiplicity of interpellations through the different discourses to which she is subjected. Her 'inner voice' is a Babel, or babble, of interpellating discourses, among which she will find her individual subjective path.

In other words, the individual becomes a fully-fledged subject when the last link in the chain, the *speech-act*, is reached. For speech-acts have two striking characteristics: they are individual (thus allowing the methodological individualism that fetishises them) and they are indefinitely multiple. Even if they come in genres (carefully described by Searle),[33] even if they conform to felicity constraints, which make them more than a little conventional, they are ascribed to an individual speaker, who assumes responsibility for them, and who may exploit them for her own expressive purposes, thus turning conventional infelicity into stylistic felicity. Clichés are an endless source of travesty, pastiche, ironic reversal, malapropistic but meaningful quotation.

So, with the speech-act, at the end of the chain, we have reached the moment of individuality and full subjectivity: the moment of expression, infinitely diversified (in an infinity of Bakhtinian 'speech genres', or language-games), whose linguistic name is *style*, a term which, even more than 'cliché', is reversible, as it denotes at the same time the linguistic idiosyncrasies of the inimitable individual subject, and the fact that this individual expression makes her belong to a community, a group, a school (Cézanne's style and the style of the post-Impressionists; not to mention the style of clothing of mods and rockers, hardly an instance of individual expression). The word 'style' encapsulates the dialectics of subjectivation as expressed in the linguistic interpellation chain: interpellation *and* counter-interpellation, constraints *and* self-expression, individual strategy *and* collective field of action, cliché as ready-made language *and* cliché as material for ironic reversal, as receptacle of those dead metaphors we live by, linguistic fetishism *and* the linguistic abstraction of the word into a concept, the point of view of totality *and* the point of view of the individual subject. Finally, the dialectical play between alterity *and* identity. What the dialectics of interpellation and subjectivation tells us is that there is no escaping the collective, which is both oppressive and liberating, and there is no escaping the individual subject *at the end of the chain*.

And please note that in arguing that ideology is linguistic, I am not merely arguing, which would be trivial, that ideological practices, like all practices, come into contact with language. Since I do not jump before the command 'jump!' is issued, bungee-jumping is a 'linguistic' sport in that sense. What I am arguing concerns the existence of a constitutive link between ideology and language, a link so close that the two are indistinguishable, and can be connected by the copula of identity, as we may question the necessity of their very distinction. The whole chain of interpellation, and not merely the end-of-chain speech-act is linguistic: institutions are collective assemblages of enunciation, the essence of a ritual is in the performatives it stages, practices are steeped in language, as language is the medium of social intercourse and its motor.

The thesis that ideology is linguistic has a converse, which states that language is ideology. What can this mean?

At a simple level, it means there is no such thing as neutral language, uncontaminated by ideology. There are no independent 'rules' of grammar, available for the whole community, or as universal as ethical norms. In other words, Stalin may have shown some common sense in deciding that language was not a superstructure, but, in adding that it was a neutral instrument, relatively impervious to historical and totally to political change, he was not a Marxist. This does not mean of course that language *is* a superstructure, as Nikolai Marr, a superficial and recent Marxist, had maintained – merely that the dogmatic dichotomy of base and superstructure is in need of deconstruction.[34] In language, as we have seen, or in ideology *qua* linguistic, the division between the two levels becomes untenable. Deleuze and Guattari's concept of collective assemblage of enunciation, their obvious dislike for the term 'ideology' in its Marxist sense, is a symptom of this: the ontological mixture of the assemblage precludes any separation between material base and ideas, discourses or institutions. And language pervades the whole assemblage.

So, in language, the form (rules of grammar, etc.) is inseparable from the contents (the 'ideas' expressed). This is another reason why the classic distinction between sentence and proposition must be questioned, which is exactly what Lakoff and Johnson do with their embodied language, and their critique of the 'propositional' theory of language (they do this as part of their overall attack on the adequacy theory of truth).[35] Language is not the instrument that transmits ideal propositions, it is made up of metaphors, and if the 'body' in question is conceived as the collective body of the social speaker (a natural metaphorical extension of the term 'body', as in 'they advanced in a body'), then the 'neutrality' of a language now firmly conceived as in and of the world becomes highly dubious: forces and *rapports de forces*, placing, subjection and subjectivation are involved, 'identity' is at stake.

The tradition, linguistic or extra-linguistic, offers us two concepts to deal with this situation. The first is the concept of *connotation*, originally proposed by Hjelmslev and developed by Barthes.[36] What it suggests is that, in natural language (as opposed to artificial languages), there is no denotation without connotation. Barthes's two canonical examples are well known. The second is a Latin sentence, culled from a Latin grammar, *quia ego nominor leo*, which at the level of denotation appears to express the proposition 'because my name is lion', but which, at the level of connotation, means 'I am an example of a rule of grammar stating predicate concord in Latin and [this is my addition] you are to conform to what I say if you wish to attempt a Latin prose.' So the proposition is in fact a command. And the first, more famous, example is pictorial rather than linguistic: a black soldier, a *tirailleur sénégalais*, is saluting the French flag on the front cover of a French weekly. The denotative utterance that the photograph explicitly conveys is the description I have just given. But there is, of course, a connotative utterance, implicit but all the more forceful, which alone can explain the choice of *this* photograph for the front cover of the journal: 'the French empire is a good and glorious thing: the natives love it'. There is a certain amount of dramatic irony here: the photograph was published in 1956, just before the collapse of the French empire. So there is a second connotative utterance involved, one not clearly expressed by Barthes: the picture has an aspect of wishful thinking, or of Freudian denial, it confesses, *a contrario*, a certain uncertainty about the future of the French empire, it is trying to intervene in a political situation where intimations of imminent collapse are not lacking, so that this third utterance is again a command, or a slogan: 'defend the French empire!'

Connotation, therefore, is the ideological aura of language: not a superfluous addition, but a necessary part of its workings, to the point that the aura is often more important than the figure it outlines. For it will soon appear that the distinction between the literal and the metaphorical, the denotative and the connotative, is itself an ideological distinction.

The second concept is the concept of the *slogan*, or *mot d'ordre*, as the primitive form of utterance, command preceding statement and proposition. It is central to the elaboration of a new pragmatics by Deleuze and Guattari. They, of course, borrow the term from Lenin, who was not a philosopher of language but who, in 1917, during a period of enforced leisure (he was threatened with arrest and hiding from the police) devoted his time to the writing of a pamphlet on the timing of slogans: not merely their performative force (as in the old Marxist formula: 'ideology moves the masses' – how or when is hardly ever said), but the temporality of their efficacy. Up to a certain day, the slogan 'All power to the Soviets' was the only efficient, or just, slogan. After that date, that is after its moment in the conjuncture had passed, it had to be replaced by another one (which called for insurrection and the immediate and violent overthrow of the government). Those clinging to the slogan after its moment, even in the Bolshevik party, courted disaster. What Deleuze and Guattari do with the concept is extend it to the workings of all language, and not merely political language (unless we suppose that language in general is a political phenomenon): hence their now well-known suggestion that grammatical markers are markers of power. This formula is still merely stipulative: the case histories that will follow shortly will make it, I hope, more precise. But first, here is a mere hint of a suggestion, a theoretical site where this apparently outrageous claim (the neutrality of grammar, under the name of the principle of immanence, is a dogma of linguistics and mainstream philosophy of language) may begin to make sense.

In his essay on the obscurity of Hegel's style, 'Skoteinos'[37] (a Greek word meaning 'obscure', the antonym of *phanos* in Plato's *Republic*) Adorno contrasts Descartes's call for 'clear and distinct' ideas, of necessity expressed in distinct and clear language, with Hegel's realisation that such clarity, which fixes objects for intellectual grasping (in the etymological meaning of 'concept') is a form of fetishism. Adorno analyses Hegel's 'anti-linguistic impulse', his consciousness that 'the moment of universality, without which there would be no language, does irrevocable damage to the complete objective specificity of the particular thing it wants to define' (p. 106), his refusal to agree that communication is the sole aim of linguistic exchange, his challenge 'to the principle of fixedness, which is indispensable for the existence of anything linguistic' (p. 119). Hegel's famous obscurity is the result of a position towards language, a stylistic strategy, that seeks thoroughly to detach itself from 'the common sense of everyday language': his aim is the construction of a philosophical idiom which, like all philosophical language, will be 'a language in opposition to language' (p. 100). We understand, in this context, why clarity involves reification:

> Once it is acknowledged that clarity and distinctness are not mere characteristics of what is given, and are not themselves given, one can no longer evaluate the worth of knowledge in terms of how clearly and unequivocally individual items of knowledge present themselves. When consciousness does not conceive them as pruned down and identified like things –photographable, as it were – it finds itself of necessity in conflict with the Cartesian ambition.

> Reified consciousness freezes objects into things in themselves so
> that they can be available to science and praxis as things for others.
> (p.100)

I am not sure that we must take this as a licence to imitate Hegel's
style. But the contrast between the stylistic positions (which are crucial
philosophical positions) of Descartes and Hegel illustrates the necessity
(in the two senses of inevitability and usefulness) of linguistic fetishism
and the urgent need to combat it as, under values of transparency and
clarity, it freezes processes into things. And we have a clear example of
the two opposed senses of 'ideology', whose separation has plagued
Marxist theories of ideology: we understand its necessity (it is ideology
that makes subjects of all of us) and its dangers (ideology mystifies, it is
false consciousness, the body of ideas produced by the operations of
fetishism).

I promised to illustrate the present thesis (that language is constitu-
tionally ideological) with two 'case histories', that is with the analysis
of two apparently innocuous utterances. Here they are.

'The cat is on the mat' is an archetypal statement, meant to warm
the hearts of traditional linguists and philosophers of language. It is a
single, and a simple, sentence, generated by elementary syntactic rules,
devoid of any syntactic or semantic ambiguities or complications. For
it is as semantically perspicuous as it is syntactically simple: a sentence
to be taken literally, expressing a proposition whose reference can be
ascertained using the correspondence theory of truth (' "the cat is on
the mat" is true if and only if the cat is on the mat': we recognise
Tarski's typical pseudo-tautology). Its very innocuousness will be
demonstrated *a contrario* when it becomes the healthy part of what is
known as 'Moore's paradox': 'the cat is on the mat, but I don't believe
it is' (the problem lies in the second part of this sentence, which
forgets that assertion presupposes belief). Perhaps, with Moore's
paradox, the slightest anxiety creeps in, since if even the most innocuous of sentences can become enmeshed in paradox, there is no
certainty that the drifting (from sense into nonsense) will stop at that.

But where does this innocuous sentence come from, where has the
philosopher found it? Not in his venerable grizzled head: in a school
primer, where its very simplicity and clarity are examples of the
reification of processes into objects (that purring tabby-coloured shape
is of course a cat, this rectangular shape is of course a mat) – and the
reification extends, which is even more important, to the perceiving
subject who is absented by language from her utterance, in order to

turn a process of perception into a series of positive facts and things (compare our sentence with: 'Poor Pussy can't come in!', or 'The bloody cat has pooed on the mat again'). Our sentence, therefore, is not as innocuous as it sounds: in fact it is entirely artificial (Culioli once remarked that the trouble with the canonical example of early Chomskyan linguistics, 'the man hit the ball', is that it is an impossible sentence: any self-respecting speaker would say something like 'See that ball? Well, the man hit it', introducing topic and focus). It is caught up in the construction of a *rapport de forces*, it forces its transparent obviousness (a symptom of ideology in the pejorative sense) on the hearer, beginning with the child who, at school, is made to read it, copy it out, illustrate it and learn it by rote. For us, it illustrates the twin aspects of fetishism, and of ideology: the necessity of naming and abstraction, and the dire effects of consequent reification.

The second sentence is equally famous for, whether we type or not, we have all encountered 'the quick brown fox jumped over the lazy dogs'. This is not an idyllic evocation of the beauties of the English countryside and the joys of the chase (of which the fox wholly partakes), not even an extract from a tale by Beatrix Potter: this is the typist's equivalent to a spelling bee, *the* sentence that contains all the letters of the English alphabet at least once. We are moving from *Peter Rabbit* to Foucault's AZERTY (the French equivalent to QWERTY), not an individual utterance but a collective social *énoncé*, rife with Barthesian connotation (in the case of our sentence, it does not so much evoke dogs and fox as remind us of the placement of the letters on the keyboard, as we painfully learn to type with more than two fingers).

The thesis that language is a social phenomenon is not without serious consequences. The main consequence is that it induces us to think of language as a series of processes, not a collection of objects or facts, a 'treasury', to use Saussure's term, of words and rules: language *qua* social is a site for competing forces and the establishment of *rapports de forces*. Even as classes do not exist outside the class-struggle that constitutes them, speakers are constituted collectively in the linguistic struggle, and their individualisation through interpellation and 'placing' does not precede their engagement with social language, but is an effect of it (this is the point of view of *agôn* as opposed to *eirene*: an anti-Habermas position). We understand why we must discard both the old ontology of base and superstructure (the role of language is not limited to the superstructure) and the common sense that excludes language from the life and struggles of a class society: why Marr was in his way a *fou littéraire*, and Stalin not a Marxist. Perhaps the time has come to reread Paul Lafargue on the language of the French Revolution: his essay, in which he tried to analyse the effect of a historical event, namely the French Revolution, on the language of the actors (on its vocabulary, on its registers, on its syntax) was dismissed as unsound by Stalin – it is nevertheless one of the rare attempts, within the Marxist tradition, to take the fact that language is a social and a political phenomenon seriously.[38]

A question looms up: how is meaning constructed, if we adopt such a social-collective point of view? Remember that at the end of the last section we accounted for historical change in language in terms of metaphorical drifting, and suggested that the synchronic construction of meaning was effected along a Markov chain, interrupted and retroactively reinterpreted at *point de capiton*, the quilting point or upholstery button (a famous Lacanian metaphor *cum* concept). A Markov chain does not work only according to the internal constraints of language, whether syntactic (a transitive verb is followed by a noun), syntactico-semantic (in French a feminine article takes a feminine noun), or semantic (such constraints are systematically ignored in Chomsky's celebrated sentence, 'colourless green ideas sleep furiously'). It also abides by the social-collective constraints that generate public meaning (and meaning is always public). Thus, in the canonical example, 'Pride comes before a –', the apparition of the last word is somewhat syntactically constrained (any noun will do), it is to an extent semantically constrained (the noun phrase must be capable of being meaningfully governed by the preposition 'before'), and it is maximally constrained by the public meaning of the proverb, a paroxystic example of constraints on what can be said, as the proverb demands that the sentence should end on a dying 'fall'. Except, of course, that the speaker, having acquired individuality in the process of interpellation by social-collective language, may counter-interpellate the language that interpellates her, and end the sentence with ' – before a vote of impeachment', thus exploiting the constraints for her own expressive purposes. Thus, the quilting point, which *re*interprets an always-already interpreted (because public) utterance, allows the speaker to recognise the meaning: so she was talking about Clinton all the time. At the quilting point, public meaning being achieved, the interpellated speaker becomes a full subject, for ideological-linguistic constraints are defeasible, and meant to be exploited, as indeed are syntactic and semantic constraints (contrary to what the mainstream linguist, for whom 'rules of grammar are laws of nature', would like to believe).

## 6   Third Positive Thesis

Language, as we saw, is a historical and a social phenomenon. It is also material and political. Hence my third positive thesis, which states that *language is a material phenomenon*. That language has a material aspect in so far as utterances are emitted by the human body is obvious. Chrysippus's pseudo-paradox ('When I speak of a chariot, a chariot goes through my mouth') and what I have called the Castafiore principle[39] (the prima donna's vocal production, if emitted at the right pitch, may break glass) are derived from this elementary fact. But it is equally obvious that language has an ideal aspect, that *phone* is nothing if not animated by *logos*. The question is: can we go beyond this linguistic dualism? The purpose of the present thesis is to suggest that we can, by insisting on the materiality of language, on its origin in the body.

But unless we wish to go back to Chrysippus and the Castafiore principle – pleasant as they are, they will not tell us much about the workings of language – we must make what we mean by 'body' a little clearer. The question then becomes: which body is responsible for the materiality of language? For bodies there are more than one.

The immediate candidate is the *biological body*. Language is, after all, physically produced by our vocal organs. We may wish to add that the ideal aspect of language is a product of the brain. Chomsky's phrase, 'the mind/brain' is an elegant attempt at disguising, or rather denying in the Freudian sense, what amounts to a reductive physicalism, or, in our Marxist jargon, the 'gross or vulgar materialism' associated with eighteenth century philosophers (I know that he denies this, but, as we saw, he has read Lange, the historian of that tradition, his only reference on the rare occasions when he broaches the question of materialism). Lakoff and Johnson's 'embodied language', even if, as we shall see, it involves another type of body, also partakes of a form of physicalism (which in their case, they claim, is not reductive, no mere determinism): their second-generation cognitive science speaks the idiom of neurone circuits, where long ago scientists talked areas of the brain (the Great War provided an endless supply of patients with pieces of metal embedded in their brains, and therefore a vast array of types of aphasia), and contemporary scientists talk genes. The problem with this is the usual: such physicalism naturalises language, and falls into the trap of methodological individualism, as it will talk in terms of the individual body (even if the biological endowment is characteristic of the species), and therefore of the individual speaker: both the historical and the social aspect of language become at best irrelevant, at worst incomprehensible. As Vygotsky insists, from the animal to the human development of the intellect, something essential changes in the very nature of the development: it goes from the simply biological to the socio-historical. 'Verbal thought is not an innate, natural form of behaviour but is determined by a historical-cultural process.'[40] The paradoxical consequence of biological reductionism, on the other hand, is that it cuts language off from the world, by imprisoning it, in the form of an ideal competence, within the individual body – gross materialism, as Althusser points out, is always accompanied by rank idealism.

Let us, therefore, examine another candidate, the *phenomenological* body. This is the body of the speaker as site of grammatical operations in enunciation theories inspired by phenomenology. It is to be found in France in the work of Benveniste and Culioli,[41] in the United States in the work of cognitive linguists like Langacker or Lakoff and Johnson[42] (I am aware that the latter explicitly distance themselves from phenomenology, as they operate with a concept of unconscious, which is however closer to Leibniz's 'small perceptions' than to the Freudian unconscious). This phenomenological body is actively conscious and consciously active. It is oriented in the world around it, its life-world (orientational metaphors are a type of Lakovian metaphor: 'the ball is behind the rock' – but the rock has no fixed 'behind', and the same place, should I walk round the rock, would become the 'front' of the rock). And it creates systems of metaphors (which Lakoff and Johnson call 'structural') through semantic drifting from the known and immediate, in other words the speaker's own body, her *corps propre*, to the less immediate and less well known. The third type of Lakovian metaphor, 'ontological metaphor', is concerned with abstraction; but such abstraction or reification (the preferred example is 'inflation', a series of processes frozen into an object graspable in language), always start from the body – this philosophy, this conception of truth and reason is firmly *embodied*. For instance, our concept of time is constructed through metaphors of the situation of our body in space, through the Time Orientation Metaphor (Location of Observer → Present; Space in front of Observer → Future, etc.), or the Time orientation Metaphor (Objects → Times; the Motion of Objects Past the Observer → the 'passage' of Time, etc.).[43]

There are serious philosophical limitations to this type of analysis, which over-simplifies our concept of time (I need only mention the elaboration of a concept of aspect in enunciation linguistics). In her analysis of inner speech and the embodied mind (see the section

'Topographical metaphor and embodied mind'), Denise Riley points out the disadvantages of a blissfully ahistorical account. But this vision of an embodied speaker, in which the object of the analysis is not the utterance as product or result (the string of words) but the utterance as process (the act of producing the utterance in a given situation: *énonciation* rather than *énoncé*) marks a progress from the physical or naturalist reductionism *à la* Chomsky. Those 'enunciative operations' (Culioli), 'psycho-grammatical operations' (the followers of Gustave Guillaume) or 'embodied metaphors' (Lakoff and Johnson) allow us, to a certain extent, to escape from the fetishism of mainstream linguistics (with its twin symptoms of naturalism and methodological individualism). And, whether this is acknowledged or not, they owe a lot to Merleau-Ponty's view on language, to his dichotomy, or chiasm, of *parole parlante* and *parole parlée*,[44] in which the distinction between process (of enunciation) and result (the utterance) is already explicit. And we note that a number of Culioli's concepts, for instance, are borrowed from *Phénoménologie de la perception*.

This phenomenological body is more relevant to us than the purely biological 'natural' body (which always turns out to be an ideal body). It allows us to avoid the 'principle of immanence' on which structural linguistics is founded, to reconnect language with the world, to forget about the ideality of the ideal system: this is the body of experience, not so very far from the body of praxis. It is the body in which consciousness (or Lakoff and Johnson's 'cognitive unconscious') emerges. But it is not the only body.

The third body is the *erotic body*, if I can so glorify the body of psychoanalysis. Here we find a real concept of the unconscious (which Lakoff and Johnson too easily dismiss as repressive), in its relation to language. Within this theoretical framework, the articulation of language and the body is at last made more precise. The phenomenological body, at least in the linguists mentioned above (Merleau-Ponty is another matter) remains somewhat vague: where are those 'enunciative operations' situated? Physical reductionism here has the advantage of clarity. But so has psychoanalysis, with its conceptual apparatus of primary and secondary processes, dream work and joke work. The early Deleuze, in *Logique du sens*, borrowed from this apparatus to produce a fully-fledged theory of language.[45] Such articulation is to be found in Freud, a better linguist than most, in the early Lacan (we have already evoked the retroactive construction of meaning from *point de capiton*; we could evoke the constitution of the subject from the point of the other and the maxims of interlocution that can be derived from this),[46] or in the work of Serge Leclaire, with the inscription of the letter on the erotic body.[47] There is a whole corpus of work, among the first circle of Lacanians, on the relations, or frontiers, between body and language, including the early work of Luce Irigaray,[48] or the ethnological work of J. Favret-Saada on witchcraft in the French *bocage* region.[49]

The problem with this erotic body is that it is theoretically unstable. The gains made on the question of language are at risk of being lost when Lacan and his followers indulge in a metaphysics of *jouissance*. The history of the concept *point de capiton* from the early to the late Lacan is a good example of such drifting. Nevertheless this erotic body is of crucial importance to us: we owe it the concept of *maternal tongue* (the phrase, of course, is old as the hills). The speaker is not an angel (as J. C. Milner describes Saussure's ideal speaker as agent of the ideal system): he has a body nurtured within the celebrated triangle, he is inhabited by a language which is his mother's language; as is only too obvious in the case of Louis Wolfson, he is spoken by his maternal tongue (even if the empirical mother is, for one reason or another, not present to do the nurturing: psychoanalysis has taught us that absent parents are as worrisome, if not more, for their offspring as the concrete incarnations that plague their daily lives).

Important as it is, the erotic body is not the only one. There is a fourth body, the *labouring body*. And here, naturally, the Marxist finds herself on familiar ground. We find an account of such a body in the work of David McNally, *Bodies of Meaning*.[50] This is how he describes his position in the introduction to his book:

> One overarching argument runs through these pages; that post-modern theory, whether it calls itself post-structuralist, deconstruction or post-Marxism, is constituted by a radical attempt to banish the real human body – the sensate, biocultural, labouring body – from the sphere of social life. As a result, I argue, these outlooks reproduce a central feature of commodified society: the abstraction of social products and practices from the labouring bodies that generate them. (p. 1)

> Central to the critical materialism that informs this book, then, is the insistence that the concrete bodies, practices, and desires, which have been forgotten by idealism, perform a return of the repressed. Invariably, these things return in devalued form, as 'the excrescences of the system', as the degraded and discarded elements of refuse which 'show the untruth, the mania of the systems themselves'. The

text of critical theory is to produce a knowledge built out of these excrescences, a knowledge derived from attending to the fragments which have escaped the imperial ambitions of linguistic idealism. And this means starting from the body. (p. 4)

Let us take this as a philosophical programme. The body as here conceived is the site from which a materialist philosophical gesture can be made: it is what linguistic idealism, which deals with angels, excludes, and it operates a return of the repressed in the 'excrescences' of actual language that subvert the ideality of the system. And the workings of the idealist view of language are indeed attributed to 'a central feature of commodified society', in which we easily recognise fetishism. At this stage, 'the body' as a concept is still a little vague, it is not entirely distinguished from the psychoanalytic, perhaps even from the phenomenological body, hence the reappearance of questions of 'ethno-racial identity' (I am aware, of course, that 'ethno-racial' differences pervade language as they pervade the whole of society: but I am wary of the language of 'identity' used to account for them, rife as it is with incipient or explicit fetishism).

But this concept of 'body' is made more precise by the introduction of a type of body so far neglected, the 'labouring body', forcefully presented in the terms of classical Marxism (with a feminist twist):

Of course, bourgeois discourses have to admit the body at some stage of the game. But they do so by 'cleansing' it of the sweat of labour and the blood of menstruation and childbirth. The bourgeois body is a sanitized, heroic male body of rational (nonbiological) creatures: it does not break under the strain of routinized work; it does not menstruate, lactate, or go into labour; it does not feel the lash of the master's whip; it does not suffer and die. The bourgeois body is, in short, an idealist abstraction. (p. 9)

I like the robust language that dares still use the term 'bourgeois' in an offhand manner. And I think we recognise the rhetoric of pathos that animates the first lines of Deleuze and Guattari's *Anti-Oedipus*:[51] it shits, it fucks, it works ... In the case of Deleuze and Guattari, this 'it', which is obviously a body, is described as a machine ('everywhere it is machines ...'), not a metaphor, but, they insist, an actual machine. And it is true that at this stage McNally's body, no longer a phenomenological, nor even a psychoanalytic body, is still indistinguishable from the Deleuzean 'body without organs' of the philosophy of desire.

And you will not be surprised to learn that the book has a chapter on Bakhtin and his carnivalesque Rabelaisian body. But this body soon becomes socio-historical:

> To talk about human bodies and the practices in which they are immersed need not entail treating the body as a timeless object of nature. The human body, as I hope to show, is inherently historical. True, bodies have a relatively fixed biological constitution. But the evolutionary history of the human body also involves the emergence of cultural practices and social history. To talk meaningfully about the human body is to talk about bodies that are the site of dynamic social processes, bodies that generate open-ended systems of meaning. It is, in other words, to talk about relations of production and reproduction, about languages, images of desire, technologies, and diverse forms of sociocultural organization. All of these things operate on the site of the body and its history. (p. 7)

There is, of course, a vast tradition which makes the same theoretical gesture.[52] This historical body is a signifying body, 'a body which generates and is shaped by systems of meaning' (p. 9). The advantages of this concept of the body over the phenomenological and the psychoanalytic concepts are now clear: such a body is no longer merely individual, it is social, shaped by social forces and relations; it is radically historical, the 'biological endowment', itself a product of history (here, evolution is treated as a form of long-term history), being modified by history; it is not only the agent of collective praxis, but also an end product of the processes which make up that praxis.

This is an explicitly materialist position, firmly grounded in the materiality of the human body (with its etymological *pathos*: the body not only as contingent site for the intellect, but as the necessary site of affects). But it enables us to envisage a wider form of materialism (encapsulated in the Marxist phrase 'historical materialism'): the materialism of institutions, and of ideas (in so far as they are incarnated in discourse, in slogans for instance, and 'move' the masses). For there is more to an English department in a university than rooms, tables and chairs, the bodies of students and staff: modules, memos, essays and dissertations, the materiality of which is only too weighty. This is, as we have seen, where Deleuze and Guattari's concept of collective assemblage of enunciation shows its usefulness. Hence also the crucial importance of the concept of interpellation for a theory of language. For interpellation does 'communicate', but in the French sense of the transmission of an impulse or a force. This force, the material force of bad words, the force that causes Wolfson something close to physical pain, is what circulates along the chain of interpellation, materially linking institutions, 'ideas' and bodies. And this is what, at the end of the chain, the subject is: a body assigned its place by linguistic interpellation, a socially and historically placed body, the 'labouring' body of praxis. Language, before it is fetishised into an ideal system for the communication and exchange of thought clothed in words, is a system of places, a site for struggle and *rapports de forces*, the site of processes of subjectivation through the ascription of places, an operation described by François Flahault in *La Parole intermédiaire*.[53]

We understand why insults leave traces: because they become material forces when they forcibly seize the addressee's body (there is a rich array of metaphors to describe the physical effect of insults on my body). What is inscribed here is not only Leclaire's letter (on the erotic body), but also insults (on the social labouring body – the choice by McNally of the ambiguous term 'labouring' body, the body of work and the body of childbirth, is particularly apt). If we generalise this to all language-games (and not merely to bad words or erotic games), we will understand why commands or slogans are primitive forms of utterance. And we shall also understand why, in Favret-Saada's account of witchcraft, the only defence against the witch's spell, which is all the more efficient (it can provoke panic, and, she suggests, in one case at least, lead to death) as it is inexistent (there is no such thing as a witch, therefore no one has actually uttered the spell), is the counter-spell that will place the supposed (but always innocent) witch under linguistic attack, an attack which may cause exactly the same physical damage as the inexistent spell. Finally, we will understand why Anglo-Saxon pragmatics, for all its talk of forces, gets it wrong. Its 'forces' are disembodied, a pretext for endless classification of speech-acts, they are neither material nor social forces, circulating along the chain, from institution to ritual, from ritual to practice, from practice to speech-act. In Anglo-Saxon pragmatics, this material grounding of linguistic forces only emerges in denial, in Austin's concept of infelicity, when a material hitch sullies the purity of the speech-act: when a horse is appointed consul (such, however, is the force exerted by institutions that, as long as the emperor has not been assassinated, the horse *is* a consul), when the bridegroom already has a wife, who is sitting, heavily pregnant, with the congregation, or when a dubious proletarian character seizes the bottle of champagne from the hand of royalty and names the ship the 'Generalissimo Stalin'. In all such cases, bodies as constrained by institutions, rituals and practices, are involved: social, labouring bodies.

Lastly, we shall understand why we do not need to solve the chicken and egg riddle of which comes first, language or work. As attributes of the social body, they are in a state of mutual presupposition: they both emerge(d), in dialectical embrace, from social praxis.

My concept of 'the remainder'[54] was an early attempt to think the inscription of materiality in language, and also to think the very materiality of language itself. It sought to name the return, within language, of the repressed social body that shatters the self-centred ideality of the linguistic 'system'. And we could make up a case for modernist, or avant-garde literature (for instance the idiosyncratic literary canons – Artaud, Bataille, Roussel, etc – defended by Foucault or Deleuze) as the reinscription of this body into language, rather than a mere matter of formalist *exercices de style*. But this is another discussion.

## 7   Fourth Positive Thesis

My fourth, and last, thesis is that *language is a political phenomenon*. Here, we must take the collectivism of language seriously. Methodological individualism fetishises the individual speaker. But language deals with collective, or, as Lucien Goldman called them, 'transindividual' subjects[55] before it deals with individual speakers. One speaks language only in so far as one is a member of a linguistic community (there is no such thing as private language), and this linguistic community is also a political community, a *polis*. We do not need the bearded prophet to be reminded of this: it goes as far back as the introduction to Aristotle's *Politics*, towards the end of which man is said to be a political animal because he is a speaking animal. Following Volosinov, I am merely suggesting that the converse is also true, that man is a speaking animal because he is a political animal, that intersubjectivity emerges from interlocution, which in turn is in a relation of mutual presupposition with social relations, of work, of the division of labour, of *rapports de force* and the ascription of places.

In the everyday life of speakers, this political aspect takes a specific form, the form of a *natural* language that is so called because it is also a *national* language (by which, following Gramsci, we understand not only a grammatical system, but the totality of a culture, a 'conception of the world', which is socially and historically, and therefore also geographically, bound). What is meant by the phrase, 'national language', a concept that goes beyond, and comes before, the historical constitution of nation-states? The answer, already suggested in Gramsci, is: the cement of what Benedict Anderson calls a nation, that is an imagined community; a machine for distributing social capital, ascribing places, but also creating communities and organising ideological consensus. We understand why Chomsky is deeply wrong, and English, as a separate entity, must exist. It involves far more than a few grammatical parameters, and a gradual passage from German through Dutch: a political entity, above the dialects, registers and jargons that constitute it. This is how a theorist of translation, Lawrence Venuti, phrases it:

> There can be no question of choosing between adhering to the constants that linguistics extracts from language or placing them in continuous variation because language is a continuum of dialects, registers, styles and discourses positioned in a hierarchical arrangement and developing at different speeds In different ways. Translation, like any language use, is a selection accompanied by exclusion, an intervention into the contending languages that constitute any historical conjuncture.[56]

We recognise the concepts of Deleuze and Guattari's critique of linguistics (in the opposition between the extraction, or abstraction, of constants and the process of continuous variation), and an echo of their crucial concept of a minor versus a standard language. And this position has the advantage of formulating the first two moments of the dialectic clearly. On the one hand, there is nothing but continuous variation, a multiplicity of dialects, etc.; but on the other hand there is also a hierarchy, which is a political hierarchy, at the top of which English as a standard language lords it over the dirty dialectal rascals, at the price of being constantly threatened with minorisation. So that 'English', a necessary fetish but a fetish, is a site of constant political struggle. What we call a 'natural' language, far from being natural, is a sedimented aggregate of past and present political struggles

And the dialectic works both ways. A national language is constituted as such by the political struggles that eventually end up in the creation of a nation-state. But it also plays a constituting part in such struggles. The role of Dante's Tuscan dialect of Italian in the constitution not only of standard Italian but of the Italian state is well known. And similar claims could be made about Shakespeare: this is a major component of 'Shakespeare' as a national myth. Again, we have a dialectical relationship: national language plays a major part in the constitution of the nation, and the emergence of the nation-state contributes to the emergence of the national language, for, such is the wisdom of the old joke, what is a language if not a dialect with an army? Two examples will illustrate this.

The first quasi-statistical survey of the state of the French language was produced at the time of the French Revolution by abbé Grégoire. The results were that out of twenty-four million inhabitants, only four or five million actually spoke 'correct' French. The rest either spoke other languages (German in Alsace, Italian in Corsica, a form of Gaelic in Brittany, Occitan in the South of France), or other dialects or patois that were closer to the French language, but often unintelligible to the speaker of standard French.[57] The history of the constitution of French as a national language, therefore, is the political history of the imposition of 'national' French on speakers of dialect, an imposition which took more than a century and was carried through by institutions such as courts of justice, an army of conscripts and the school apparatus (this is the object of Renée Balibar's book, which seeks to substantiate Althusser's thesis that the school apparatus is the main ideological state apparatus under the capitalist mode of production)[58].

The second example is chosen for scientific, but also for biographical reasons. It takes the form of a question: is Corsican an independent language? The question, with the implied preference for a positive answer, is recent: for decades, almost for centuries, one took it for granted that Corsican was a dialect of Italian, closer to the Tuscan dialect that became standard Italian than most, but hardly better than the unwritten patois of illiterate peasants. And the linguist has to confess that Corsican and standard Italian are mutually intelligible, have parallel morphologies and similar syntax, and share a great part of their vocabularies. The differences belong mainly to phonology (with the suspicion that they might be simply a matter of accent: nobody would claim that Geordie is not a form of English), and of lexicon.

But the fact that the question, in the last thirty years, has been raised and answered positively cannot be ignored. Nor can it be ignored that it was raised contemporaneously with the rise of Corsican nationalism. So a language may not be a dialect with an army (Corsican is singularly deficient in this, unless you count bombs), but it may be a dialect promoted into a language because an imagined community has decided to find its unity in it, or to found its unity on it. And the irony is that as a language, Corsican is indebted to the French language and to the French school apparatus. To the French language: Corsican has now been separated for more than two centuries from standard Italian, which used to be the written official language (in deeds and other documents: Corsica is the only aspiring nation whose national anthem is sung in another language than its own), and is now only taught in schools as a foreign language. It has consequently evolved away from standard Italian and towards French, through heavy lexical borrowing and syntactic *calque*. As a result of this, Corsican is now an independent language, almost equidistant from French and Italian (the 'almost' is an exaggeration: the mutual intelligibility is still with Italian). And the language is also indebted to the French state apparatus, in the shape of the school. For the sad fact is that fewer and fewer people speak Corsican: in the last eighty years the agricultural way of life that was dominant in the island has vanished (the massacres of the First World War were a contributing factor), and urbanisation has struck. Half the population now lives in the two main cities, where the younger generation no longer speaks Corsican. So, as a vernacular, Corsican is threatened with death – its only chance of survival is through compulsory teaching in the school apparatus, a major political demand of the nationalists, and one that the French state has so far refused to accept, although Corsican as a regional language has received a certain amount of support (a body of specialised teachers funded by the state, the creation of bilingual schools, etc.).

So the history of a language, and its very constitution as a language, are inextricably bound up with political events. If you are an optimist, you will analyse this in terms of mutual presupposition; if a pessimist, as a form of vicious circle: for Corsican to emerge as a 'natural', that is as a national language, Corsica needs to be a nation; but Corsica, in order to be a nation, needs the existence of Corsican as a national language.

The relationship between language and politics in the broadest sense, however, goes much further, or much deeper, than the contribution of language to the constitution of the nation-state. It permeates the whole of civil society, it is a constitutive factor in the fabric of everyday life. This is Gramsci, the great historicist, on the 'spontaneous philosophy', not of the scientist, but of the man in the street, for according to him, every human being is a 'philosopher'. Such philosophy is to be found:

1. In language itself, as a set of determinate ideas and concepts, and not merely a treasury of words empty of contents; 2. in common sense and good sense; 3. in the common people's religion, and therefore in their system of beliefs, superstitions, opinions, ways of seeing things and sources of action which usually go by the name of 'folklore'.[59]

Here, language, the language of the *polis*, is seen as the repertory of the common folks' reasons to believe, and to act according to such beliefs: it is the inscription and sedimentation of folk-policy, the policy of the common people, hence the nexus language/common sense/religion. Language it is that turns the individual agent, with her idiosyncratic and inimitable point of view on the world, into a collective agent, sharing with the rest of the national/linguistic community a 'conception of the world', a form of common sense, a 'natural' philosophy (a highly cultural and historical construct), a religion. For the linguist, the interest of this, Gramsci's concept of language, is that it is clearly linked to metaphor, so that Lakoff and Johnson's concept of 'metaphors we live by' was anticipated by Gramsci by half a century, with the added advantage that, in Gramsci, such metaphors are firmly cultural, grounded in the political/ historical conjuncture:

> Generally, when a new conception of the world succeeds an older one, the old language remains in use, but in the form of metaphors. The whole of language is a continuous process of metaphorisation, and historical semantics is a part of the history of culture: language is both a living thing and a museum where the fossils of life and older civilisations are exhibited.[60]

At this point we need a specific concept to capture the intricacy and mutual presupposition of language and politics. Tradition suggests the concept of *linguistic imperialism* (the blunt statement that English is the language of imperialism usually provokes a *frisson* of excitement mingled with indignation in academic audiences). This goes further, and is more complex than L. J. Calvet's concept of *glottophagy*,[61] which describes the absorption and disappearance of the language of a politically dominated people, at the hands of a colonial or imperialist power, armed with their overbearing language. If language death is not only a phenomenon to be deplored, but also one which, according to the linguists who study it, occurs every fortnight,[62] the existence of a glottophagic form of imperialism can hardly be in doubt. But the situation, as history has repeatedly shown, is more complex than this. Linguistic imperialism is more insidious, no less affirmed, but also more fragile than plain political and economic imperialism. The history of the relationship between Latin and Greek, when the all-powerful Roman empire adopted Greek as the language of the elite, but also the flourishing of Latin among the ruins of the empire are cases in point. Rather than glottophagy, we shall turn to Deleuze and Guattari's concept of a minor language, or rather, since they always think in terms of process and becoming, of the minorisation of a standard language by a host of minor dialects – the fortunate paradox that the concept (obviously imported from the field of politics) embodies is that the domination of the standard language is precisely due to the constant process of minorisation which it undergoes at the hand of minor dialects, registers and styles. So that at the very moment that English is acquiring world dominance as the one and only global language, it is splitting up into a multiplicity of New Englishes, or being debased to the dubious status of a *lingua franca*, where the purist, brought up in the admiration of Addison, if not Carlyle, would feel indignantly lost.

So a standard language, that historical/political construct, is both the vector of linguistic imperialism, killing smaller languages in its triumphant wake, imposing its grammatical markers of power (from the modal auxiliaries to the grunts uttered by Lara Croft) on hapless foreigners on the other side of the planet, and a constantly minorised dialect, always in danger of being debased (the metaphor of the coin is particularly apt) or watered down if not swamped (where the metaphor becomes cataclysmic). We understand the interest of the concept of style both in Volosinov and in Deleuze and Guattari. Linguistic imperialism, like the common and garden variety, is always resisted, and this resistance, which the concept of minorisation captures, is embodied in the style of discourse, not as the acme of individual originality, but as the inscription in the utterance of the clash of competing dialects. What Volosinov calls the 'pluriaccentuality' of the word, or the better-known concept of polyphony developed by Bakhtin, are ways of describing the linguistic (class) struggle. In all of this, of course, we hear echoes of our old friend, interpellation.

An example, taken from the sexual politics of language, will illustrate this. In the summer of 2002, the British press reported the following question, asked in the course of an interview for a civil service job involving much travel from a woman applicant: 'What will your husband do for sex when you are away?' The mainstream philosophy of language treats questions as genuine demands for information, the model of which is the innocuous question asking the time. True, some questions are loaded, and presuppose a type of answer, if not a precise answer ('Aren't you coming?'): but it can be claimed that if they do not exactly ask for information, at least they seek confirmation of what the speaker believes. But our question, a brutal ascription of place of a blatantly reactionary type (being an irredeemable optimist, I should have thought such explicit vulgarity was a thing of the past, but it clearly is not), is not asking for any answer, and the only response to the male speaker, a fully deserved one, would have been another question: 'What does your wife do for sex when you are away?' (unless, of course, she answers 'Would you like me to give you his phone number?'). Such a response, however, is of course precluded by the local *rapport de forces*. So some questions are merely the conveyors of bad words, with the added sins of perfidy or hypocrisy (at least a plain insult is frank in its aggression). Some questions do require answers, but one that the questioner already knows and that he will use to reward or damn the answerer – you have recognised the professional discourse of the academic *qua* examiner. In normal life, such a low trick would trigger the indignant rejoinder: 'if you knew, why (expletive) did you ask?' In our example one function of the question is to exclude (the applicant from what is obviously a male preserve) and to ascribe a place on the sexual/cultural divide. In short, it is a political speech-act, where our concepts of linguistic imperialism and linguistic class-struggle find application in everyday life – if the function of ideology is to interpellate individuals into subjects, the operation of the ideological struggles concerns every individual in her everyday existence. We may note that the political result of the operation of language here is to fetishise gender, which is a way of politicising it and opening up a space for the struggle of counter-interpellation. Even if the applicant was not in a position to make the rejoinder I suggested, the possibility remains open: the very fact that the exchange was reported in the national press shows that a *rapport de forces* can always be contested, and eventually overturned. But perhaps this is naïvely optimistic: the exchange has news value only if it is presented as a joke – the interviewer's remark is not so much an aggression as a snigger, a joke always uttered for the benefit of the audience (which now includes the readers of *The Guardian*).

The thesis, 'language is a political phenomenon' brings together a number of related propositions.

(i) Man is a political animal because a speaking animal. Language is the necessary, even the constitutive, medium of politics. *Agôn*, that 'generalised athleticism',[63] is the archetypal form of political relationship. For Deleuze, it is the essence of democracy, in the form of the democratic debate; for a Marxist, it is the essence of the (class-) struggle, in so far as it inevitably takes a linguistic form. Were I to adopt the political philosophy of Carl Schmitt, I would add that language, being the only way whereby friend and foe can be distinguished, or even constituted, is the essence of politics.

(ii) But the reverse is also relevant: man is a speaking because a political animal. Political action is the canonical form of *praxis* (at least for a tradition that goes from Aristotle to Habermas, via Hannah Arendt), and linguistic *praxis* is the archetypal form of *praxis*. Whence the conviction that language and politics are inextricably mixed. Language is in fact both the expression and the means of the constitutive collectivity of humankind, of the fact that the individual never comes first, but always as a part of a *socius*, from which (on the background of which) she emerges as an individual. The umbilical cord, which is also the social bond, uniting individual and *socius* is language. We understand why Marxists do not shun the mythical problem of the origin of language, for which they, inevitably, offer diverging solutions, from communal hunting (Tran Duc Thao) to the division of labour (Marx).

(iii) Ideas become material forces when they capture the masses. And they do so because they are incarnated in language: in political propositions, in calls to action and slogans. And it is important to understand that political ideas are not 'translated' into slogans, that they do not precede the linguistic expression that might transcribe and sometimes betray them: they *are* the slogans that inscribe them on the body of the *socius*. In his early writings, Marx insists on the materiality of language as a reality of the senses: the ideas that capture the masses obtain their efficacy from this material existence as words and slogans, from their insertion into Deleuze and Guattari's 'collective assemblages of enunciation', assemblages characterised, as we saw, by their ontological mixture. So ideas 'become material forces' not through a process of transformation, but because they are material from the very start, being the words that 'express' them (here, the vocabulary of the dominant philosophy of language betrays us, as usual). We understand why Lenin, in that moment of enforced leisure just before the October Revolution, devoted some of his no doubt precious time to the composition of his pamphlet on slogans. The justness of a political line is not a question of abstract theory, but the practical result of the enunciation of the right slogans in the right conjuncture.

(iv) If the origin of language is to be sought in the division of labour, it follows that language is still concerned with the division of society into antagonistic classes, and closely involved in their struggle. For language is the source of the illusory generality (or ideology in the pejorative sense) in which humankind disguises the real relations between families, tribes and classes that make up society and that are fetishised into the state: it is itself fetishised into what Marx in *The German Ideology* calls 'an independent realm'.[64] But language is also the battleground on which such struggles are fought, and the task of a revolutionary critique is to take down language from its illusory philosophical heights (Marx is scathing about the philosophical pretensions of Max Stirner, with his sub-Hegelian play on words which passes for the construction of concepts) into the materiality of the real world – this is what he ultimately means by 'the language of real life'.

So there is such a thing as the linguistic class-struggle. By which we do not merely mean that the class-struggle is carried *through* language, which is obvious, but also *in* language. Let us attempt to give this phrase more detailed positive contents.

To do so means developing the old Marxist tautology, 'the dominant ideology dominates'. For the class-struggle in language has one striking characteristic: its agents, or rather its mouthpieces, are not necessarily aware that it is being waged, at the very moment when, as speakers, they are actively involved in it. The following sentence was part of a news item on the national news in the mid-1980s:

The dispute by the health workers is now in its third week.

This is a blatant case of solecism. The grammar of the noun 'dispute' demands that it take a prepositional phrase beginning with 'between', not an agent beginning with 'by', as its complement. And this sole-cism, of course, is not politically innocent. It exonerates the other side in the dispute from the inconvenience to the general public caused by the strike; it ascribes the sole responsibility of the strike and its contin-uation to the workers; and it even manages to avoid the word 'strike', as emotionally and politically charged. In other words, our sentence isolates the striking health workers and interpellates us, the audience, into consumers and tax-payers potentially incensed by the breakdown of a public service. The interesting point about this analysis is that, being conducted strictly at the level of language, it does not presup-pose the darkest intentions on the part of the journalist who wrote it – whether he or she was aware of the exact implications of the sentence, whether the solecism is deliberate or not, while not an entirely irrele-vant issue, is certainly not an essential matter. The passive, with its ascription of agency, is a weapon in the ideological struggle, *whether or not the speaker is aware of it*. The political unconscious has its own symptoms and slips of the tongue.

It is all, of course, a question of alliances and exclusion, of who will be placed in the position of the scapegoat. And language, which unites the community of speakers, also separates and excludes – this is the function of 'bad words'. But it is important to note that such separation is not always operated through hostile and insulting naming: it is already present in the grammatical core of language, for instance in the structure of personal pronouns (the 'inclusive' 'we' is also an instrument of exclusion; the 'you' of insult – 'you idiot!' – is a mark of separation; and Benveniste is right to call third-person pronouns 'pronouns of non-person'). In an article published in a linguistics journal, Todorov accounts for the structure of sexual jokes according to Freud in similar terms:[65] A, a man, makes a pass at B, a woman; being repulsed, he takes his revenge by sharing with C, another man, an obscene joke of which B is the victim. The exclusion is achieved by the combined use of shifters (the referent of 'you' is no longer B, but C, even though she is still the indirect addressee of the joke) and pronouns of non-person (by being referred to as 'she', B is excluded from any participant role in the linguistic exchange, reduced to the status of an object – of discourse). We understand why comedy programmes on television are sites for the linguistic class-struggle, on both sides of the divide. The list of the butts of the two Ronnies' 'news item' jokes reads like a roll-call of minorities in the sense of Deleuze and Guattari : women, trade-unionists, gays, foreigners, not to mention the Irish or the Scot. And we understand why Trevor Griffiths, the Marxist playwright, wrote a play entitled *Comedians*,[66] and why left-wing comedians appeared on our screens towards the end of the Thatcher era. The political 'war of attrition', as Gramsci called it, is notoriously waged in language.

The description of the linguistic class-struggle as a war of attrition would take up a whole volume. The brief mention of two fields of battle will have to do here. The first field is that of the minorisation of the standard language by 'dominated' dialects. This, as we saw, is a major problem facing English in its new capacity as the only global language, or the language of imperialism. Being outstretched, as the Roman empire once was, the linguistic empire of English is subjected to all sorts of centrifugal forces, whereby the struggle of the dominated cultures and languages (which is also the political struggle of the periphery against the centre, of the colonial against the imperial) makes itself felt. This takes many forms: new Englishes, international English as *lingua franca*, the struggle within Britain of regional or class dialects and accents against BBC English and the Received Pronunciation.

The second area is the area of education. The classic studies of Renée Balibar on the emergence of French as a national language and on the division of the two educational dialects that correspond to primary and secondary or higher education respectively show that under the ideal of a unitary language (for the needs of untrammelled exchange and circulation), the class division, and therefore the class-struggle, persist.[67] What is interesting in this is not that the dominant ideology dominates in the field of language (it is easy to contrast the elementary simplicity of school grammars destined for what the French aptly call 'elementary' education with the complexity of the 'secondary' language as exemplified in the 'great' literature that is the privileged object of study in higher education) – it is rather the political struggle that takes place not only *through* but also *in* language: a process of contradictory alliance and distinction between the bourgeoisie and the petty-bourgeoisie, the linguistic creation of a 'people' through 'universal' education (this was the explicit ambition of the French Third Republic). All this is conducted *in* language, that is through the use of grammatical or stylistic markers. Balibar's account of 'school' French is conducted through an analysis of the style of Camus's *The Outsider* (the stylistic 'difference' of which is its unexpected – and striking – conformity with elementary rather than literary French). The merest glance at the two following *incipit* shows the difference:

(i) Pendant un demi-siècle, les bourgeoises de Pont Lévêque envièrent à Mme Aubin sa servante Félicité. (For half a century, the ladies of Pont Lévêque were envious of Mme Aubin because of Félicité, her maid)
(ii) Under certain circumstances, there are few hours in life more agreeable than the hour dedicated to the ceremony known as afternoon tea.

The first is the opening of Flaubert's 'Un coeur simple'. It sounds like a dictation exercise out of a primary school textbook, a possible corpus for a battery of grammatical substitutions (time adjunct v. adverb; plural v. singular; feminine v. masculine gender, etc.). Only in the replacement of 'cinquante ans' with 'un demi-siècle' can we hear an individual voice speaking, through the power of rhetorical modulation. The second is the opening of Henry James's *Portrait of a Lady*. It, too, begins with an adjunct, but of a deliberately vague kind (is it an adjunct of time? or of manner?). The rest of the sentence, however, is vastly different: syntactic complexity (dedicated by whom? known to whom? – the agent is deliberately left out) and the rhetorical effect of point of view (who is it that calls that homely occurrence a 'ceremony'?) – all this marks another stylistic strategy, another dialect, in which the necessities of simple exchange are forgotten, and perhaps despised.

We could develop this with the help of the concepts with which Pierre Bourdieu accounts for language.[68] The main thrust of his account is not only, as we saw, the passage from internal to external linguistics, but also the realisation that a speech-act is a conjuncture, that grammar is at best a part determinant of meaning, that meaning is fully realised only on the marketplace of linguistic exchange – as a result of which the relevant concept for the analysis of language is no longer Saussure's *langue* but, as we have just demonstrated, *style*.

The advantage of this account (conducted with the help of quasi-Marxist concepts: official language, linked to the state, versus the various dialects; standard language as the product of a history of class-struggle; symbolic domination; linguistic capital, etc.) is not merely that it is based on the linguistic class-struggle: it avoids the pessimism of the Frankfurt School, where reification is so prevalent as to preclude any hope of resisting the domination of the dominant ideology.[69] Bourdieu's analyses of linguistic domination through intimidation and symbolic capital allows for strategic and tactical, collective and individual action on the part of all those who enter the field of linguistic exchange. Minority speakers of the world, unite –that is the slogan of the linguistic class-struggle, the pervading nature of which should now be apparent.

## 8   End Thesis

My last example takes me, after the preliminary thesis that language is a form of praxis and the four positive theses just developed, to my *end thesis*: *language is the site, and the instrument, of subjectivation/subjection*. After linguistic conjuncture, linguistic imperialism, linguistic (class-) struggle, *linguistic interpellation and counter-interpellation* is the fourth Marxist concept I propose to introduce. Its origin, in Althusser's late theory of ideology, as developed by Judith Butler in *Excitable Speech*, is clear. Again, the object of the exercise is to replace the traditional concept of 'the subject', that reified entity, by the process of which it is the result, an end-of-chain result, as appears in the Althusser inspired linguistic chain of interpellation (institution → ritual → practice → speech-act). We cannot be content with the reflexivity and vicious circularity of a fetishised subject contemplating itself as centre of consciousness and discourse, as speaker and individual site of the operations of language, with the consequent psychologisation of the whole process, even if it goes under the name of an 'unconscious'. This must give way to a process, which is historical, social, material and political: the process of subjectivation, in which the subject is at best a secondary, end-of-chain product, which must not overshadow the primary process of interpellation by, and counter-interpellation through, language. Not only is there no individual subject without the operations of language, but the subject, at best a dubious concept, is the privileged site of linguistic fetishism. We are not surprised to find metaphors of the subject and the self among Lakoff and Johnson's metaphors we live by.[70] They are characterised by a double form of fetishism: the self is conceived as a thing, the subject as an essence. The philosophy of language that we need, and that I have been trying to sketch, defetishises the concepts. Both self and subject are treated not as thing or essence but as process (of struggle); not as origin or centre, but as end-of-chain product; not through spatial, but through temporal metaphors. In short, the static analysis of self and subject as bearers of consciousness and owners of language has been replaced with a dialectics of subjectivation, where language and the subject interpellate and counter-interpellate each other.

# Notes

## 1 'A voice without a mouth': Inner Speech

1. Samuel Beckett, 'Texts for Nothing', XIII, in *Collected Shorter Prose 1945–1980* (London: John Calder, 1984), p. 152.
2. Sigmund Freud, 'The Ego and the Id', trans. James Strachey, Pelican Freud Library Vol. II: *On Metapsychology* (Harmondsworth: Penguin, 1984), pp. 362–3.
3. V. N. Volosinov, *Marxism and the Philosophy of Language*, Leningrad, 1929, 1930, translated from the 1930 edition by Ladislav Matejka and I. R. Titunik (New York and London: Seminar Press, 1973), p. 14. Volosinov was the author of incisive work on the philosophy and psychology of language; some scholars have identified him as Bakhtin but most hotly dispute this, convinced that Volosinov was the true author, working in dialogue with Bakhtin and others. See Carl Brandist, *The Bakhtin Circle: Philosophy, Culture and Politics* (London: Pluto Press, 2002).
4. He continues, 'The hallucinatory voices serve the purpose, among other things, of warning the sick person of the danger of being overpowered by the id.' (I thank Steven Connor for referring me to this.) Otto Isakower, 'On the Exceptional Position of the Auditory Sphere', *International Journal of Psycho-Analysis*, 20 (1939), pp. 345–6.
5. Maurice Merleau-Ponty, *Phenomenology of Perception*, trans. Colin Smith (London: Routledge and Kegan Paul, 1962), p. 183.
6. William James signed a contract for the book in 1878, although it was only completed later and published in 1890.
7. Louis Althusser's account of subjection is set out in the chapter 'Ideology and Ideological State Apparatuses' in his *Lenin and Philosophy* (London: New Left Books, 1971).
8. Ludwig Wittgenstein, *Philosophical Investigations*, I, trans. G. E. M. Anscombe (Oxford: Basil Blackwell, 1963), p. 220e.
9. Henry Head, *Aphasia and Kindred Disorders of Speech*, Vol. I (Cambridge: Cambridge University Press, 1926), pp. 317ff.
10. Or, *Inner Language and the Different Kinds of Aphasia*. G. Ballet, *Le langage intérieur et les diverses formes de l'aphasie* (Paris: Bibliothèque Nationale de France, 1888).
11. John Hughlings Jackson in *Brain*, 38 (1915), pp. 113ff.
12. Pierre Marie, 'Revision de la question d'aphasie', in *La semaine médicale*, 17 October 1906, Paris, pp. 7ff.
13. Roman Jakobson, 'Aphasic Disturbances', in *Fundamentals of Language, Pt. 2. Two Aspects of Language and Two Types of Aphasic Disturbances* (The Hague: Mouton 1971).
14. James Mark Baldwin, chapter 14, 'The Mechanism of Revival: Internal Speech and Song', in *The Mental Development of the Child and the Race*, 3rd edn (New York: Macmillan and Co, 1906), pp. 409–28.

15. Kurt Goldstein, *Language and Language Disturbances* (New York: Grune and Stratton, 1948) drew on the earlier work on aphasia, adding an organicist interpretation.
16. L. S. Jacyna, *Lost Words: Narratives of Language and the Brain, 1825–1926* (Princeton: Princeton University Press, 2000) offers a history of aphasia.
17. *Diagnostic and Statistical Manual IV* (Washington: American Psychiatric Association, 2000).
18. Antonio Damasio, *The Feeling of What Happens: Body and Emotion in the Making of Consciousness* (London: Heinemann, 1999).
19. Alain Morin, 'On a Relation Between Inner Speech and Self-awareness: Additional Evidence from Brain Studies', 1999, in *Dynamical Psychology, an Electronic Journal*, www.goertzel.org/dynapsych.
20. R. Cubelli and P. Nichelli, 'Inner Speech in Anarthria: Neuropsychological Evidence of Differential Effects of Cerebral Lesions on Subvocal Articulation', *Journal of Clinical and Experimental Neuropsychology*, 14, 4 (1992), pp. 499–517.
21. Psychosis Research Group, Institute of Psychiatry Research Report, 1997–1998 (London: King's College London, 1998).
22. See Jerry A. Fodor, *RePresentations: Philosophical Essays on the Foundations of Cognitive Science* (Cambridge, Mass.: MIT Press 1981).
23. William James, *The Principles of Psychology*, Vol. I (London: Macmillan, 1901), p. 253.
24. Joseph Butler, *The Works of Bishop Butler*, ed. J. H. Bernard, Vol. II, *The Analogy of Religion* (London: Macmillan and Co, 1900) ch. 3, p. 8.
25. Merleau-Ponty, *Phenomenology of Perception*, p. 177.
26. Bible, King James Authorised Version, 1 Kings 19: 11, 12.
27. Plato, *The Phaedrus*, trans. Walter Hamilton (London: Penguin Classics, 1973), p. 101.
28. Among whom, each very differently, Nietzsche, Derrida and Wittgenstein. For a discussion of traditions of viewing language as systematically misleading, see my *The Words of Selves: Identification, Solidarity, Irony* (Stanford: Stanford University Press, 2000), pp. 38–44.
29. Tristan Tzara, *Sept Manifestes Dada*, 1924; trans. Barbara Wright as *Seven Dada Manifestos and Lampisteries* (London: Calder Books, 1988).
30. George Steiner, quoting Fritz Mauthner's *Beitrage zu einer Kritik der Sprache* (Leipzig 1923). In Steiner, *After Babel: Aspects of Language and Translation* (Oxford and London: Oxford University Press, 1975).
31. Roland Barthes, 'To Write; An Intransitive Verb', in *The Rustle of Language* trans. Richard Howard (Oxford: Basil Blackwell, 1966), p. 123.
32. See Russell B. Goodman, *Wittgenstein and William James* (Cambridge: Cambridge University Press, 2002).
33. See the discussion of Echo and narcissism in 'Lyric Selves', ch. 3 of my *The Words of Selves*.
34. Merleau-Ponty, *Phenomenology of Perception*, p. 179.
35. The French psychiatrist and neurologist Pierre Janet (1859–1947) was known for his research on hysteria and theories of dissociation. Judge Schreber, whose case Freud analysed, wrote *Memoirs of My Nervous Illness*, trans. Ida MacAlpine and Richard A. Hunter (Cambridge, Mass.: Harvard University Press 1988).

36. The Haswell Lodge branch of the Durham Miners' Association, from about 1890.
37. Bible, Hebrews 11: 4; 'and by it [Abel's sacrifice] he being dead yet speaketh'.
38. Ludwig Wittgenstein, *Philosophical Investigations*, trans. G. E. M. Anscombe (Oxford: Basil Blackwell, 1963), p. 211e.
39. Samuel Beckett, 'Texts for Nothing', XIII, p. 152.
40. Antoine Meillet, *Grammaire du Vieux-Perse*, 2nd edn enlarged and ed. E. Benveniste (Paris: Librairie Ancienne Honoré Champion, 1931), pp. 137–8.
41. Were I to interrupt the sacrifice by taking the knife, and to execute the action (and the goat) for myself instead, this would resemble the modern use of 'to write', fast becoming a middle verb. See Roland Barthes, 'To Write; An Intransitive Verb', pp. 18–19.
42. Volosinov, *Marxism and the Philosophy of Language*, p. 13.
43. Jean-Jacques Lecercle discusses Deleuze's idea of the impersonality of style in his *Deleuze and Language* (Basingstoke: Palgrave Macmillan, 2002), pp. 219–46.
44. V. N. Volosinov, *Freudianism: a Marxist Critique*, trans. I. R. Titunik, ed. I. R. Titunik with N. H. Bruss (New York: Academic Press, 1976), p. 114.
45. Volosinov, *Marxism and the Philosophy of Language*, p. 33.
46. Volosinov, *Marxism*, p. 39.
47. Roland Barthes, *Writing Degree Zero and Elements of Semiology*, 1968, trans. Annette Lavers and Colin Smith (London: Jonathan Cape, 1984). p. 12.
48. Barthes, *Writing Degree Zero*, p. 12.
49. Barthes, *Writing Degree Zero*, p. 13.
50. Volosinov, *Freudianism*, p. 114.
51. Volosinov, *Marxism*, p. 10.
52. Volosinov, *Marxism*, p. 11.
53. Volosinov, *Marxism*, p. 11.
54. Volosinov, *Marxism*, p. 11.
55. Volosinov, *Marxism*, p. 13.
56. Volosinov, *Marxism*, p. 14.
57. Volosinov, *Marxism*, pp. 28–9.
58. Michel Henry, *The Genealogy of Psychoanalysis*, trans. Douglas Brick (Stanford: Stanford University Press, 1993), p. 302.
59. Henry, *The Genealogy of Psychoanalysis*, pp. 262–3.
60. This is traced in Milad Doueihi, *A Perverse History of the Human Heart* (Cambridge, Mass.: Harvard University Press, 1998).
61. Nicolas Malebranche, *The Search After Truth*, trans. and ed. Thomas M. Lennon and Paul J. Olscamp (Cambridge: Cambridge University Press, 1997), p. 574.
62. Henry, *The Genealogy of Psychoanalysis*, p. 326.
63. Henry, *The Genealogy of Psychoanalysis*, p. 327.
64. Hannah Arendt, *The Life of the Mind* (San Diego: Harcourt Inc., 1978), p. 185.
65. Arendt, *The Life of the Mind*, p. 193.
66. Wittgenstein, *Philosophical Investigations*, p. 222e.
67. Wittgenstein, *Philosophical Investigations*, p. 220e.
68. Wittgenstein, *Philosophical Investigations*, p. 223e.
69. Our sense of the privacy of our inner speech is not, of course, the same topic as that of the concept of a 'private language', which Wittgenstein demolishes in his *Philosophical Investigations*.

70. Baldwin, ch. 14, 'The Mechanism of Revival: Internal Speech and Song', in *The Mental Development of the Child and the Race*, p. 416.
71. Baldwin, 'The Mechanism of Revival', p. 419.
72. This is elaborated in my *The Words of Selves*, pp. 15–16.
73. Gilles Deleuze, *The Logic of Sense* (London: Athlone Press, 1990), pp. 132–3.
74. William James, *The Principles of Psychology*, p. 301.
75. Michel Foucault, 'The Thought of the Outside', in *Aesthetics, Method, and Epistemology: Essential Works of Michel Foucault Vol. 2*, trans. Robert Hurley et al. (London: Allen Lane, Penguin, 1998), p. 152.
76. Maurice Blanchot quoted by Foucault, 'The Thought of the Outside', p. 166.
77. Foucault, 'The Thought of the Outside', p. 168.
78. Foucault, 'The Thought of the Outside', p. 152.
79. Foucault, 'The Thought of the Outside', p. 149.
80. Samuel Beckett, 'Texts for Nothing', p. 154.
81. Aimée Gasston, 'The Textual Resistance to Failure in Samuel Beckett's Shorter Fiction', unpublished MA dissertation, School of English and American Studies, University of East Anglia, Norwich, 2001, p. 55.
82. George Steiner, *After Babel*, p. 39.
83. Nicolas Malebranche, *The Search After Truth*, p. 575.
84. Elizabeth Closs Traugott, 'Conventional and Dead Metaphors Revisited', in *The Ubiquity of Metaphor*, ed. Wolf Paprotté and René Diven (Amsterdam: John Benjamin Publishing Company, 1985), p. 49.
85. I. A. Richards, *The Philosophy of Rhetoric*, 1936 (Oxford and New York: Oxford University Press, 1965), pp. 108–9.
86. Mark Johnson, *The Body in the Mind: the Bodily Basis of Meaning, Imagination, and Reason* (Chicago and London: University of Chicago Press, 1987), p. 125.
87. Doueihi, *A Perverse History of the Human Heart*, p. 12.
88. Steiner, *After Babel*, p. 289.
89. James, *The Principles of Psychology*, p. 251.
90. James, *The Principles of Psychology*, pp. 251–2.
91. Wittgenstein, *Philosophical Investigations* p. 219e.
92. James, *The Principles of Psychology*, pp. 252–3.
93. Wittgenstein, *Philosophical Investigations*, p. 154e, §589.
94. Thomas Carlyle, *Sartor Resartus*, ed. P. C. Parr (Oxford: Clarendon Press, 1913), p. 51.
95. Carlyle, *Sartor Resartus*, p. 51.

## 2   Bad Words

1. See ch. 5 of my *The Words of Selves: Identification, Solidarity, Irony* (Stanford: Stanford University Press, 2000).
2. Joan Scott, writing about history's phantasms, notes that 'retrospective identifications, after all, are imagined repetitions and repetitions of imagined resemblances'. In 'Fantasy Echo: History and the Construction of Identity', *Critical Inquiry*, Winter 2001, pp. 284–304 (p. 287).
3. *The Words of Selves*, pp. 84–9. For an introduction to the history of pragmatics, which does differently consider the forcefulness of language, see B. Nehrlich

and D. Clarke, *Language, Action, Context: the Early History of Pragmatics in Europe and America, 1780–1930* (Amsterdam: John Benjamins, 1996).

4. In, for instance, some psychiatric classifications used in South America.

5. As Joan Scott writes, 'the fantasy also implies a story about a sequential relationship for prohibition, fulfillment, and punishment (having broken the law that prohibits incest, the child is being beaten)'. Scott, 'Fantasy Echo', p. 290.

6. Jean Laplanche has remarked on the 'message' which always comes to me from another, as an impingement on me of the other's unconscious, formative for my own, and has raised the question of how to take account of that constitutive alterity. 'Confronted with this enigmatic message, a message compromised by any number of unconscious resurgences, the child translates it as best as he can, with the language at his disposal.' Jean Laplanche, *Essays on Otherness*, ed. John Fletcher (New York: Routledge, 1998), pp. 158–9.

7. A burden of his sustained discussion of pain and scepticism about its reporting, in his *Philosophical Investigations*, I, trans. G. E. M. Anscombe (Oxford: Basil Blackwell, 1963).

8. From 'Adagia' in *Wallace Stevens, Collected Poetry and Prose*, ed. Frank Kermode and Joan Richardson (New York: Library of America, 1997), p. 907.

9. Jacques Lacan, 'The Signification of the Phallus' in *Ecrits: a Selection*, trans. Alan Sheridan (London and New York: Routledge, 2001), p. 315.

10. The Russian word 'ideologiya' has, like ideology, debated meanings. As one glossary on Bakhtin's terms, by Graham Roberts, asserts 'The Russian ideologiya is less politically coloured than the English word "ideology". In other words, it is not necessarily a consciously held political belief system; rather it can refer in a more general sense to the way in which members of a given social group view the world. It is in this broader sense that Bakhtin uses the term. For Bakhtin, any utterance is shot through with "ideologiya", any speaker is automatically an ideologue'. (*The Bakhtin Reader*, ed. Pam Morris (London: Edward Arnold, 1994), p. 249.

11. V. N. Volosinov, *Marxism and the Philosophy of Language*, trans. from the 1930 edn by Ladislav Matejka and I. R. Titunik (New York and London: Seminar Press, 1973), p. 39.

12. Volosinov, *Marxism*, p. 29.

13. G. W. F. Hegel, *Phenomenology of Spirit*, trans. A. V. Miller (Oxford, Oxford University Press, 1977), p. 187.

14. Hegel, *Phenomenology*, p. 188.

15. Jacques Lacan, *The Signification of the Phallus*, pp. 86–7.

16. '… through all the techniques of moral and human sciences that go to make up a knowledge of the subject'. Gilles Deleuze, *Foucault*, trans. Sean Hand (London: Athlone Press, 1999), p. 103.

17. Hegel, *Phenomenology*, p. 308.

18. Hegel, *Phenomenology*, p. 116.

19. Marcus Aurelius, maxim 20, Book 9, *Meditations*, Penguin Classics, trans. Maxwell Staniforth (London and NY, Penguin Books, 1964), p. 142. See also, again in the spirit of Epictetus, his remark 'That men of a certain type should behave as they do is inevitable. To wish it otherwise were to wish the fig tree would not yield its juice.' Book 4, maxim 6, p. 65.

20. A recall of the title *Love's Work*, by Gillian Rose (London: Chatto and Windus, 1995).
21. Hegel, *Phenomenology*, p. 116.
22. 'Just as the individual self-consciousness is immediately present in language, so it is also immediately present as a universal infection; the complete separation into independent selves is at the same time the fluidity and universally communicated unity of the many selves; language is the soul existing as soul.' Hegel, *Phenomenology*, p. 430.

## 3   A New Philosophy of Language

1. K. Marx and F. Engels, *The German Ideology* (London, Lawrence and Wishart, 1965), p. 37.
2. Tran Duc Thao, *Recherches sur l'origine du langage et de la conscience* (Paris: Editions Sociales, 1973); M. Merleau-Ponty, *Signes* (Paris: Gallimard, 1960).
3. J. Butler, *Excitable Speech* (London: Routledge, 1997).
4. S. Leclaire, *Psychanalyser* (Paris: Seuil, 1968).
5. J. C. Milner, *De la syntaxe à l'interprétation* (Paris: Seuil, 1978).
6. A. Banfield, 'Narrative Style and the Grammar of Direct and Indirect Speech', *Foundations of Language*, 10 (1973), pp. 1–39.
7. J. Habermas, 'What is Universal Pragmatics', in *Communication and the Evolution of Society* (London: Heinemann, 1979), pp. 1–68.
8. A. Culioli, *Cognition and Representation in Linguistic Theory* (Amsterdam: John Benjamins, 1995).
9. G. Deleuze, *Logique du sens* (Paris: Minuit).
10. C. Panaccio, *Le Discours intérieur* (Paris: Seuil, 1999).
11. V. Volosinov, *Marxism and the Philosophy of Language* (Cambridge, Mass.: Harvard University Press, 1986); L. S. Vygotsky, *Language and Thought* (Cambridge, Mass.: MIT Press, 1962); G. Steiner, *After Babel* (Oxord: Oxford University Press), 1975.
12. G. Deleuze and F. Guattari, *L'Anti-Oedipe* (Paris: Minuit); *Mille plateaux* (Paris: Minuit, 1980).
13. J. Searle, *Intentionality* (Cambridge: Cambridge University Press, 1983).
14. G. Deleuze and F. Guattari, *Mille plateaux*.
15. See J. J. Lecercle, *Interpretation as Pragmatics* (Basingstoke: Palgrave Macmillan, 1999).
16. The limitations of the analogy must also be noted: Chomskyan deep structure is conceived as a rational calculus, which has little to do with the Freudian unconscious (see I. Fonagy, *Languages within Language* (Amsterdam, John Benjamins, 2000), p. 616).
17. P. Macherey, *Pour une théorie de la production littéraire* (Paris, Maspéro, 1966), p. 66.
18. G. Deleuze, *Spinoza et le problème de l'expression* (Paris: Minuit, 1968).
19. N. Abraham and M. Torok, *L'Ecorce et le noyau* (Paris: Flammarion, 1978).
20. J. J. Lecercle, *The Violence of Language* (London: Routledge, 1990).
21. C. Lévi-Strauss, *Tristes tropiques* (Paris: Plon, 1955).
22. See Deleuze and Guattari, *Mille Plateaux*.

23. V. Volosinov, *Marxism and the Philosophy of Language*; and *Freudianism: a Marxist Critique* (New York: Academic Press, 1976).
24. J. P. Brisset, *Les Origines Humaines* (Paris, Baudoin: 1980), p. 135. Quoted in W. Redfern, *All Puns Intended: the Verbal Creation of Jean-Pierre Brisset* (Oxford: Legenda, 2002), p. 162.
25. R. Wallace, *The Agony of Lewis Carroll* (Melrose: Gemini Press, 1990).
26. R. Wallace, *Jack the Ripper, 'Light-hearted friend'* (Melrose: Gemini Press, 1997).
27. See J. J. Lecercle, *Philosophy of Nonsense* (London: Routledge, 1994).
28. On the distinction between affects and quasi-affects (involved in make-believe), see K. Walton, *Mimesis as Make-Believe* (Cambridge, Mass.: Harvard University Press, 1993).
29. Louis Wolfson, *Le Schizo et les langues* (Paris: Gallimard, 1970).
30. See R. Harris, *Saussure and His Interpreters* (Edinburgh: Edinburgh University Press, 2001).
31. J. J. Lecercle, *Interpretation as Pragmatics* , ch. 1.
32. G. Deleuze and F. Guattari, *Kafka* (Paris: Minuit, 1975).
33. I. Fonagy, *La Vive voix* (Paris: Payot, 1983).
34. J. J. Lecercle, *The Violence of Language*, pp. 85–94.

## 4 The Concept of Language We Don't Need

1. N. Chomsky, *Propaganda and the Public Mind*, interviews with David Barsamian (London: Pluto Press, 2001); N. Chomsky, *Necessary Illusions: Thought Control in Democratic Societies* (London: Pluto Press, 1989).
2. Chomsky, *Propaganda and the Public Mind*, p. 210.
3. R. L. Gregory (ed.), *The Oxford Companion to the Mind* (Oxford: Oxford University Press, 1987).
4. Chomsky, *Propaganda and the Public Mind*, p. 207. Similar formulations can be found in Chomsky's recent collection of philosophical essays, *New Horizons in the Study of Mind* (Cambridge: Cambridge University Press, 2000).
5. Chomsky, *New Horizons*, p. 35.
6. Chomsky, *New Horizons*, p. 120.
7. Chomsky, *New Horizons*.
8. G. Lakoff and M. Johnson, *Metaphors We Live By* (Chicago: University of Chicago Press, 1980); *Philosophy in the Flesh* (New York: Basic Books, 1999).
9. Chomsky, 'Language: Chomsky's Theory', p. 421.
10. D. Biber et al., *Longman Grammar of Spoken and Written English* (London: Longman, 1999), p. 347.
11. The example is adapted from J. M. Saddock, *Toward a Linguistic Theory of Speech Acts* (New York: Academic Press, 1974), p. 25. See also S. C. Levinson, *Pragmatics* (Cambridge: Cambridge University Press, 1983), pp. 247–51.
12. J. R. Ross, 'Constraints on Variables in Syntax', unpublished PhD dissertation, MIT, 1967. Extracts published in G. Harman (ed.), *On Noam Chomsky: Critical Essays* (New York: Anchor Books, 1974).
13. R. Hull, *Excellent Intentions* (Harmondsworth: Penguin, 1938), p. 15.

14. R. Wingfield, *Hard Frost* (London: Corgi, 1996), p. 223.
15. S. S. Van Dine, *The Benson Murder Case* (London: Hogarth, 1988, first published, New York, 1926), p. 77.
16. C. Holme, *Beautiful End* (Oxford: Oxford University Press, 1935, first published, 1918), p. 192.
17. L. Althusser, *Philosophie et philosophie spontanée des savants* (1967) (Paris: Maspéro, 1974).
18. Chomsky, *Horizons*, p. 167. F. A. Lange, *The History of Materialism* (London: Routledge & Kegan Paul, 1925).
19. G. Sampson, *Educating Eve* (London: Cassell, 1997).
20. See J. Elster, *Making Sense of Marx* (Cambridge: Cambridge University Press, 1985); J. Roemer (ed.), *Analytical Marxism* (Cambridge: Cambridge University Press, 1986).
21. See J. J. Lecercle, *Deleuze and Language* (Basingstoke: Palgrave Macmillan, 2002).
22. G. Lukács, *History and Class Consciousness* (London: Merlin Press, 1971).
23. R. Barthes, 'Le mythe aujourd'hui', in *Mythologies* (Paris: Seuil, 1957).
24. Lukács, *History and Class Consciousness*, p. 130.

## 5  The Concept of Language We Need

1. L. S. Vygotsky, *Thought and Language* (Cambridge, Mass.: MIT Press, 1962, first published, 1934), p. 124.
2. Vygotsky, *Thought and Language*, p. 125.
3. G. Lakoff and M. Johnson, *Philosophy in the Flesh* (New York: Basic Books, 1999), p. 80.
4. Tran Duc Thao, *Recherches sur l'origine du langage et de la conscience* (Paris: Editions Sociales, 1973).
5. Tran Duc Thao, *Phénoménologie et matérialisme dialectique* (Paris: Editions Minh-Tân, 1951).
6. Vygotsky, *Thought and Language*, p. 118.
7. L. Althusser, *Pour Marx* (Paris: Maspéro, 1965), p. 167 (my translation).
8. C. Marazzi, *Il Posto dei Calzini* (Bellinzona: Casagrande, 1994).
9. K. Marx and F. Engels, *The German Ideology* (London: Lawrence & Wishart, 1965), pp. 41–2.
10. Marx and Engels, *The German Ideology*, p. 56.
11. Marx and Engels, *The German Ideology*, p. 37.
12. Marx and Engels, *The German Ideology*, p. 492.
13. Marx and Engels, *The German Ideology*, p. 491.
14. H. Lefebvre, *Le Langage et la société* (Paris: Gallimard, 1966).
15. See R. L. Trask, *Mind the Gaffe* (Harmondsworth: Penguin, 2002).
16. P. Fussell, *The Great War and Modern Memory* (Oxford: Oxford University Press, 2000).
17. A. Gramsci, *Il Materialismo storico e la filosopfia di Benedetto Croce* (Turin: Einaudi, 1978), p. 146 (my translation).
18. Gramsci, *Il Materialismo*, p. 156.
19. Vygotsky, *Thought and Language*, p. 51.
20. Vygotsky, *Thought and Language*, p. 64.
21. Vygotsky, *Thought and Language*, p. 67.

22. Vygotsky, *Thought and Language*, p. 74.
23. Gramsci, *Il Materialismo*, p. 3 (my translation).
24. See, for instance, Owen Barfield, *History in English Words* (London: Faber and Faber, 1953), or his *Poetic Diction* (Hanover and London: Wesleyan University Press, 1973).
25. R. Williams, *Marxism and Literature* (Oxford: Oxford University Press, 1973).
26. R. Williams, *Culture and Society 1780–1950* (London: Chatto & Windus, 1958).
27. R. Williams, *Keywords* (London: Fontana, 1976).
28. J. J. Lecercle, *The Violence of Language* (London: Routledge, 1991).
29. P. Macherey, *Pour une théorie de la production littéraire* (Paris: Maspéro, 1966), p. 66.
30. L. Althusser, *Pour Marx* (Paris: Maspéro, 1965), pp. 238–43.
31. A. Badiou, 'Le Balcon du présent', lecture given at the 'Returns to Marx' colloquium, London, French Institute and Tate Modern, May 2002.
32. L. Althusser, *Sur la Reproduction* (Paris: PUF, 1995); J. J. Lecercle, *Interpretation as Pragmatics* (London: Macmillan, 1999).
33. J. Searle, *Speech Acts* (Cambridge: Cambridge University Press, 1969).
34. That is precisely what happens to it in Derrida's *Spectres de Marx* (Paris: Galilée, 1993). There is, however, nothing new in this: it already occurs in the famous passage on the persistence of Greek art in Marx's *Grundrisse*, or in his letter to Annenkov of 28 December 1846.
35. Lakoff and Johnson, *Philosophy in the Flesh*, p. 99.
36. R. Barthes, *Mythologies* (Paris: Seuil, 1957).
37. T. Adorno, *Hegel: Three Studies* (Cambridge, Mass.: MIT Press, 1993), pp. 89–148.
38. P. Lafargue, 'La langue française avant et après la Révolution', in *Critiques littéraires* (Paris: Editions Sociales Internationales, 1936), pp. 35–86.
39. See Lecercle, *The Violence of Language*.
40. L. Vygotsky, *Thought and Language*, p. 51.
41. E. Benveniste, *Problèmes de linguistique générale*, 2 vols (Paris: Gallimard, 1966, 1974); A. Culioli, *Pour une linguistique de l'énonciation*, 3 vols (Gap: Ophrys, 1990 (vol. 1) and 1999 (vols 2 and 3)); *Variations sur la linguistique* (Paris: Klincksieck, 2002).
42. R. Langacker, *Foundations of Cognitive Grammar*, 2 vols (Stanford: Stanford University Press, 1987, 1991); Lakoff and Johnson, *Philosophy in the Flesh*.
43. Lakoff and Johnson, *Philosophy in the Flesh*, pp. 140–3.
44. M. Merleau-Ponty, *La Prose du monde* (Paris: Gallimard, 1969); *Le Visible et l'invisible* (Paris: Gallimard, 1964).
45. G. Deleuze, *Logique du sens* (Paris: Minuit, 1969), series 34.
46. J. J. Lecercle, 'The Misprision of Pragmatics in Contemporary French Philosophy', in A. Phillips Griffiths (ed.), *Contemporary French Philosophy* (Cambridge, Cambridge University Press, 1987), pp. 21–40.
47. S. Leclaire, *Psychanalyser* (Paris: Seuil, 1968).
48. L. Irigaray, *Parler n'est jamais neutre* (Paris: Minuit, 1985).
49. J. Favret-Saada, *Les Mots, la mort, les sorts* (Paris: Gallimard, 1977).
50. D. McNally, *Bodies of Meaning: Studies in Language, Labor, and Liberation* (New York: State University of New York Press, 2001).

51. G. Deleuze and F. Guattari, *L'Anti-Oedipe* (Paris: Minuit, 1972), p. 11. For a detailed analysis of this text, see J. J. Lecercle, *Deleuze and Language* (Basingstoke: Palgrave Macmillan, 2002), ch. 1.

52. See M. Fraser, 'What is the Matter of Feminist Criticism?', *Economy and Society*, vol. 31, 2002, pp. 606–25, which has an impressive bibliography.

53. F. Flahault, *La Parole intermédiaire* (Paris: Seuil, 1978).

54. See Lecercle, *The Violence of Language*.

55. L. Goldman, *Marxisme et sciences humaines* (Paris: Gallimard, 1970).

56. L. Venuti, *The Scandals of Translation* (London: Routledge, 1998), pp. 29–30.

57. R. Balibar and D. Laporte, *Le Français national* (Paris: Hachette, 1974), p. 32. On the Grégoire report, see also M. de Certeau, D. Julia and J. Revel, *Une Politique de la langue* (Paris: Gallimard, 1975).

58. L. Althusser, *Sur la reproduction*.

59. Gramsci, *Il Materialismo*, p. 3 (my translation).

60. Gramsci, *Il Materialismo*, p. 146 (my translation).

61. L. J. Calvet, *Linguistique et colonialisme* (Paris: Payot, 1974).

62. D. Crystal, *Language Death* (Cambridge: Cambridge University Press, 2000); D. Nettle and S. Romaine, *Vanishing Voices* (Oxford: Oxford University Press, 2000).

63. G. Deleuze and F. Guattari, *Qu'est-ce que la philosophie?* (Paris: Minuit, 1991), p. 10.

64. Marx and Engels, *German Ideology*, p. 491.

65. T. Todorov, 'Freud sur l'énonciation', in *Langages*, 17 (Paris: Didier-Larousse, 1970), pp. 34–41.

66. T. Griffiths, *Comedians* (London: Faber, 1976).

67. Balibar and Laporte, *Le Français national*; R. Balibar, *Les Français fictifs* (Paris: Hachette, 1974).

68. P. Bourdieu, *Ce que parler veut dire* (Paris: Fayard, 1982).

69. On this, see F. Vandenberghe, *Une Histoire critique de la sociologie allemande*, vol. 2 (Paris: La Découverte, 1998).

70. Lakoff and Johnson, *Philosophy in the Flesh*, pp. 235 sqq.

# Index